Praise for *Night Fighter*

"*Night Fighter* is unique. It is a most revealing documentary account and living history of the Special Ops, and I know of no other book that offers so complete and objective a glimpse within the organization. By the end, you will know and feel what it was like to be a night fighter from Korea all the way to SEAL Team 6."

—Chimp Robertson, author of *POW/MIA: America's Missing Men*

"It is my opinion that without the commitment, passion, ingenuity, and ruthlessness of Hamilton and (Roy) Boehm there would have been no SEAL teams as we know them."

—John Weisman, co-author of Richard Marcinko's Rogue Warrior series and coauthor of *Shadow Warrior*

"Through your efforts we have been made aware of a significant threat to the development and construction of a strategic defense system (SDI, 'Star Wars')."

—Lieutenant General James A. Abrahamson

"This idea of Bill Hamilton . . . and others into airborne delivery (Helicopter cast-and-recover) was the genesis of the Navy SEALs—SEALs standing for Sea, Air, Land."

—Orr Kelly, author of *Brave Men, Dark Waters*

"You (Hamilton) are the father of the U.S. Navy SEALs."

—Sedgwick Tourison Jr., author of *Secret Army, Secret War*

"Hamilton was also the man responsible for forming SEAL Team Six. (He) did the country a great service in forming what is now one of America's finest professional warrior units."

—Rudy Enders, retired CIA officer

NIGHT FIGHTER

Books by Charles W. Sasser

NIGHT FIGHTER

AN INSIDER'S STORY OF SPECIAL OPS FROM KOREA TO SEAL TEAM 6

CAPTAIN WILLIAM H. HAMILTON JR., USN

AND

CHARLES W. SASSER

WITH A NEW FOREWORD BY CRAIG ROBERTS

Arcade Publishing • New York

Copyright © 2016 by William H. Hamilton Jr. and Charles W. Sasser
Foreword copyright © 2020 by Skyhorse Publishing, Inc.

All rights reserved. No part of this book may be reproduced in any manner without the express written consent of the publisher, except in the case of brief excerpts in critical reviews or articles. All inquiries should be addressed to Arcade Publishing, 307 West 36th Street, 11th Floor, New York, NY 10018.

First Paperback Edition 2020

Arcade Publishing books may be purchased in bulk at special discounts for sales promotion, corporate gifts, fund-raising, or educational purposes. Special editions can also be created to specifications. For details, contact the Special Sales Department, Arcade Publishing, 307 West 36th Street, 11th Floor, New York, NY 10018 or arcade@skyhorsepublishing.com.

Arcade Publishing® is a registered trademark of Skyhorse Publishing, Inc.®, a Delaware corporation.

Visit our website at www.arcadepub.com.

10 9 8 7 6 5 4 3 2 1

Library of Congress Cataloging-in-Publication Data

Names: Hamilton, William H., Jr., 1927–2016 author. | Sasser, Charles W., author.
Title: Night fighter : an insider's story of special ops from Korea to Seal
  Team Six / Captain William H. Hamilton Jr., USN and Charles W. Sasser.
Description: New York, NY : Arcade Publishing, 2016. | Includes
  bibliographical references and index.
Identifiers: LCCN 2016029663 (print) | LCCN 2016035170 (ebook) | ISBN
  978-1-62872-680-0 (hardcover : alk. paper) | ISBN 978-1-950691-10-4 (paperback) |
  ISBN 978-1-62872-683-1 (ebook)
Subjects: LCSH: Special operations (Military science)—United States—History. |
  Special forces (Military science)—United States—History.
Classification: LCC UA34.S64 H356 2016 (print) | LCC UA34.S64 (ebook) | DDC
  359.9/84 [B] —dc23
LC record available at https://lccn.loc.gov/2016029663

Cover photo: iStockphoto

Printed in the United States of America

*This book is dedicated to
the American warriors of Navy, Army,
and Air Force Special Forces.*

FOREWORD

by US Army LTC W. Craig Roberts (Ret)

WHEN MY FATHER, A US Marine, returned from World War II, he had a large red book entitled *The Marines* that contained possibly the first account in United States military history of a very special operations unit known as Carlson's Raiders. Their mission was to go ashore on enemy-held islands, destroy enemy assets, communications, equipment, and, when possible, enemy officers, then pull back to their rubber boats to return to a submarine or surface craft offshore.

Other elite units followed into US military history—Army Rangers, US Army Special Forces (Green Berets), elite Army airborne units, and others that are used in high-risk and clandestine operations. One of these units, the US Navy SEALs (standing for "Sea, Air, Land"), developed a reputation for skill and daring and are considered modern-day Raiders. Each member must pass a rigorous and demanding selection course that pushes trainees to their limits. Many can't take it and "ring the bell" to be dismissed.

Those who pass the course are awarded the badge of the SEALs, the Trident, and are sent out to teams at three locations—on the East Coast at Little Creek, Virginia; the West Coast at Coronado Island, San Diego; and Virginia Beach, Virginia, home base for SEAL Team Six, the famed special-missions and counterterrorism unit.

Underwater Demolition Teams (UDTs) were predecessors of SEALS. They were used extensively as combat swimmers during

World War II and the Korean War, and subsequently evolved into SEALs. Navy Captain William H. Hamilton Jr. is credited with forming the SEALs, along with Lieutenant Roy Boehm. Both saw battle action as navy divers in the Pacific and clandestine operations in Korea.

Hamilton's military career after graduation from the US Naval Academy began in the Air Wing as a Navy jet pilot flying Grumman F9F Panther jets, the first jet produced by Grumman, designed for carrier operations. His squadron was assigned to the *USS Valley Forge* (CVA-45) then cruising offshore of the Korean Peninsula. He flew combat missions using a photo recon aircraft to film enemy positions, troop movements, and other potential targets for armed aircraft.

While aboard ship in Korea he was impressed by a tough group of men who performed dangerous behind-the-lines operations. They looked rough and every bit of what he considered commandos or "night fighters." Interested in their operations to the point of unofficially accompanying a team on a mission ashore, he decided to switch from aviation to UDT operations. He considered these "frogmen" everything he imagined a "super warrior" to be.

Hamilton requested UDT training, passed the rigorous selection, and set his course in UDT and Special Warfare. Through the following years, he and other hand-picked officers and NCOs, such as Roy Boehm, began a course of action and activities that eventually led to the formation of America's Sea, Air, and Land (SEAL) warriors.

Night Fighter tells this remarkable story of the development of, and Hamilton's important role in, what today are considered the best Special Warfare fighters in the world—from World War II through Korea, Cuba, Vietnam, Grenada, Panama, and other ops worldwide, where these magnificent fighters, often led by Hamilton, put their lives on the line in combat as well as in behind-the-scenes politics, both inside and outside the Navy, to justify their very existence, and to grow, expand, and prepare today's modern US Navy SEALs to accomplish missions throughout the world: the night fighters.

AUTHOR'S NOTE

As a professional writer, I am privileged to help bring to life the remarkable story of retired U.S. Navy Captain William H. Hamilton Jr. Now eighty-eight years old with a mane of white hair and striking blue eyes, he still bears on his six-four frame the broad shoulders and lean profile of the man declared to be the "father of Navy SEALs."

It was Hamilton more than any other single figure in U.S. military history who not only forged the Navy SEALs but also stamped his indelible brand upon U.S. special operations forces and upon modern counterterrorism efforts. From the Bay of Pigs to the Cuban Missile Crisis, from chasing Che Guevara to thwarting Fidel Castro, from the deltas of Vietnam to the intrigues of European capitals, from the Iran hostage crisis to Nicaragua and the Middle East, Captain Hamilton *lived* the history of the late twentieth century, a period of action and adventure in one of the most vital and dangerous eras of the American experience. His incomparable career spanned tours as a combat fighter pilot in Korea; commander of ships on covert assignments; missions with Underwater Demolition Teams (UDTs) and SEALs; top secret assignments with the CIA in Africa, Latin America, and Europe; experiments for the exploration of space and for unorthodox new methods of counter-subversion, such as the training of dolphins; advisor on security for SDI (President Ronald Reagan's Strategic

Defense Initiative, "Star Wars"); Pentagon consultant, and advisor for U.S. counterterrorism strategies.

He felt it his inexorable duty to help build the most effective and feared unconventional military organization ever conceived. His story unfolds behind the scenes and in the shadows as the United States takes the concept of unconventional warfare and molds it into the one force in the world capable of combating terrorists, international criminals, and tyrants on their own turf—a story that continues today with the rise of ISIS in the Middle East and the chilling prospect of a nuclear World War III.

The information in this book is based upon a variety of sources: interviews with Captain Hamilton and his wife Barbara; personal observations and the recorded observations of witnesses; official U.S. Navy, U.S. Army, and government documents; personal diaries and autobiographies; and newspapers and other published accounts. In addition, I drew upon my own thirteen-year experiences in U.S. Army Special Forces (the Green Berets) and on friendships and associations with those in the SpecOps community such as Commander Roy Boehm, an old friend and the "First SEAL"; Command Sergeant Major Galen Kittleson of the 7th Special Forces Group; Sergeant Carlos Hathcock, Marine sniper during the Vietnam War; Navy SEAL sniper Chris Kyle; Army Ranger Joseph Kapacziewski; Marine Colonel Craig Roberts; Army chopper pilot Colonel Ron Alexander; Marine Silver Star recipient Ray Hildreth; and many others during my twenty-nine-year military career (active duty and reserve) in both the U.S. Navy and the U.S. Army. A special thanks goes to Rudy Enders, the former CIA agent who directed me to this project. These special men enriched my life and added to my own understanding of Special Operations, unconventional warfare, and counterterrorism.

I would also like to express my gratitude to the following authors and their published works, from which I also drew in co-writing this book: *The Hunt for Bin Laden* by Robin Moore; *Terrorism* by John Pynchon Holms with Tom Burke; *Special Forces* by Tom Clancy and John Grisham; *First SEAL* by Roy Boehm and Charles W. Sasser; *Counterterrorism in Modern Warfare* by Daniel Marston and Carter Malkasian; *Delta Force* by Colonel Charlie A. Beckwith and Donald Knox;

Guerrilla Strategies by Gerard Chaliand; *Encyclopedia of Navy SEALs* by Charles W. Sasser; *SEAL Team Six* by Howard E. Wasdin and Stephen Templin; *Bay of Pigs* by Peter Wyden; *Thirteen Days* by Robert F. Kennedy; *Pieces of the Game* by Colonel Charles W. Scott; *Killer Elite* by Michael Smith; *60th Anniversary of Special Forces*, where I drew in particular on my chapter, "The History of Special Forces"; *Combat Swimmer* by Captain Robert A. Gormly; *The Man Who Killed Osama bin Laden* by Jacob Gleam; *No Easy Day* by Mark Owen; *Shadow Warrior* by Felix I. Rodriguez and John Weisman; *Requiem in the Tropics* by Jack Cox; *An American Life* by Ronald Reagan; *Navy SEALs: Their Untold Story* by Dick Couch and William Doyle; *Rogue Warrior* by Richard Marcinko and John Weisman; *Shadow Warriors* by General Carl Stiner and Tony Koltz; *Iran-Contra Affair* by *The New York Times*; and *Brave Men Dark Waters* by Orr Kelly.

Actual names are used throughout except in those rare instances where names were lost due to either lack of memory or lack of documentation, where privacy is requested, or where public identification would serve no useful purpose and might cause embarrassment.

In various instances dialogue and scenes have necessarily been re-created. Time has a tendency to erode memories in some areas and selectively enhance it in others. Where re-creation occurs, we strive to match personalities with the situation and the action while maintaining factual content. The recounting of some events may not correspond precisely with the memories of all involved. In addition, all data has been filtered through the authors. We must therefore apologize to anyone omitted, neglected, or somehow slighted in the preparation of this book. We take responsibility for such errors and ask to be forgiven for them.

While we may have made interpretational mistakes, we are assured that the content of this book is accurate to the spirit and reality of all the brave men who participated in the events described in it. Our objective was to present a true account of one man's selfless duty to country and to his fellow warriors.

CHARLES W. SASSER

PREFACE

I'M EIGHTY-FOUR YEARS OLD and no longer able to run the missions. It's May 2, 2011. I received a telephone call from a contact at the Pentagon. Some people from the old days still remember me.

"Bone," the caller said. "You're going to want to be in on this. Stay by the phone. I'll call back and let you know how it comes out."

"Bone" is a nickname from a different time. It started at Bullis School, where I played football. I don't recall exactly, but "Bone," I think, is a contraction of "Hambone" or "Bone Crusher." I was a big kid and I hit hard and often.

I'm waiting. Waiting for that call back. Wondering what the hell my guys have got themselves into this time. I know one thing, always. You can depend on them, depend on them to kick ass and get a job done. I helped make them that way.

* * *

Halfway around the globe, twin Blackhawk helicopters—"stealth" versions with sharp "Transformer" angles to deflect enemy radar—slide over the crests of the Sarban Hills and ride black after-midnight downdrafts toward a scattering of lights flung across the bowl-like Orash Valley. Abbottabad, Pakistan.

"Three minutes!"

The alert warning crackles through the two troop compartments. Two dozen U.S. Navy SEALs from DEVGRU (Special Warfare Development Group, better known as SEAL Team Six) grip weapons, adjust night vision goggles, check equipment. They tap each other on the shoulders or helmets and receive a muted "hoo-yah" in response. They have trained and rehearsed for this special mission these past weeks using mock-up compounds back in the States and then at the staging area on Bagram Air Base in Afghanistan.

"Go" had been ordered by highest authority, the president of the United States. Within the next hour, if everything goes according to plan, al Qaeda's Osama bin Laden, the FBI's Most Wanted Terrorist, with a $25 million bounty on his head, the mastermind behind the 9/11 attack on America, sought by a dozen other countries for international crimes, will be reaching room temperature.

Chief Petty Officer Robert "Rob" O'Neill, thirty-four, is a member of the "kill" element. Like every other SEAL on the mission, he is a seasoned veteran who served two previous combat tours in Iraq and participated in more than four hundred missions, including the rescue of the hijacked crew of the *Maersk Alabama* from Somali pirates in 2009.

"The more we trained on it," O'Neill would say later, "the more we realized . . . this is going to be a one-way mission. We're going to go and we're not coming back. We're going to die when the house blows up . . . when he blows up."

SEALs expect the house to be possibly wired with explosives.

"Or," O'Neill said, "we are going to be there too long and we'll get arrested by the Pakistanis and we're going to spend the rest of our short lives in a Pakistan prison. [But] it's worth it to kill him. He's going to die with us."

* * *

My phone jangles inside a residence in a gated community at Virginia Beach even as the airborne element of *Trident Spear* streaks out of Pakistan with bin Laden's bullet-mangled corpse aboard. It's the call I'm expecting.

"Bone," a voice says. "Bone, your SEALs did it. *They did it!*"

NIGHT FIGHTER

CHAPTER ONE

MEMORIAL STADIUM AT THE U.S. Naval Academy, Annapolis, Maryland, erupted with throaty cheering as eight hundred newly graduated midshipmen sprang to our uniformed feet and flung hats—*covers*, in Navy parlance—high into the air. It was a tradition at the academy; tradition in the U.S. Navy is a tradition itself. The storm of caps caught the June sun above Chesapeake Bay like a roiling summer cloud.

Midshipmen hats rained back to earth to be claimed by younger siblings, girlfriends, and proud parents, who snatched them joyfully out of the air for keepsakes or, in the case of younger siblings, for the traditional dollar or two tucked into their linings. Warren S. Parr Jr. and I made our way toward the stands where his family had joined mine and were all on their feet with the rest of the noisy stadium. At twenty-one years old, I was probably topped out to my max height at six-four, which meant I towered over most of my peers in the graduating class of 1949.

My roommate Parr was several inches shorter, with eyes almost black, an aftershave shadow he had to scrape down to blood in order to pass inspection, and a perpetual mocking grin. Twenty-six years earlier, my dad and Parr's had undergone this same rite of passage when they graduated from Annapolis. Hamilton Sr. and Parr Sr. had been roommates in 1923. Old blocks and chips, Parr Jr. called us.

Commodore William Hamilton Sr. was a pioneering naval aviator and a squadron commander in the South Pacific prior to and at the beginning of World War II. He was pulling a command tour at Fleet Air Wing in London when Ambassador Joe Kennedy's aviator son, Joe Jr., was shot down in a bombing mission over Germany. It was Dad's duty to inform the ambassador of his son's disappearance. Dad was still in England when the dropping of atom bombs at Hiroshima and Nagasaki ended the war.

In the stands someone had caught the cap with my name in it. I had tossed it in the direction of my little brother, Frank, who was sixteen. He finally ended up with it after an exchange of prisoners. As Parr Jr. and I made our way toward our families, I tried to consider what Dad might be thinking were he able to be here today.

Three things I had grown up with, being the son of a seafaring man—war, the sea, and Dad's frozen seawater countenance. The Navy had made us a gypsy family. I barely got settled in one school when the old man got orders for somewhere else. Even before I reached high school, I attended grammar schools in Coronado, Norfolk, Long Beach, Jacksonville, and Cristobel in the Canal Zone.

I completed my last two years of high school at Greenbrier Military Academy, a boarding school in Lewisburg, West Virginia. It was the longest period I had ever spent at any one school.

"Where do you want to attend college?" my old man had asked.

I didn't have to think about it. The old man had already made up my mind for me. "Annapolis, the Naval Academy," I said.

Dad nodded solemnly the way he did. Mom looked concerned. "Are you sure that's what you want to do, honey?"

All through my growing up, Dad was that stern stranger who seemed to pop up from time to time between sea duty. He was a good man, I knew that, even perhaps a great man. But it was Marjorie, my mom, who reared us kids, who taught me how to swim, how to cook, reviewed our report cards, and dished out punishment when rambunctious boys deserved it.

More than Frank, I took after Dad in looks and temperament. When I made up my mind about something, I was bound to do it, come hell or high water.

"Yeah, Mom. I'm going to Annapolis."

I graduated Greenbrier at sixteen, too young for Annapolis. Dad sent me to a one-year Naval Academy prep school at Bullis in Silver Springs, Maryland, where I chased girls, played football, earned my "Bone" nickname, and generally got into mischief. The only thing that saved me was good grades and Mom's urging school officials to "crack down" on me.

I left Bullis for the Naval Academy in 1945, just as Adolf Hitler and Eva Braun were committing suicide in a Berlin bunker and nuclear tests were being conducted in Nevada preparatory to dropping "the Bomb" on Japan.

"There will always be wars and rumors of wars," Dad predicted. It was in the Bible. "A military career is always a good bet. Wars will be different but also the same—only getting more brutal with time and technology."

That stuck with me—the part about wars getting more brutal with time. Perhaps even to the point that technology like the atom bomb would wipe out humankind.

Somewhere along the way between childhood and early youth, I developed a fascination with the emergence of what was known as "guerrilla warfare." Perhaps the old man planted the seed with his talk about Tito's guerrillas in Yugoslavia, American major Bob Lapham, who led guerrillas against the Japanese in the Philippines, General Wingate's exploits in Burma. . . .

"Men will have their wars," Dad said. "But we don't have to wipe out whole cities and kill everybody back two generations in doing it. What we can do is choose up sides and send guerrillas out to some godforsaken place nobody wants anyhow and let them kill each other off for us."

"Like Roman gladiators?" I said.

"And may the best men win."

Between the school year while I was still at Greenbrier, I landed a summer job helping construct the foundation for a radar tower from which to spot German U-boats that prowled the Atlantic coast off the United States. Whenever I took a break to wipe sweat and arch my aching back, I gazed out to sea across the rollers marching in from the Gulf Stream. I scanned for periscopes or sharklike shapes lurking beneath the surface.

Once when Dad came home on leave from fighting in the South Pacific, he told me about new units called Underwater Demolition Teams (UDTs) and swimmers who referred to themselves as "Frogmen." I read an account from the American Civil War about a man who must have been the first American Frogman. On the night of October 23, 1864, Navy Commander William Cushing led a daring commando raid to sink the Confederate ironclad CSS *Albemarle*, which dominated the Roanoke River. Raiders sent the ironclad to the bottom, although they blew up their own boat in the process. Two of Cushing's men drowned and eleven were captured. Cushing swam ashore and hid out until he was able to steal a small skiff to complete his escape.

Why couldn't commandos also be used against submarines? It was a far-out idea, I conceded that, but still, there had to be unconventional methods of dealing with conventional threats.

At Annapolis, my mind turned down other avenues while my classmates pondered conventional naval tactics of position and counter-position, beach assaults and mass fleet tactics. I read about Merrill's Marauders, the Swamp Fox and Leathernecks of the Revolutionary War, Devil's Brigade, the OSS, and, of course, the Alamo Scouts, Rangers, and UDTs. I imagined small bands of trained "special warriors" able to command earth's elements—sea, land, air—as they infiltrated enemy positions, rescued POWs and hostages, blew up enemy command posts, sank enemy submarines, assassinated terrorists. . . . Any damned thing.

"Bone? *Bone?*"

Parr shook me. We were at our desks that evening studying when I found myself staring into space.

I looked at him. "What do you want, asshole?"

That was how best buddies talked to each other.

"So the Prodigal Son is dreaming of launching himself into the world to seek adventure, fame, and fortune? Bone, you know you're sometimes more like Don Quixote than Admiral Farragut?"

"You're saying I'm jousting windmills thinking they're giants?"

"All that's missing is the Lady Dulcinea and a fat man on a jackass."

"That makes you either the fat man or the jackass."

So now fresh ensigns were leaving Bancroft Hall to meet the challenges of the fleet. World War II and the Great Depression were over, the Cold War began after Winston Churchill dubbed the Soviet Union's communist isolation an "iron curtain," and America was on a roll. The economy was booming and folks were ready to kick up their heels and get back to the good times like in the Roarin' Twenties.

President Harry Truman and his "Fair Deal" Program were in the White House after President Roosevelt died in office. In this year of 1949, the first Volkswagen Beetle arrived in the United States, the B-50 Superfortress *Lucky Lady II* made the first nonstop around-the-world airplane flight, NATO was formed in Europe, and the "Red Scare" unsettled the nation.

Albert the Monkey became the first primate shot into space, "Tokyo Rose" was convicted of broadcasting propaganda for Japan during the war, *Hopalong Cassidy* aired on NBC-TV as the first western, Los Angeles received its first recorded snowfall, the last American troops from World War II pulled out of Korea, and Grady the cow got stuck inside an Oklahoma silo.

Over below the bleachers at Memorial Stadium, a group of graduates minus their covers struck up "Navy Blue and Gold," the Naval Academy's alma mater.

Four years together by the bay where Severn joins the tide,
And by the service called away we scatter far and wide.
But still when two or three shall meet and old tales be retold,
From low to highest in the fleet, we'll pledge the Blue and Gold.

The Hamiltons and Parrs waited for Warren and me in the bleachers, Mom wiping her eyes and Frank waving with both hands, one of which clutched my cover. Dad would have been proud of me, whether he was here or not. I could almost see the softening of the lines in his face that made all my academic efforts worthwhile.

As Parr and I worked our way through the wildly celebrating cadets to join our folks, the heavy thunder of an aircraft engine stopped us. Out over the bay, the Academy's N3N open cockpit seaplane labored low over the water, its gray-blue fuselage and wings gleaming in the sun. The Academy used it in aviation familiarization for midshipmen inclined toward becoming pilots.

"I suppose you're following your old man's webbed feet into naval aviation?" Parr said. "You're going to be a flyer, right?"

The seaplane dropped a wing and turned back toward the upper end of the bay. I watched it until it swept out of sight.

"Yeah," I said. "Time to give up the windmills and go to work in the real world."

CHAPTER TWO

A s REQUESTED ON MY "dream sheet," I received orders on June 30, 1949, for preflight training at Naval Air Station, Pensacola, Florida. Parr elected to go with the fleet. The next time I saw him he would be riding a destroyer off Korea in 1952.

By this time, the Cold War, the standoff between communism and what we in the West termed the "Free World," was into its fourth year. The USSR called off its blockade of West Berlin in May 1949, after nearly a year—during which time the only access the U.S. had to the divided city was by air. America might be on a roll, but the rest of the world was jittery, as though countries were anticipating something dark and uncertain lurking in the future.

"It won't be long until the Russkies have the Bomb," the Admiral predicted. Dad had his sources. "We should have listened to George Patton and taken out the Soviets while we had the upper hand. We wouldn't be in the crap we're in now if we'd dropped Little Boy on Moscow."

In August 1945, I was a first-year plebe at Annapolis, a tall, gawky kid with big ears and blue eyes exactly one week away from my eighteenth birthday when the world entered the nuclear age. A senior engineering instructor came into the classroom wearing dress whites, gold braid, and a constipated expression.

Warren Parr leaned across the aisle toward me. "Maybe Commander Murdock ought to loosen his tie and his belt," he whispered.

Rumors had been circulating through Bancroft Hall since early that morning. It seemed Commander Murdock was about to confirm them; he was dressed for a formal announcement. The classroom fell dead silent as the commander unfolded the morning's *New York Times* and, without preamble, read a statement issued by President Harry Truman:

> Sixteen hours ago an American airplane dropped one bomb on Hiroshima and destroyed its usefulness to the enemy. That bomb had more power than 20,000 tons of TNT. It had more than two thousand times the blast power of the British "Grand Slam," which is the largest bomb ever yet used in the history of warfare. . . .
>
> It is an atomic bomb. It is a harnessing of the basic power of the universe. The force from which the sun draws its power has been loosed against those who brought war to the Far East. . . . We are now prepared to obliterate more rapidly and completely every productive enterprise the Japanese have above ground in any city. We shall destroy their docks, their factories, and their communications. . . . If they do not now accept our terms, they may expect a rain of ruin from the air the likes of which has never been seen on this earth.

I called Mom as soon as I could; it took me about an hour to get through to Norfolk. All the lines were tied up by relatives of sailors, soldiers, Marines, and airmen telephoning around trying to pick up some news about their loved ones in the Pacific.

"Your dad is in London, last I heard," Mom reported.

"He wasn't flying?"

"I rang Buck at the Pentagon. He told me there were no reports of U.S. casualties. Don't worry, darling. Your dad's a tough old bird. You'll be just like him."

Japan announced her surrender after one more bomb and my eighteenth birthday. Germany had capitulated on May 8. World War

II was over. The Admiral and all the other "boys" would be coming home.

I later looked upon the construction of the atom bomb and its employment against Japan as a major influence in developing my viewpoint on limited war. Dropping "the Bomb" was necessary in order to save American lives that would be lost in an invasion of Japan, including possibly the life of my own father. Still, as the Cold War advanced into a bomb-rattling standoff between the "Iron Curtain" countries and the "Free World," I began to consider the threat of nuclear war too awful to contemplate.

"There must be an alternative," I insisted to Parr and some of our midshipmen buddies. "There *has* to be."

Parr shrugged. "Like the *super* warriors you're always talking about?"

"So the alternative is for nations to go around killing off each other to let God sort 'em out?"

Call me a softie, but I was profoundly touched by accounts of how children, women, and the elderly suffered at Hiroshima and Nagasaki. The two bombs killed about 130,000 people, a toll almost incomprehensible in only two explosions. A piece I read about Toshika Saeki personalized that number, brought it down to where you could imagine something like that happening to your mother or your aunt, your girlfriend, sister, or wife if circumstances had been reversed and Japan and Germany got the Bomb first.

Toshiko Saeki lived on the outskirts of Hiroshima with her children while her husband, like husbands in the United States, was away fighting. She looked up and saw two enemy airplanes flying so high over the city that no anti-aircraft guns fired on them.

"There came a flash of light. I can't describe what it was like. . . . I lay flat on the ground, trying to escape from the heat. I forgot all about my children for a moment. Then, there came a big sound, sliding wooden doors and windows were blown off into the air. I turned around to see what had happened to the house, and at one part of the ceiling, it was hanging in the air. At some parts, the ceiling was caved in, burying my sister's child and my child as well."

Thirteen of her family members were killed instantly.

"I couldn't identify people by their faces. Trying to find my family, I had to take a look at their clothing. . . . I couldn't find any of my family, so I went to the playground. There were four piles of bodies and I stood in front of them. . . . If I tried to find my beloved ones, I would have to remove the bodies one by one."

Reaction in America to the devastation was mixed. Most accepted it as necessary, a human anomaly that ended the war, saved lives, and would never be used again. Others became frightened and uneasy about their personal fortunes and mankind's ultimate fate.

"It looks as if humanity is moving inexorably toward Armageddon and into the limbo of forgotten things," they said. "An oblivion of our own making . . . and this time destiny plays for keeps."

Others were more optimistic. "This menace can turn into the most powerful deterrent to future wars of aggression."

No one was even thinking of such consequences in October 1941, two months before Pearl Harbor, when President Franklin Roosevelt approved a crash program to develop an atomic bomb. Scientists had already discovered the secret of fission and the power it unleashed. Roosevelt appointed Brigadier General Leslie R. Groves Jr. director of what became known as the Manhattan Project. Groves in turn selected a brilliant theoretical physicist from the University of California, Berkeley, to head the project's secret weapons lab. J. Robert Oppenheimer was thirty-eight years old, emaciated at 125 pounds, and had a chronic cough.

Three years later, on July 16, 1945, he oversaw the world's first test explosion of an atom bomb. Brigadier General Thomas Farrell was among 425 observers who waited for code-name "Trinity" to go off in the predawn of the Jornada del Muerto desert on the Alamogordo Bombing Range in New Mexico. The desert's name, ironically, can be translated as "Journey of Death."

Farrell waited with Oppenheimer in the control bunker during the countdown.

"Doctor Oppenheimer," he recalled, "grew tenser as the last seconds ticked off. He scarcely breathed. He held on to a post to steady himself. For the last few seconds, he stared directly ahead and then when the announcer shouted 'Now!' and there came this tremendous burst of light followed shortly thereafter by the deep growing roar of the explosion, his face relaxed into an expression of tremendous relief. The damned thing actually worked!"

"Trinity" exploded with the equivalent of twenty kilotons of TNT. It left a crater in the desert five feet deep and thirty feet wide. People felt the shock wave over a hundred miles away as the mushroom cloud, which soon became the symbol of mankind's doom, rose to a height of seven and a half miles.

"The whole country was lighted by a searing light with the intensity many times that of the midday sun," Farrell said. "It was golden, purple, violet, gray and blue. It lighted every peak, crevasse, and ridge of the nearby mountain range with clarity and beauty that cannot be described but must be seen to be imagined."

Oppenheimer's reaction became gravely famous: "We knew the world would not be the same. A few people laughed, a few people cried. Most people were silent. I remembered the line from the Hindu scripture, the *Bhagavad Gita*. Vishnu is trying to persuade the Prince that he should do his duty and, to impress him, takes on his multi-armed form and says, 'Now I am become Death, the destroyer of worlds.'"

Nazi Germany might well have dropped the first bomb on the Allies had the timeline been somewhat altered. In 1939, only months after the discovery of nuclear fission, Hitler approved a clandestine scientific effort to develop atomic weapons. The war might well have ended quite differently had not events turned against him before his program matured.

Russia likewise had entered the nuclear race. Only five months after Pearl Harbor and America's entry into the war, a Soviet nuclear physicist named Georgy Flyorov wrote a letter to Josef Stalin warning him that the U.S., Britain, and Canada were conducting scientific research on the atom, the results of which "will be so overriding [that] it won't be necessary to determine who is to blame for the fact that this work has been neglected in our country."

Stalin launched a Soviet program of his own to build a weapon, which proved initially unsuccessful. At the end of the war, allies began scrambling all over Austria and Germany to identify and exploit

Germany's nuclear research. The United States and Britain brought 1,500 scientists, technicians, and engineers to the West to continue their work. Stalin did the same sort of "requisitioning" for the Soviet Union.

Aided by his seizure of Nazi scientists and by a communist spy ring operating inside the Manhattan Project, and spurred on by desperation in the wake of Hiroshima and Nagasaki, Stalin quietly accelerated his research and development. Military nuclear reactors and research facilities sprouted up all over the USSR. United States intelligence warned that the Soviets were on the verge of a breakthrough that could upset the balance of Cold War power and threaten all mankind well into the future.

Dad said World War III would last less than thirty days.

By now I had begun the twenty-two-week primary training program for naval pilots at Naval Air Station, Pensacola, the successful completion of which led on to training in props, helicopters, or jets, the latter of which were just coming online in numbers.

NAS Pensacola was my first active duty station. It was just as I remembered it from when I was a kid bouncing around all over the Navy following Dad: white-painted World War II barracks, classroom buildings, hangars, and other construction, all seemingly presided over by lawned BOQ quarters and stately officers' and senior enlisted family housing on North Avenue, some of which had been built shortly after the Civil War. Everything was clean and orderly and dress-right-dress squared. The sun reflected off the wings of trainer aircraft as advanced students made touch-and-gos or practiced carrier landings on the runways. Everything was as bright as the Florida sun in the aspirations of young naval aviators at the start of our careers.

Ground school came first. Actual flying followed later. We future aviators filled our days in classroom studies of engineering, aerodynamics, air navigation, aviation physiology, basic instruments. . . . In little groups, like chicks trailing after a mother hen, we gathered around our instructor and the blue-gray stubby SNJ trainers on nearby Whiting Field and went over pre-flight and start-up procedures. We were even allowed to *sit* in the cockpit and buckle in. I lifted my head so I saw nothing but sky through the top of the canopy and pretended I was soaring at 10,000 feet, patrolling for bogies. *Ace* Hamilton, fighter pilot.

The United States had no active enemy at that moment, a condition of relative peace in a world pausing to catch its breath after the latest championship bout. Such a state wouldn't last long if the Admiral was right—and he was always more right than wrong. War, not peace, was the natural condition of mankind.

I chafed to get on with it and move out into the fleet and test my wings on an aircraft carrier. Mom always said I had the patience of a hungry vulture: "Patience, hell! Let's go *kill* something!"

For me it had to be jets.

Evenings, some of us got together after study time and caroused over to the O Club to sip a sud or two, smoke cigarettes, and trade scuttlebutt. Classmate Lieutenant (junior grade) "Rico" Rifkin and I hit the books until after dark on August 28, 1949, a date memorable in that it was the night before the world changed again, even more significantly than it did after Fat Man and Little Boy fell on Japan.

Rifkin knocked on my door. "Let's go, Bone Head. I hear a beer calling your name."

The night was exceptionally warm, the dog days of summer when the snowbirds up north stayed home and waited for the weather to cool before their annual migration to Florida to lie on the beaches, sip mint juleps, and complain about high taxes.

A first-phaser named Collins joined us. He was a wide-shouldered kid with black cropped hair and a temper to go with his crooked nose. We discovered the O Club full of second-phase students training to become helicopter pilots.

"Bus drivers," Collins sneered loud enough to be overheard.

One of the chopper trainees took umbrage and swaggered over to our table. "Who you calling a bus driver, asshole?"

Rico was a little shorter than I, lanky, and long-armed. A challenging grin crossed his face as he and Collins pushed back their chairs and slowly stood up. I dropped my chin on my chest. "Oh, shit!"

I rose to my feet as two or three other bus drivers pushed around the table.

Collins's lip curled, which made the crook in his nose even more pronounced. "*Real* men light their afterburners," he said. "Our *grandmothers* drive helicopters."

The confrontation among "officers and gentlemen" might have turned into a healthy brawl had not the bar manager called the Shore Patrol. I probably would not have remembered the incident at all except the next day was the day the Soviet Union tested its first implosion-type nuclear device and amped up the stakes by becoming the second power to obtain the Bomb.

Chapter Three

Aircraft carrier USS *Valley Forge* (CV-45) rolled gently in the Sea of Japan off the Korean Peninsula. A red sun rising flamed through thin morning mist that left dew on the canopy of my F9F Panther fighter jet as a deck crew hooked me to the catapult cable and I sucked it up for the launch. I had received my wish out of flight school—jets. In plenty of time for Korea.

I was still training in jets when North Korea invaded South Korea in a mass surprise attack on June 25, 1950, that turned the peninsula into the first hot clash of the Cold War and a testing ground of will between the Iron Curtain and the Free World. Resolution 82 authorized the United Nations to assist South Korea in repulsing the action. President Harry Truman selected General Douglas MacArthur, the aging World War II commander of U.S. Pacific Forces, to lead the UN command. Within three months, he landed at Inchon and pushed the NKs back to the Pusan Peninsula, from which they had launched.

On November 24 he flew the front lines in his C-54 Skymaster. What he saw concerned him greatly. The entire line, he informed President Truman, was "deplorably weak."

China entered the fray the next day, mass-attacked, and drove UN forces into full retreat all the way back to Seoul. The Soviet Union supported the counteroffensive with war supplies—and with the threat of "First Lightning," the nuclear bomb it had developed and tested fifteen months before.

Each side had its finger poised on the nuclear trigger.

Joint Chiefs of Staff (JCS) Chairman General J. Lawton Collins requested from MacArthur a list of possible targets inside the Soviet Union to strike in the event Stalin should actively enter the war. In April 1951, JCS drafted orders authorizing MacArthur to use nuclear weapons against Manchuria and the Shantang Peninsula if the Chinese launched airstrikes from those locations. At the same time, President Truman arranged to transfer nine Mark 4 nuclear bombs from the U.S. Atomic Energy Commission to military control. A nuclear war with China and the Soviet Union became a very real option.

If two such weapons could destroy entire cities and wipe out tens of thousands of people, as at Hiroshima and Nagasaki, what might an exchange of hundreds of such weapons do?

Still, MacArthur warned, the Free World must not back down, regardless of consequences. "The communist conspirators have elected to make their play for global conquest," he wrote in a letter to Truman. "If we lose the war to communists in Asia, the fall of Europe is inevitable. Win it and Europe most probably would avoid war and yet preserve freedom. . . . We must win. There is no substitute for victory."

I had so far lived much of my young life under war clouds of varying density—vicariously through Dad, as a bystander while atomic bombs were developed and used, as a student during the first uneasy peace of the Cold War. And now I was right in the middle of it, flying war planes and getting my hands dirty along with everyone else.

As a kid I made bean flips—slingshots—out of forked branches and strips of tire inner tube with which to shoot stones at squirrels and birds—and the windows of crotchety old Mrs. Parnell who lived next door when we were stationed at Norfolk. Being launched off a flight deck in an airplane was a lot like being the stone shot from a bean flip.

I caught my breath as the catapult slung my airplane down the deck. Momentum sucked me back into the seat. The engine throbbed with power that vibrated throughout the Panther and my helmeted body. The sleek craft, nearly the same deep blue hue as the ocean, sank off the end of the flattop, but lifted almost immediately with its engine afterburner growling as I raised the nose and streaked into the sky, heading on a bearing north toward the Pusan Peninsula and MiG Alley.

I glanced over my shoulder from inside the pressurized all-around-vision canopy as the carrier and her destroyer escorts receded to toy boats bobbing on calm water.

"See you soon, Elinor," I recited jauntily for good luck. Combat pilots all had their little rituals or tokens that we hoped helped keep us safe. *See you soon, Elinor*, was mine.

I had married Elinor McHale in San Diego only months before I shipped out with VC-61 for Korea. I tried to warn her, God knows I did, tried to warn her hard, that Navy life was no life for a woman. How many times during my "Navy brat" youth had I watched Mother standing at dockside with tears welling in her eyes as Dad went to war, never knowing if he would return alive?

Sweet little Elinor with the long luxurious hair, only twenty-one years old and standing at her first dockside with Mom and Dad as I departed on my way by troop transport to the Philippines, where I would link up with *Valley Forge*. Tears fell. I even had to bat them back myself. But we were in love, and Elinor was poetic and philosophical about it.

"Love has to be seized like a fragile bird before it flies away," she recited. "Or before it dies."

"Don't worry," I reassured her. "I won't be in direct combat."

I kissed her hard. Then I turned and walked away and forced myself not to look back. Not even at poor Mom, who had gone through this so many times before.

Direct combat depended upon interpretation. VC-61 (Composite Squadron 61) was a reconnaissance outfit operating off a carrier. Attached Panthers went out scouting, generally alone, unarmed except for cameras mounted in their noses with which to catch images of roads, bridges, railroad tracks, troop concentrations, movements, and other possible targets and strategic locations for the benefit of war planners. This ability to spy downward on the enemy provided the UN alliance a major advantage in fighting and defeating the Red NKs.

Aerial recon aircraft confronted the same missiles, anti-aircraft ground fire, and the occasional bogie as *real* fighters. The difference was that fighters could shoot back. Our only defense was to *run*. Run and evade.

Dangerous business either way. During this autumn of the second year of the war, Naval Air Group Five, to which VC-61 was temporarily attached, lost twenty-seven airplanes and eleven pilots.

"It's a hell of a way to fight a war," my sometimes-wingman, Lieutenant "Tex" Baker, liked to say in his big Texas drawl, "but, damn, man, it's the only war we got."

Valley Forge disappeared in mist and distance as I punched the Panther out through haze that dissipated as I approached Pusan. Yellow bands of sunlight splashed across terrain below that resembled green-and-brown construction paper crushed in the hand of a giant. I kept a sharp eye peeled for bogies and for dam construction on a river that Operations wanted photographed.

I suddenly became aware that I might not be alone in the sky: a sixth-sense feeling stimulated by a flitting, winged shape in the clouds. Like a prowling shark hunting prey on a shadowy ocean reef.

Adrenaline surged as I scanned the surrounding cloud-mottled skies, head rotating, eyes darting as the Panther screamed through another slash of cloud at nearly 600 mph. Even though I was looking for the bogie, the silver MiG nonetheless surprised me as it flashed into sight at my nine o'clock and below at a distance of less than a mile. It closed fast into cannon range.

Heart pounding, I poured in power and nosed into a shallow dive, pushing the sleek blue bird to its max. The MiG latched on and opened up with a burst of cannon fire. Tracers snapped past my canopy.

Panther pilots had outflown and outmaneuvered MiGs before, had claimed a number of kills without a single loss of our own. Those were our *fighters*. I could get this sonofabitch now if I could kill with a camera. Poor Mom, and Elinor, were going to miss me.

The MiG zipped underneath, a shimmer of silver, and executed a sweeping turn for another pass. I nosed into a steeper dive to attain more speed. My teeth clacked from vibration as the aircraft exceeded its limitations, wings clattering. It seemed a matter of which I lost first—my teeth or my wings.

A pilot could live without his teeth.

The MiG made another run, guns blasting. Rounds snapped into the Panther's rear fuselage.

I pulled G's in a deceptive, gut-wrenching climb to the left. The MiG lost speed. I threw in the coal and streaked through the sky in a deep plunge toward the blue of the Sea of Japan and my mouse's hole aboard *Valley Forge*. I doubted the commie pilot would follow into a certain barrage of anti-aircraft fire from our destroyers.

Valley Forge's nickname, *Happy Valley*, had never seemed so appropriate. I bounced once and glued the bird to the deck to tailhook the arresting cable. A landing aboard a carrier was never much more than a controlled crash. The Panther pulled up hard on the cable, thrusting me forward in the harness before movement curtailed. I noticed my hands shaking.

Tex Baker was below decks in the pilots' ready room debriefing his own flight when he heard my radio exchange about the bogie. He met me on deck while I was inspecting a bullet hole through my horizontal stabilizer.

"Damn!" he cracked. "The bastards are shooting at us out there! It just ain't fair when all we want to do is take their pictures."

My hands stopped shaking and my breath returned to normal. I spotted a bunch of ratty-looking seafarers on the fantail as we made our way to the ladder leading below decks. Tex said they had just come aboard after being extracted from a mission on the North Korean mainland. They were awaiting further transport to their mother ship, a high-speed APD transport located in the flotilla to the south.

"Aren't we lucky, pard?" Tex drawled. "While we're up there in the wild blue yonder comfy in our clean pressurized bubbles, these guys are down here rooting around in the mud behind enemy lines blowing up shit and scaring the snot out of us Glamour Boys."

This was my first face-to-face encounter with UDT. Four of them garbed in filthy camouflage uniforms, faces blackened, armed with pistols, knives, carbines, and stubby submachine guns. They were laughing and playing grabass, as men in closely-knit units will do in relieving tension following a dangerous mission.

The sight of them instantly brought back my old fascination with naval unconventional warfare. These guys *looked* the part of night fighters, like they could go anywhere, anytime, and pull off any damned thing asked of them. At that moment I would have exchanged my F9F Panther, my last pair of clean socks, and my roadway to career success in the Navy for a chance to join them.

CHAPTER FOUR

"I N THE TEAMS YOU go places and do things most men in the world would never think about," one of the UDTs said to me before a launch arrived to rescue them from *Happy Valley*.

Tex Baker laughed. "Oh, Bone *thinks* about it."

The leader of the band looked me over. He could have been either an officer or enlisted. None of them wore rank or identification. Also, from appearance they might have been hobos, farmworkers, a gang of thieves and robbers, or the Bowery Boys.

"Bone?" The Frogman chuckled at the nickname. "*Bone*, you look crazy enough to be a Frog."

I had devoured everything I could find about UDTs and Frogmen from the time I was a little kid and Dad came home on leave from the South Pacific and told me about them. They seemed to be raw material for the super warriors my young and impressionable mind thought possible. Only after I reached Annapolis and the war ended was I able to put together their history, since most of it had been kept secret during the war.

Before World War II began, the United States Navy had no underwater capability other than hard-hat divers used principally for ship repair and salvage. Pearl Harbor and the subsequent demand for men to recon and clear beachheads led to the Scouts & Raiders—and to Lieutenant Philip Bucklew.

A muscled-up ex-football left end for the Cleveland Rams, Bucklew was a physical training instructor at Naval Station, Norfolk, Virginia, when he learned of plans to create "amphibious commandos." He volunteered immediately as a trainer, along with heavyweight prizefighter Gene Tunney. The first class of ten Scouts & Raiders recruits began in May 1942, their mission to recon landing beaches, mark obstacles and defensive construction, and guide assault troops to the beachhead.

Scouts saw their first action in November 1942. Hitler's armies, supplemented by traitorous Vichy French, had descended on North Africa like a plague of sand fleas. Americans planned to land 100,000 assault troops to drive them from North Africa and free the way for an invasion of Europe. Big Bucklew and seventeen of his Scouts & Raiders led the way.

Shortly after dark, the small band launched a Higgins boat from an offshore warship and set out silently to penetrate the Wadi Sebou River, their mission to cut cables and anti-shipping nets so American destroyers could fight their way upstream to the harbor and cover infantry moving in to seize the Port Lyautey military airfield. The team passed directly underneath the machine guns of a Vichy fort on higher ground overlooking the river.

Squalls of rain buffeted the small wooden boat and its sodden crew and, along with the darkness, cut visibility to almost zero. Groundswells from tide and wind swept the boat upriver as though it were a wild, uncontrollable carnival ride.

Red flares muted by heavy rainfall arced from the fort and burst over the boat, revealing the Scouts to machine gunners on the walls. Tracers cut through the drenched night. Scouts turned tail and retreated, their first mission as a unit ending in failure. Miraculously, they suffered not a single casualty.

Undaunted, Bucklew and his men returned the following night, this time undetected. They blew up cables supporting the anti-shipping nets and afterward fought their way back out to sea against an incoming tide. A hail of machine-gun fire from the fort drilled thirteen bullet holes in their boat. Again, none of the team was hit.

The American troop landing proved a success. The Vichy fort and the airfield surrendered.

By June 1943, having discerned a need for water demolitions against enemy beachheads, the Navy established Naval Combat Demolition Units (NCDUs), which began training next door to an old casino at Fort Pierce, Florida. Bucklew had moved his Scouts & Raiders to Fort Pierce in January. In November, six men of NCDU-11 and four Scouts were dispatched to England under Bucklew's command to begin preparations for the Normandy invasion.

Operating from small rubber boats, NCDU and Scouts spent weeks snooping the French coast, sketching and mapping it in anticipation of the pending invasion. Bucklew might be considered the first invader of German-occupied Europe after he crawled ashore one night to bring back a bucket of sand so army experts could study its capacity to support tanks and other heavy vehicles.

By D-Day in June 1944, NCDU and Bucklew's Scouts & Raiders had expanded to number several hundred men. In the predawn on the morning of the invasion, swimmers from the units, under heavy enemy fire, blew gaps in German defenses on Omaha and Utah beaches and cleared yards of the beachheads in advance of Allied landings. Of 175 NCDU and Scouts on Omaha, thirty-one were killed in action and sixty wounded. Four on Utah Beach were killed and eleven wounded.

In the meantime, the momentum toward naval guerrilla warfare continued with the activation of Amphibious Roger, a collection of NCDU and S&R volunteers to fight the Japanese in China with the Sino-American Cooperation Organization (SACO). While some Scouts trained Nationalist Chinese guerrillas, others disguised as coolies employed sampans and small steamers to survey the Yangtze River and Japanese-controlled coastlines from Shanghai to Kitchioh Wan near Hong Kong. Bucklew was involved in the operation along with preparing for the Normandy invasion. Because of his large size and his inability to speak Chinese, partisans disguised him as a slump-shouldered deaf-mute. Japanese who heard of the large-bodied American spy dubbed him "Big Slump."

Over 1,300 men ultimately trained to serve in Scouts & Raiders.

In the Pacific Theater, similar evolutions were occurring in naval special warfare, stimulated by "Terrible Tarawa" in November 1943, where inadequate invasion preparation led to the loss of more than a thousand U.S. Marines and the wounding of 2,500 others on the beachhead. Commander Draper Kauffman was assigned the responsibility of creating a blend of Scouts and NCDUs into Underwater Demolition Teams with an expanded mission. UDTs would operate more clandestinely by taking the mission underwater, a further step toward all-around, all-purpose commandos.

Training and operating out of Waimonalo Amphibious Training Base in Hawaii, UDT teams led by Kauffman participated in every major landing action in the Pacific from their first assignment to the Marshall Islands in January 1944 until the end of the war in 1945. Frogmen caused a stir wherever they appeared.

Following the successful invasion of Saipan, Kauffman and a UDT lieutenant hailed a lift on an amtrac to the sand for consultation with the landing master. A Marine stuck his head up from a foxhole and spotted the two Frogmen garbed in swimming trunks and sneakers with green stripes painted on their near-naked bodies.

"Christ, I've seen everything," he exclaimed in mock surprise. "We ain't even got the beach yet, and the tourists are already here."

Draper Kauffman's foresight may have created the Underwater Demolition Teams, but Francis Douglas Fane's insight prevented their extinction. Fane could not even swim when World War II broke out, was in fact actually afraid of water after having almost drowned as a child. He took a crash course in swimming and soon assumed command of UDT-13.

After the war ended, most of the thirty-four UDTs in service with their 3,500 swimmers were reduced to a skeleton crew of seven officers and forty-five enlisted men. While most officers with stars in their eyes moved on to "the real Navy," Commander Fane, better known as "Red" or "Red Dog" until after his hair turned white, took charge of what remained of the dying UDTs on the East Coast and fought to preserve and expand them into his vision of naval special warfare. The UDT fighting song, patterned after that of the Georgia Tech football team, was attributed partially to Fane and his struggle to build unconventional warriors.

When the Navy gets into a jam
They always call on me
To pack a case of dynamite
And put right out to sea. . . .

Out in front of the Navy
Where you really get the heat
There's a bunch of crazy bastards
Pulling off some crazy feat. . . .

"I realized," Fane preached, "that if we were going to come in, in future wars, we would have to be better prepared. I thought of working underwater all the way. Working with submersibles out of submarines. Coming in surreptitiously at night. Of being dropped by helicopters into the water. I envisioned the whole system."

His guidance had already moved UDT a long way toward forming underwater warriors of tomorrow. While I was flying Panthers off *Happy Valley*, he and UDT-3, a detachment of eleven men, were operating with the CIA out of bases in Japan. He and Lieutenant Commander Bucklew, who joined Fane from time to time, added UDT-1 and UDT-5 to make three teams and three hundred men clandestinely giving the NKs headaches in their own territory.

But the man whose path I would soon cross, and who would eventually share with me the most direct impact on the development of Navy commandos, arrived off the Korean coast a month after the war kicked off. The light cruiser USS *Worcester*, the *Wooster*, the *Big Woo*, had pulled out of Greece with orders to join the Seventh Fleet. Grizzled twenty-eight-year-old Bos'n Mate First Class Roy Boehm was in charge of the vessel's Third Division, which included half the *Big Woo*'s gun mounts.

Boehm had encountered UDTs while fighting the Japanese in the Pacific as General MacArthur's and Admiral Chester Nimitz's "island hopping" campaign proceeded toward Japan. He was immediately captivated by them. A seed began germinating in his mind—undersea warriors who could be used in a variety of ways to revolutionize warfare.

Now, a decade later and after surviving my engagement with the Soviet MiG, I stood on *Happy Valley*'s catwalk with Tex Baker and watched the tough-looking UDT men spring into a ship's launch and breeze away across the ocean. At that moment, I had no way of knowing how my destiny would become entwined with theirs and with bold and visionary men like Draper Kauffman, Phil Bucklew, Red Fane, and Roy Boehm as naval special warfare began to emerge ready and tailor-made for the twentieth and twenty-first centuries.

Korea would prove to be the turning point.

CHAPTER FIVE

I NEEDED TO GET A firsthand look at Navy commandos in action by participating in one of their missions. Linking up with the team was verboten. But with a little jockeying, I latched on with a U.S. Marine squad that went in ahead of the Frogs to set up security.

"Hellfire and dumplings, man, if you're crazy enough to fly a fucking unarmed jet into MiG Alley," the Marine captain reasoned, "I guess you're loco enough to get your butt shot off with us. If you don't come back, we'll tell your commander we never knew ye."

Tex Baker shook his head. He always looked like he should be wearing a ten-gallon hat with a grass stem stuck out of his mouth. "Bone, you are one crazy sonofabitch. So you got a bullet hole in your plane, so now you go out and get a bullet hole in *you*. What do you want me to tell your wife?"

"Tell her it was destiny."

Things weren't that hunky-dory anyhow between Elinor and me. Letters I received from my new bride sounded like she found life with a Navy pilot on deployment less glamorous than she supposed. It appeared her mama was talking to her, like Mama thought the Navy wasn't paying me enough to keep her daughter in the style to which she aspired. Wasn't much I could do about it from halfway around the globe.

The UDTs of Korea were not the same as their forerunners in the previous war, who were largely confined to the role of amphibious recon and the clearing of beachheads. Aside from Inchon, there hadn't been any beachheads in Korea to seize. As a result, their mission capabilities expanded to include activities such as demolition raids on enemy shipping and supply lines, sabotage of port and harbor facilities, clearing of sea and shipping lanes, intelligence gathering from behind enemy lines, and other classic commando- and guerrilla-like activities.

Tonight's mission was to infiltrate enemy country fifty miles north of the battle line, blow a section of train rail over which Chicoms— Chinese communists—transported troops and war materiel to the front, and then slip out again. UDTs continued to venture farther and farther from the high water line to which they were restricted during World War II.

"Contact is not only possible, but probable," the UDT commander said as his rowdy-looking bunch, along with the Marines and me, crowded into the ops room for briefing aboard their "lily pad," a high-speed transport. He was the same man who decided upon our first meeting aboard *Valley Forge* that I might be crazy enough to be a Frog.

He was lean and sharp-featured, with his face painted black and green. He wore what appeared to be the same filthy camouflage as when I first saw him. His men were likewise fierce-looking bastards, scary even, laden as they were with knives, pistols, submachine guns, and leather demo bags. He raised a brow as he studied me, the tall stranger in their midst. It was obvious that I didn't quite belong, although I had blackened my own face and borrowed a set of utilities and a boonie hat from the Marines.

"Action on objective," he said, addressing his team and Marine security, "is to get in quick, do the job, and get out quick." His eyes returned to regard me. "*Bone?* That's what they call you? You're too big to carry out. You're on your own if you get fucked up."

I couldn't tell if he meant it or not.

"Bone, you do know how to shoot?"

He handed me an M-1 carbine, short and stubby with a box magazine. I took it and pretended to know exactly what I was doing. One of the Marines handed me a full ammo belt. I buckled it around my waist.

Most pilots carried the .45 pistol as part of their standard survival gear. Otherwise, the only guns most sailors needed to be familiar with were anti-aircraft machine guns and the big cannon aboard ship. Navy brought Marines with them to do the ground fighting.

This was my first time thrust into circumstances that might entail personal combat *mano a mano*. I found a bit daunting the prospect of venturing out of my element into the dark sea where savage little men lurked to do me in if they got the chance. The cavalry was not apt to bugle in to save the day if we got caught in a jam.

I tightened my grip on the carbine. My mouth felt and tasted like a porcupine had crawled inside and taken a leak. My respect grew for those bold men who dared take such risks.

The patrol boat, with all lights extinguished, steamed north and pulled up in black waters, north of the battle line drawn across the narrow waist of the Korean peninsula. I assisted the six-man Marine security detail in lowering an inflatable boat by rope. The Marine patrol leader tapped me to go over the side of the APB into the raft. Which I did, rather clumsily. It was a bit more chancy than climbing into the stable cockpit of an F9F.

Armed with the carbine and my .45 in a web holster, I crunched into the wet bottom of the raft while two alert Marines with weapons ready rode shotgun at the prow and the other four dipped paddles into the surf for the short, silent ride to shore. White-foamed breakers shone in the dim starlight, spray hissed cold into my face, and I sniffed the rancid scent of danger.

Land appeared in a black outline wedged between the lighter sky and the sea, low near the water but rising sharply into hills beyond. I heard rollers lapping against sand and rock as Marines paddled the rubber boat through the surf. Everyone went silent and watchful. The oily snick of a Bren gun selector switch clicking off *safe* made a startling sound as the forward lookouts prepared to spring ashore.

The boat nudged land with a rubbery bump. Lookouts disappeared. The rest of us followed. Cold seawater rose to my shins as I helped drag the boat out of the water. Waves licking and splashing the rocky shore covered any sounds we made.

Among the competent night fighters I felt like a toddler taking his first steps. I merely tagged along and did what they did, dropping down among a field of boulders to listen and look with them, trying not to embarrass myself with incompetence and maybe bring down the entire Red Army on our asses.

The railroad lay about a half mile inland, according to the briefing map. That was a long damned way to run in the dark over this terrain should we make unintended contact with enemy troops. *Happy Valley* had lost several pilots forced to bail out over enemy country; now I knew how they must have felt.

One Marine remained behind with the raft to guide the Frogs ashore when they arrived. They were about two minutes back. I followed the others across the beach and through a field of short sea-grasses and into a copse of trees. Beyond, terrain rose to a low plateau bisected where rails glistened like parallel lines in the rising moonlight. A birdcall gave me a start, made me think of Old West movies in which Apaches surrounded John Wayne and communicated with each other in birdcalls just before the first arrow pierced a cavalryman's back.

Otherwise, nothing appeared to move out there. What we counted on was Chicoms, Chinese communists, not being able to guard every mile of their supply lines, and that this was one of those unguarded miles. Air recon photos from today revealed no activity in the area, a good sign.

The patrol leader fanned out target security up-track and down-track, two Marines on each point to watch for enemy approaches. They disappeared silently into the darkness. The patrol leader and I watched until he thought they were in place before he and I slipped farther uphill to obtain a high-ground view of the objective. No alien sounds or movement other than a night bird that jumped up ahead of our approach. Perhaps the same one I had heard before. He was unarmed.

I sprawled on my belly behind a rock, rifle ready, and squinted into the surrounding night, my mouth dry and my heart pounding against the sand. After what seemed at least three days but might have been only three minutes, my Marine received a predetermined signal by radio squelch. Shortly thereafter, stealthy shadows emerged from the night to our rear. UDTs passed on through to lay explosives along a section of the rails.

I waited for another eternity until the Frog team returned to retrace our steps back to the rubber boats. Security Marines closed in to cover the rear of a rather anticlimactic withdrawal.

We were on our rafts and halfway back to the APB when the sabotage explosion went off. A flashing series of detonations slashed the night sky. Fiery light reflected off our faces. Explosions rumbled through the hills, reverberating like approaching thunder.

Damn! What a rush! Men clapped each other on the back and hooted with laughter as we clambered back aboard the lily pad.

"Another kick in the Chink's drawers," the Frog commander cheered. He pounded my back. "What do you think now, Fly-Fly Boy?"

Before I had time to respond, a heavy machine gun from somewhere out there began to saw out rounds. Shooting at shadows, proving that the enemy had been present all the time, even though unseen and not confronted. It was a blow for me to accept how close the enemy had been all the time without our even knowing about it—and how close we had been to them without *their* knowing it.

* * *

Such missions were becoming standard fare for Korea-stationed Underwater Demolition Teams. While many high-ranking officers in the traditional Navy objected to the expansion, others saw it as a necessary move in the right direction.

Six weeks after the U.S. entered the war, Vice Admiral C. Turner Joy, Commander of U.S. Naval Forces in the Far East, tasked UDT-3 with its first clandestine mission to blow up a critical railroad bridge at Yosu forty-five miles behind enemy lines and about three hundred yards from the sea.

On the night of August 5, 1950, Lieutenant (JG) George Atcheson and his team in a rubber raft infiltrated from the USS *Diachenko*

(APD-123). Atcheson and Bos'n Mate Third Class Warren "Fins" Finley scout-swam ahead of the boat in swift current and scrambled up a seawall a short distance from the target to conduct a hasty recon.

Finding the area apparently secure, they signaled the rest of the team to bring in explosives. Just as the Frogs began work, a squad of North Korean soldiers pumping a railroad handcart emerged from a tunnel overlooking the bridge, spotted the intruders, and opened fire. A bullet struck Finley's thigh and knocked him off the ledge along which the rails ran. He fell twenty-five feet and shattered his kneecap to become the first U.S. Navy casualty of the Korean War.

Carrying the wounded operator with them, team members returned fire and tossed hand grenades to cover their withdrawal to the sea.

A week later, UDT-3, with Lieutenant Atcheson again in command, embarked against a second pair of tunnels and a railroad bridge at Tanchon, 160 miles up the North Korean coastline. This time the detachment succeeded in blowing up the tunnels and bridge with a ton of TNT.

By the time I reached Korea with VC-61, UDTs were in the process of acquiring all sorts of new commando tasks—inserting and handling spies, sabotaging enemy shipping, rescuing our downed airmen from behind enemy lines, destroying NK fishing nets to deprive the enemy of a major food source, prisoner snatches, hit-and-run ops. . . . Korea was changing the nature of war and the Navy was adapting.

CHAPTER SIX

S HOOTING PICTURES WAS A helluva way to fight a war. At least when I went with UDT-5 to blow the railroad I had the option of shooting back with real bullets. All I could do from the cockpit of an unarmed Panther was dodge flak, avoid and evade MiGs, and take pictures.

"I'm beginning to think I'm pushing my luck," I confided in my wing mate, Tex Baker. We were smoking and having coffee together in the galley, coming down off our afternoon missions.

Mine had been a hairy one. Exploding flak peppered the sky in a blazing panorama starting at the Sea of Japan and spreading across the Korean peninsula to the Yellow Sea. Flying through it was like dodging raindrops—or hailstones that exploded if they hit you.

"Man, this war can't last much longer," Tex drawled, blowing cigarette smoke at me across the narrow table bolted to the deck. "Stick out the tour, Bone, and we're on our way up the ladder. We'll both be admirals by the next war."

"All we have to do is stay alive and not go down with the airplane, right?"

Pilots kept failing to return from sorties. We Glory Guys launched from the flattop decks with our jaunty put-on grins and cocky salutes— and then those who *did* return waited on the catwalks and anxiously scanned the sky for those of us who did *not* return.

Commander Paul Gray of VF-94 was having a run of bad luck. He ditched three damaged Panthers at sea and crash-landed another ashore and had to be rescued. Other pilots with typical graveyard humor erected a sign in the ready room: *Use caution when ditching damaged airplanes in Wonsan Harbor. Don't hit Cdr. Gray.*

"Bone," Tex said. "You and me, we're like cats. We got nine lives."

"Cats don't fly," I pointed out.

Naval aviation was relatively new and small, but it was a rapidly growing field that promised an exceptionally bright future. It was definitely the right career path to advancement for ambitious young officers. It appeared that pilots and former pilots might dominate the upper echelon of the Navy and run it at least for the rest of the twentieth century.

"It just don't get no better than this," naval aviators cheered.

I wasn't sure about that.

"Your fresh little bride have anything to do with your new attitude?" Tex asked slyly.

"Leave her out of it."

Leaving Elinor out of it wasn't so easy.

I had met her at a private party while attending aerial photo recon training in California. Young, eligible women around naval air stations looked upon dashing young pilots as trophy catches. In full dress uniform, I sauntered into an upscale two-story residence in suburban Del Mar with several other aviators from nearby Miramar Air Station who were invited to the party by local girls. Booze flowed, cigarette smoke swirled, and the wonderful laughter of young ladies on the make was enough to swell the chest of any testosterone-stoked god of the skies.

A slight brunette with big brown eyes and an inviting smile waltzed up to me. I caught the sweetness of her scent, the lure of not-quite-cleavage not-quite-exposed by her full party dress. She wore a pink ribbon in her long hair. The top of her head barely reached my chest. She had to take a step back to look up and meet my eyes.

"You're a big one," she said admiringly. "I'm surprised they have an airplane your size."

I grinned back. "I have a pocket you'll fit in if you want to see my plane."

We were married three months before I shipped out for Korea. From the tone of her letters, the romance of being married to a naval aviator had failed to live up to her expectations.

Tex Baker shook his head with a wry look and took a big draught of coffee. "So, Bone, you think she'll like you going *under* water any more than you flying *above* water?"

"She wants me to resign my commission and leave the Navy."

"And what's your response?"

"Navy is the only thing I've known my entire life. I grew up around saltwater."

I was *born* almost on the sea in 1927 while Dad was stationed at North Island Naval Air Station, Coronado, California. Near the Naval Amphibious Base that would train UDT men for war in the Pacific. In a manner of speaking, Mom was likewise from the sea. Reared in and around San Francisco, Marjorie developed into a great swimmer who had won several swimming awards and once competed in the race across the Bay, a feat attempted only by accomplished and courageous swimmers.

Mom, unlike Elinor, was meant to be a Navy wife. She understood that a woman signs on for the Navy when she marries into it. All those years I never once heard her complain about the Admiral going to sea.

"Billy, are you sure you're doing the right thing, marrying Elinor?" Mom asked, looking concerned. "It takes a different sort of woman to be a Navy wife."

But, damn it, I was in *love*. What was that old saying about love conquering all, including, I suppose, bad breath, flatulence, and old age?

Funny, though, for all that I was almost born on the sea, I was once afraid of the water, like Doug Fane. I was wading in the surf at Naval Air Station, Pensacola, when I was three years old and something unseen brushed against my ankle and nipped me. I shrieked and fled to safety, flapping my arms like a seagull with a broken wing.

It took Mother a month to get me off the sand and into the water again. But once she got me back in, she couldn't get me out. I spent much of my free time in the sea from then on. One of Dad's old Annapolis classmates, commanding officer of the USS *Seal*, even took me for a cruise in his submarine when we were stationed at Panama. At Greenbrier and at Bullis I competed in both football and swimming.

I returned to *Happy Valley* after my first UDT mission exhilarated and with a new direction for my career. My flying buddies considered me foolish. In a letter, Elinor accused me of having completely lost my mind. Senior officers tried to dissuade me, pointing out that voluntarily changing a career path was looked upon in a negative light. Dad's letters expressed his disappointment. He couldn't understand why a young officer with a good record would consider jumping ship for a tiny nondescript outfit destined to remain underwater and metaphorically out of sight.

"For the last several months," read my last fitness report from *Valley Forge*, "this officer has noticed an uneasy feeling while flying; this has caused him to consider seriously the thought of terminating his career as a naval aviator. . . . It is conceivable that a recent change in marital status [my getting married before deployment] and the occurrence of several accidents involving [other pilots in] the F9F type aircraft have precipitated the decisions which this officer has been contemplating for some time."

Any decisions I made had little to do with flying. My mind had simply gone elsewhere, to a field that appeared more challenging. I submitted an official response for my decision: "Undoubtedly a sure aid to promotion in the present day navy is adherence to conventional career paths, but I am not entirely convinced that non-adherence precludes advancement. There must be a place in the navy for officers, although perhaps for only a few, motivated along UDT/EOD/diving lines in addition to the more conventional motivations, and I want to be one of these."

Chapter Seven

Elinor had moved in with her folks at Rancho Santa Fe, California, when I shipped out for Korea. We were actually on the same continent together for less than four months total of the first eighteen we were married. That was the way things were in the Navy. You often missed important family occasions like birthdays, anniversaries, family reunions, the birth of children. . . . I remembered the emptiness I felt—and my brother, Frank, must have felt as well—every time Dad shipped out for new ports or wars. But we always had Mother, and Mom wasn't the bitching sort. She took it in stride, and, of course, that made it easier for Frank and me.

I gave up flying in Korea, but that didn't mean I stayed home with Elinor. I requested UDT training and headed back out to sea for a year while awaiting orders—first as operations officer aboard the destroyer USS *Buckley* and then on the patrol ship USS *PCE*. Elinor met me once when the *PCE* docked in Norfolk. She traveled from the West Coast to the East Coast by airplane and bus, even though she was six months pregnant; obviously, my thirty-day postwar leave hadn't been wasted. She waited at the bottom of the gangplank among a boisterous gaggle of wives, children, girlfriends, and parents when ship's company, laughing and calling out to happy faces in the crowd, jostled our way ashore into waiting arms.

I was a full lieutenant by this time and easy enough to spot, what with my height and the new bars glinting on the shoulder boards of my dress whites. Elinor proved harder to spot, being tiny like she was and enveloped in the throng. She was also the only female, I noticed, who was not ecstatic with delight and waving her arms and shouting. That took the cocky grin off my mug.

She looked tired when she dutifully embraced and kissed me. She wore a drab-gray maternity blouse and, as though in afterthought of the occasion, a red ribbon in her hair. I put my arms around her and protectively helped her out of the crowd.

"How long's your visit this time?" she asked. "Visiting" was how she referred to our time together. "Will you be with me when the baby's born?"

"I—"

I still hadn't told her about applying for UDT.

I rented a hotel room for the week. We did all the things reunited families on shore liberty are supposed to do—like eat out and go to the movies, get together with shipmates and their families, attend a party. . . . What we didn't do was a lot of talking. I mean *real* talking, like new husbands and wives do when they're about to start having and raising children and discussing future plans.

Elinor seemed distracted, withdrawn, when we were alone together. It occurred to me that I had been unfair and selfish in marrying her. I recognized this same kind of *bitterness* in some of the other wives. Several of my fellow officers had already given up their careers in deference to their women, had moved on to Dubuque or Chicago to settle down as sales reps or corporate engineers.

I took Elinor's hand across the restaurant table. "Elinor? Elinor, we can work it out."

I owed her that much.

A tear squeezed from the corner of one big brown eye. "I-I . . . Oh, God, Bill, I'm so—"

She didn't say it. But I knew. *Unhappy*. And it was my fault.

I was out to sea when our daughter, Linda Jean, was born. But I called her on the ship-to-shore.

Shortly thereafter, I received orders for Underwater Demolition Team Replacement (UDTR) School, which included a "travel" week. I spent it getting acquainted with our new baby and reacquainted with my wife at her parents' home in Rancho Santa Fe on my way to Coronado Naval Amphibious Base, located across the bay from San Diego.

She exploded on me when I finally revealed my new duty station. She first went into that dead cold silence that you knew, just *knew*, was a short fuse burning. Then she opened up with a blistering broadside that scorched my timbers fore and aft.

"Bill, we have a beautiful little girl. Don't you know what that means? It means Linda Jean has a right to expect her father to be here with her when she takes her first step, when she goes off to kindergarten, here to give her first date the father's once-over. Not off to some war or gone to a dark corner of the world. Bill, for God's sake! We want you home with us. That's where you belong."

Was that *really* where I belonged? She knew who and what I was when she married me. I also knew who and what she was. But . . . but we had been in love.

"Honey, I'll only be down the coast from you and Linda Jean and across the bay."

I may as well have been on my way to the other side of the world. There would be no time off to see her and the baby. UDT training required that a trainee consider nothing beyond each grueling day. The outside world—Elinor and little Linda Jean, the continuing war in Korea, my Mom, Dad, Frank, all of it—must cease to exist if I was going to survive the next twelve weeks.

"I thought we were married," Elinor sobbed. "You know, husband and wife and baby makes three. But we're only ever *visiting*."

"Honey—?"

"Which comes first, Bill? Me or the Navy?"

Every good Navy career man had an answer for a question like that: "Maybe you shouldn't ask me that, babykins. Hell, darling, there's only *one* Navy."

But no good Navy career man ever actually said it if he valued his marriage.

I stood at the door as I left with a packed sea bag dragging from one hand and my face hanging out, brain locked, and balls sucked up. How could a six-four naval officer turn into a little boy when confronted by a five-three woman with a baby in her arms? For God's sake, it wasn't like I was deserting them.

"Love both of you more than anything," I murmured before I slung the sea bag on my shoulder and started to walk off.

Her shrill response stabbed me in the back. "More than *anything*? Is that all you're going to say? Is that all?"

History stretching back to the beginning of civilization was full of men who were not content to simply grow roots and moss, work a nine-to-five, and wait for a pension and grandkids. Odysseus took to the sea. So did Columbus and Magellan and the Vikings.

From childhood Dad and my brilliant mother instilled in me a strong sense of history. I was fascinated by the way history played out over time. Dad also cursed me with his sense of restlessness.

CHAPTER EIGHT

I SUPPOSE I MIGHT HAVE been tagged as one troubled young lieutenant (JG) when I alighted from the yellow cab at the gate to Naval Amphibious Base Coronado in February 1953. I stood outside the entrance with my sea bag while the cab turned around and headed back up the Silver Strand toward Coronado and San Diego.

What kind of man left his family to endure the torture of pain, fatigue, humiliation, cold and heat, and mental and physical exhaustion of the toughest training in the entire United States military? And for what? A vision of a commando force? Sounded like some pipe dream by a kid who had read too many superhero comic books.

From where I stood at the gate to the Amphib base, seeing the shimmer of the Pacific Ocean that stretched from here all the way to Asia, smelling the salt in the crisp air, feeling it in my bones and in my blood . . . I was *born* for this.

I drew in a deep breath, resigned to my destiny, and hoisted the sea bag to my shoulder. The Marine outside his little guard shack watched me. I nodded at him and produced my ID. He saluted crisply.

"Good luck, sir," he said.

I walked on through the gate.

Men, it seems, have always been drawn to the prospect of swimming with the fish and exploring the vast areas of Earth covered by water. Underwater diving can be traced back more than five thousand years. Divers were active in military exploits at least back to 500 B.C. when a Greek named Scyllias used a hollow reed as a snorkel in order to swim in undetected and cut the mooring lines of an enemy Persian fleet.

Alexander the Great, conqueror of much of what was then known as the "civilized world," was undoubtedly aware of using swimmers in battle. In 333 BC, he faced enemy combat swimmers himself after laying siege to Tyre. The city on an island managed to hold out against Alexander for seven months by attacking his shipping. Swimmers at night cut anchor ropes to smash Alexander's ships and their soldiers and sailors onto shoals and rocky shores.

Although no record exists of Alexander himself using divers in his conquests, he was nonetheless intrigued by the idea. Legend has it that he foreshadowed SCUBA—Self-Contained Underwater Breathing Apparatus—when he constructed a crude diving bell from a barrel and remained at the bottom of the sea for a full day.

While a hollow reed or a barrel allows a swimmer to submerge and still breathe, it is virtually impossible to suck air through any tube more than two feet long, and breathing in a barrel turns to deadly carbon dioxide in a very short time. Therefore, adventurers and enterprising "frogmen" over the centuries experimented with various other methods to live underwater, such as air-filled "breathing bags" or pumps on long surface-to-diver air hoses.

Besides being a master painter, Leonardo da Vinci, born in 1452, was one of the most versatile geniuses in history. His ideas and designs included a flying machine, a parachute, a diving bell, and a self-contained underwater breathing contraption that could have been a prototype of SCUBA systems invented centuries after his death.

Between 1500 and 1800, diving bells led to crude, one-man diving outfits, which eventually led to German-born Augustus Siebe developing the first practical deep-sea "hard-hat" diving suit.

In 1866, Benoit Rouquayrol designed a regulator that adjusted the flow of air from a tank to the diver, a necessary prerequisite for SCUBA. Jacques-Yves Cousteau, a French naval lieutenant, and engineer Emile Gagnon improved upon the concept in the midst of World War II by redesigning a car regulator to provide compressed air automatically to a diver upon demand. The two Frenchmen attached their demand-valve regulator to hoses, a mouthpiece, and a pair of compressed-air tanks to invent the first workable "open-circuit" demand-type SCUBA. They patented it in 1943 as the Aqua-Lung.

This simple device fundamentally altered diving and was eventually adapted for military purposes, both in its original form and "closed-circuit," which emitted no bubbles and made the approach of underwater swimmers virtually undetectable. Underwater breathing was not extensively used by UDTs until after Doctor Christian J. Lambertsen invented and tested his own form of SCUBA in 1942 while still working on his MD degree from the University of Pennsylvania.

In between the end of World War II and the start of the Korean War, Lambertsen collaborated with Commander Doug "Red Dog" Fane to keep Fane's cherished UDTs alive. His diving research and developments in oxygen and mixed-gas-circuit rebreathing for military use earned him recognition as the father of U.S. combat swimming. It was not until 1947 that the Navy's acquisition of Aqua-Lungs and Lambertsen's designs gave impetus to diving as an aspect of UDT operations.

Fane encouraged UDT deployment to new frontiers in the American peacetime fleet. Although UDT numbers had been drastically reduced postwar to a barely sustainable size, they could at various times be found working and training in the frigid waters off Point Barrow, Alaska, in the Antarctic, in the Bering Sea, off the China coast, in the Philippines, and in Latin America. Three months before the outbreak of the Korean War, a few team members took part in atomic bomb tests at Bikini Atoll.

The Korean War recorded the first use of the Aqua-Lung in combat diver operations when UDT Frogman William Giannotti dove down to locate the minesweeper USS *Pledge*, which the enemy had sunk off Wonsan Harbor. Soon, Frogmen not only became comfortable underwater but also began to leave the tracks of their webbed feet on land. By the time I reported to Coronado for UDTR, the Korean War had stalemated in the Hill Fights along the 38th Parallel and the U.S. military establishment was beginning to show more interest in using commandos in an increasingly dangerous world.

At Coronado, we UDT trainees were assigned to World War II–era Quonset huts with curved steel walls and wooden floors. Heads and showers were in separate buildings. First order of business that followed sign-in and billeting was the issuance of training uniforms and pairing off into swim buddies. Uniforms consisted of green cotton utility tops and bottoms, heavy boondocker boots, and red-painted helmet liners with the students' billet numbers painted on them. I became Billet No. 88. No name, no rank. Officers and enlisted were treated exactly the same. Everybody was a mere number.

"What's your boot size, Eighty-eight?"

"Twelve, *sir*."

"I ain't no *sir*, shithead. I work for a living."

The instructor cadre, called Black Hats, paired us off. I looked down on top of my new buddy's head—a stocky little bos'n third class with a heavy jaw that made his face look out of balance. A pair of amused brown eyes anchored a crooked, bony nose between them. Billet No. 65 was from "New *Joisey*," so "Joisey" became his nickname. Everybody had nicknames in the military. My old moniker followed me. *Bone.*

Wearing the red helmet liners was mandatory, except inside classrooms and to bed. All a student had to do to quit was take off his liner and place it on the ground. He would be out of there and back to the fleet before the sun set.

Formal classrooms lay behind our billets, but the real classroom was the ocean and the sand and the boiling-down sun. Instructor cadre were apparently selected as much for brawn as for brains. They were fit-looking specimens with broad shoulders and narrow waists who sometimes ran *backward* on long runs, not even breathing hard while they blistered us with a torrent of abuse.

"You're a bunch of puke pussies. You're slow, you're lazy, your breath stinks and you don't love Jesus. Come on, ladies, get with the program or your sorry ass is out of here. How did we ever get such a herd of worthless kikes, spics, niggers, and honkies?"

The reasoning behind it was to ride the trainees so hard that those with any quit in them at all would quit. If a man had "quit" in him, it was better it come out now.

"If you're a quitter, we don't need you in UDT," snarled the instructor we called Little Hitler. "You'd bug out when the shit came down and we really needed you."

The first month was mostly physical conditioning and harassment. Hard, pounding runs in heavy boondockers, sweaty utilities, and helmets that bounced on heads of hair skinned down to flesh. Six or eight miles at a time in formation along the surf line, carrying wet sand bags and tortured by Black Hats.

"Run, shitbirds, run, *RUN*! Are you men or pussies?"

The most minor transgression called for a penalty. Duck waddles or push-ups. "Get down. Get down. Give me fifty. Knock 'em out, shit-for-brains."

The first guy dropped out on the second day. Removed his helmet liner and he was gone. That started the exodus.

"This class will graduate in a phone booth at this rate," instructors predicted.

"Joisey," I said, "me and you will still be going strong when the rest of these pogues are gone. It takes brains and balls—and you and me have 'em. They're just testing to see if we can take the bullshit."

"I'm used to bullshit," Joisey said. "My old man's a politician."

I was wrong about officers and enlisted being treated the same. Black Hats were senior enlisted who seemed bent on proving the officer class a bunch of pussies who couldn't hack it with the Bluejackets. They came down especially hard on Academy graduates when they had a chance to make us crawl in the mud. In spite of the harsher treatment, the attrition rate among officers was lower than among the enlisted. Perhaps it was because those of us who got into Frogman training had more sand in our craws than the general run of fleet brass occupied with their fitness reports and promotions.

"You're a fucking lowlife ring-knocker, Eighty-eight, *sir*," Black Hats raved. "Lower than whale shit, flyboy. It's my personal mission, *sir*, to make you crawl. You won't be in the phone booth when what's left of this fucked-up class graduates."

"I'll be there if all that's left in it are you and me and Joisey."

"*Sir*, wipe that grin off your face. Get down! Get down! Knock 'em out."

"How many, Instructor?"

"Do 'em until I get tired, ass wipe."

I shrugged. Joisey sighed and dropped to the ground with me. Buddies did everything together. We pumped out push-ups until we were red-faced and panting.

"Reckon he's tired yet, Bone?" Joisey gasped.

Empty bunks in the Quonsets increased. Fewer and fewer trainees showed up for morning formations while red helmet liners filled up the "Quit Zone." One morning, before sunup as usual, we rushed to the beach to do our daily dozens—more like daily one hundreds—whereupon Little Hitler marched us to the main classroom instead.

"You pukes will keep your pie holes shut and listen. One of you so much as sneezes, I'll personally heave your ass in the bay and chum for sharks."

Trainees snapped to sitting attention in our seats when the NAB commander marched in and introduced a speaker. We had had lectures but rarely a *speaker*. Legendary Commander Francis Douglas "Red Dog" Fane's pale eyes sparked as he stepped briskly to the podium. He was a ruddy-faced man in his forties, of average height, with a round Scottish face, short red hair turning gray, and a thick neck bunched into muscular shoulders. He wore Navy browns minus his jacket.

"You men," he rumbled in a measured, aggressive tone, "are on the precipice of a new era in international warfare. Exciting things are happening as we enlarge our training to include not only the sea—on it and below it—but also land operations. I foresee a time in the very near future when the Frogs of UDT will become the spearhead for clandestine ops against tyranny around the world, when we will deploy to carry out missions that no other unit in the world is qualified to undertake. We are already conducting daring missions of the sort in Korea. From what I've heard"—he paused and his straight gaze stopped on me—"one or two of you may already have gone on some of these missions."

Oh, shit! Black Hats would rain down fire and brimstone on my tadpole ass if they found out about that.

Fane explained how the UDT world was changing, webbed feet developing land calluses as UDTs added elements to their arsenal and worked their way up to becoming the unconventional night fighters he had been working to create for the past decade. All kinds of new tools were appearing—closed-circuit underwater breathing, new and faster boats, "skim boats," submersibles with electric engines that pulled swimmers beneath the waves twice as fast as the swiftest Frog could swim.

An expression somewhere between pride and expectancy appeared on Fane's Irish face. His chin and eyes lifted toward the heavens.

"We now have the elements of sea and land in our repertoire bag," he said. "Next, we need to get ready for the sky."

Sea, land, and sky.

Trainees were really pumped up when we filed out of the classroom. It was on our sunburned faces. I paused at the doorway where Fane was standing, waiting for us to exit.

"Whattaya think you're doing, Eighty-eight?" Little Hitler growled. "Move! Move!"

I snapped Fane a salute. A slight grin touched the corners of his lips. He returned the salute, along with a sly wink. "See you back in Korea soon, Lieutenant Hamilton." The smile broadened. His voice lowered so Little Hitler wouldn't overhear. "This time you'll be official."

* * *

Fane's appearance marked the beginning of so-called "evolutions," each of which seemed designed to bust a trainee's ass and wash him out of the course.

The *Death Trap* consisted of two perpendicular ropes suspended horizontally fifteen feet above a muddy pond. We attempted to make our way hand over hand across the water on the ropes while explosions below shattered the air, vibrated the ropes, and splattered us with mud and water.

"If you fall down there, shitbirds, you'll come back up with the next charge of dynamite."

No one wanted to test him.

Joisey lost his grip on the *Slide for Life,* a tall wooden tower from which trainees slid on a long rope across a wide pond of stagnant water.

He plunged into the pond and came up spluttering with moss and mud dripping from his head and face.

"Try it again, Instructor? I ain't quitting."

Around the World happened in the dark with seven-man crews paddling, pushing, or carrying an IBL (Inflatable Boat, Large) over hundreds of yards of mud and sand, through barbed wire, ditches, and mud flats, across and around obstacles, racing to beat the other crews to a sea wall bordering the entrance to the bay. Joisey and I with our team came in second after our guy from Portland sprained his ankle and we had to carry him in the boat.

Both *Murder Ball* and the *Obstacle Course* were ballbusters. The *Obstacle Course* was a series of torture devices consisting of lines of elevated logs, barbed-wire crawls, water-filled ditches, and climbing walls—all of which had to be negotiated at breakneck speed. *Murder Ball* exceeded all other evolutions for sheer physical brutality. It was like sandlot football between criminals and savages. The objective was to *win*. Biting, gouging, wrestling . . . almost anything went except shooting an opponent.

A Bluejacket from Texas broke his leg and had to be recycled to the following class.

The Circus required nothing beyond pure stamina and determination. It was simply ass-busting burnout PT that ended only when the last man collapsed from exhaustion.

There was little order in how the various evolutions played out. Apparently, whim and randomness determined the pattern. In between the events, of course, came swimming. Mile-long ordeals in the bay with masks and rubber fins called "duck feet." Navigation exercises on long swims out to sea and then back again to a designated landmark ashore.

"Not this dune, you idiot, *sir. That* one. Now, do it again until you get it right. But, first, knock out fifty push-ups."

"Which arm?" I panted.

"Fifty with each, smartass, *sir.*"

"Bone, you *are* an idiot," Joisey wheezed as, resembling a thoroughly drowned rat, he dropped down on the sand to do penance with me, as was his buddy duty.

Eventually, SCUBA was introduced, along with *Cast and Recovery*, a technique for getting in and out of the water rapidly. Swimmers rolled—*cast*—out of an IBS (Inflatable Boat, Small) tethered to the side of a speeding motor launch. *Recovery* was just the opposite. A snare man in the IBS used a figure-eight loop to snatch swimmers out of the brine as the launch pulling the rubber boat barreled past.

At last came the apocryphal seven days to weed out those who were just hanging on by their fingernails and teeth—*Hell Week*. Days and nights of one evolution after another all condensed by lack of sleep during which we were pounded into a near-catatonic state of severe mental and physical exhaustion. Less than one quarter of the 125 men who began training eight weeks ago survived Hell Week.

Joisey and I hung in and hung tough. We were still there when training moved into its final phases, where we learned the real war skills—demolitions, explosives charges and formulas, hydrographic beach recons, small unit training in patrolling, weapons, raids and ambushes, five-mile swims, simulated real-world missions. . . . Trainers evaluated and graded us both as individuals and members of detachments. It was necessary that men think on their own but act as a team.

Finally, on the last day surviving members, who had lost an average of twenty pounds each, were marched to the Amphib School main classroom to graduate. Like special military men before us, we had all learned something vital. Men you could depend on when the shit came down were those who hung in there and worked hardest to get what they wanted. The tough exposure to UDT created a band of brothers, elite operational rogues willing to sacrifice everything for each other, including their lives.

Joisey breathed with relief when we entered the main classroom to graduate. We removed for the last time the red helmet liners with the numbers on them that served as our names during training.

"There were times, Bone," Joisey confessed. "There were times. . . . But, Eighty-eight, we did it!"

CHAPTER NINE

I BARELY HAD TIME TO go home—rather, go to Elinor's parents' home in Rancho Santa Fe—and kiss my unhappy wife and baby daughter, Linda Jean, hello and good-bye before I found myself back in the Korean theater, where my combat career had begun.

"Bye, honey. It'll soon be over."

"Bill, *no*—!"

My new assignment was as research and development officer for UDT-5, headquartered at Camp McGill outside Yokosuka, Japan. I could have dreamed of no better slot from which to extend the operating arm of UDTs.

The war was winding down. That was the general feeling as our forces and theirs stalemated along the 38th Parallel. Peace negotiations dragged on as they had for the past two years while the shooting continued. Nonetheless, everyone seemed encouraged that the war was only months, perhaps only weeks, away from an armistice. It seemed the world might escape the cocking of the nuclear hammer for the first time after World War II.

President Harry Truman had fired General Douglas MacArthur in 1951 as commander of UN forces because of his aggressiveness and willingness to go nuclear and replaced him with General Matthew Ridgway. Ridgway was, as politicians like to say, more *circumspect*.

Pilots in *Valley Forge's* ready room and crews throughout the ship fell stone silent that day when the carrier's skipper played MacArthur's farewell speech over the intercom. Dad, who knew the general, had told me thrilling stories about General Mac in the South Pacific. Chills broke out down my back as I listened with other pilots to that controlled voice fill the ready room.

"I am closing my fifty-two years of military service," he said. "When I joined the army, even before the turn of the century, it was the fulfillment of all my boyish hopes and dreams. This world has turned over many times since I took the oath on the plain of West Point, and the hopes and dreams have long since vanished, but I still remember the refrain of one of the most popular barracks ballads of that day which proclaimed most proudly that 'old soldiers never die, they just fade away.'"

I was determined that I not "just fade away," at least not until I had contributed my best.

For my second Korean tour, I was lodged at Camp McGill in a former officers' quarters built by Germans for the Japanese during World War II. My roommate was UDT Lieutenant John Reynolds, a lean, mean slab of a man a little older than me and a few inches shorter. Reynolds had dark eyes and a darker sense of humor—"If I were God, I'd have made octopuses and platypuses, but I'd never have made people."

In response to peace talks, UDT-5 began shutting down its activities against the NKs.

"Sonsofbitches are starting to send out patrols against us," Reynolds complained. "Bastards are actually *shooting* at us when we try to go ashore."

Shortly before I checked in, UDT-5 took significant combat casualties when North Koreans and Chicoms cornered a detachment and the detachment's accompanying South Korean guerrillas behind enemy lines.

"We need to be more invisible when we insert," I suggested.

"Parachutes?"

"Yes, that too. But more invisible."

"You're the new genius at Research and Development," Reynolds replied.

The Korean War ended with a ceasefire on July 27, 1953, four months after Josef Stalin died, to be eventually replaced by Nikita Khrushchev. Some fifty-four thousand American military had died on that cold, dreary trash pile. But while *this* war may have ended, I was sure more than ever that we needed commandos in a dangerous nuclear world. The ceasefire allowed Reynolds and me the opportunity to work on some of our ideas.

I remembered Commander Fane talking about how, back in 1947, he explored using early-day helicopters to deploy UDT operators. Reynolds and I batted the idea off each other and then decided to revive his efforts. I directed a confidential memo to Commander, Underwater Demolition Unit One (COMUDU-One), UDT-5's parent command, with a copy to Fane at UDT-1 explaining what we had in mind:

> A complete operation might be conducted in the following manner: helicopters, each carrying six swimmers could proceed at low altitude to an objective area from a remote sea or shore base. Swimmers would be dropped and the planes could then retire. The helicopter would later return, lay a protective smoke screen, and pick up the swimmers.
>
> It is believed that the particular advantage in this type operation lies in the ability to conduct reconnaissance operations in normally inaccessible areas with an element of secrecy and surprise not possible with present methods. There need be no surface units within visible distance of the objective area.

I persuaded helicopter pilots from nearby Atsugi Airfield to help Reynolds and me try out our scheme in a series of exercises off the Japanese coast. Reynolds promptly dubbed them "Bud Abbott and Lou Costello Meet Poseidon." Abbot and Costello were a popular comedy duo starring in such movies as *Abbot and Costello Meet Frankenstein* and *Abbott and Costello Meet the Mummy*.

A half-dozen Frogmen volunteers from UDT-5 waited with some degree of amused skepticism while pilots and flight crew chiefs under our direction removed cargo seats from a Sikorsky HRS-3 and installed a solid aluminum bar to which we might attach a Jacob's ladder. The ladder was for recovery purposes.

"It might have been safer if we'd kept the war going," one of the Frogmen cracked.

Casting looked simple enough. The chopper flew out over the water at the height of a three-story building and at about 40 knots true airspeed. Swimmers jumped out wearing full combat gear—pack, knives, weapons, ammo, fins, and face mask. Equipment exploded in all directions when we struck the water. We ended up half-drowned with perhaps one fin remaining and the rest of our gear sinking beneath the waves.

I gasped my way to the surface and quickly counted heads to make sure no one was missing or badly injured. Reynolds swam over.

"Bad idea, Coyote," he managed around a lung full of salt water. "Maybe we ought to slow that chopper down."

But not too much. It was necessary the helicopter maintain some speed during infiltration in order that enemy radar not smell a rat and guess what we were up to.

During the next few jumps we bundled individual equipment around flotation bladders and dropped them first. Not too bad. A few men bounced off the water and skipped across the waves like flying fish. One was knocked unconscious. A trailing safety boat plucked him out of the drink.

"Maybe we *should* slow it down a tad," I conceded.

We finally got it right after about a hundred jumps without losing a swimmer. The fastest safe drop speed seemed to be around 30 knots at an altitude half that of a three-story building. Optimum body posture was feet first, legs together, arms tucked across the chest, and body bent slightly forward at the waist to allow it to knife smoothly into the water.

A helicopter or two could slide in fast under cover of darkness or a smoke screen, slow to a safer speed, and dump their human loads into the ocean near shore without the land-bound enemy being any the wiser. It was UDT's first successful foray into becoming airborne.

Now for the recovery.

It was the same principle as recovery by boat at sea, in which a retriever with a loop in a rubber raft towed by a fast boat snatched a swimmer out of the water and flopped him like a netted fish into the IBS. The procedure sounded simple enough to use with a helicopter pickup.

Instead of to a rubber raft, we attached the loop to a flexible Jacob's ladder, whose other end was secured to the aluminum bar on the floor of the HRS-3 using bungee cord. Theoretically, the bungees took up slack and cushioned the swimmer below when he grabbed the loop as the chopper flew by.

Reynolds discovered what happened when a swimmer was too slow monkey-climbing the ladder to the chopper door. He was halfway up the ladder when the next man grabbed the loop as it passed by. The bungee cord took the shock, stretched like the rubbers on a slingshot, and launched Reynolds off the ladder like a stone.

I laughed. "You looked like a bullfrog thrown out of a mop bucket."

With a few modifications we now had a workable helicopter cast and recovery system.

"Parachutes next?" I mused.

Reynolds rolled his eyes.

I was, after all, UDT-5's research and development officer. So I needed to continue researching and developing. I talked the South Korean Air Force, now more or less in peacetime mode, into providing a C-46 platform for parachute training. We barely got started before COMUDU and the Pentagon stepped in and closed us down.

"War's over," I was informed. "You're going home."

CHAPTER TEN

SEA DUTY, WAR, AND long separations lurked in the shadows of every Navy marriage. After Korea, for the first time since we were wed, Elinor and I and toddler daughter Linda Jean lived under the same roof for a period of more than a few days or weeks at a time. I tried, honestly tried, to live the conventional life—wife, family, Ford station wagon in the garage, mortgage.

Elinor and Linda Jean followed me to the East Coast and the Norfolk area while I continued pursuing unconventional training in Army Chemical Warfare and Underwater EOD (Explosives Ordnance Disposal). The schools weren't that demanding, certainly nothing like UDT. About like a nine-to-five job. I savored home-cooked meals and evenings spent on the carpet playing little games with my daughter. Elinor seemed . . . seemed *almost* happy.

"Bill, you're *preoccupied*," she would say whenever I became too involved in study and work. "You're home now. Let's enjoy being a family and together."

Sometimes guilt for not being totally involved with family almost ate out my heart. I damned me for that seductive salt air in my nostrils, for the wandering bug Dad planted in my genes, for my warrior mentality. I seemed to be always planning the next step forward in my preoccupation with the idea of sea commandos.

Several times Elinor caught me on the phone with Reynolds or Joisey or one of my other like-minded Frogman buddies. She would frown disapprovingly over my end of the conversation: "Army Special Forces is expanding. They're way ahead of us in many areas. We have to train with the Army, learn from them if we ever expect to seize the Golden Fleece."

Guerrillas and unconventional warfare, already as old as history, were rapidly returning since the end of World War II as the predominant form of armed conflict in the world. The development of nuclear weapons and missiles with which to deliver them made conventional war not only prohibitive in terms of money and resources but also unthinkable because of its destructive power. Conventional war in the twentieth century was being priced off the market.

David of the Old Testament waged an unconventional campaign against King Saul. Two centuries before Christ, Rome fought drawn-out unconventional wars in Spain and North Africa. Jewish freedom fighters at the time of Jesus used irregular tactics against occupying Romans. Fabian Maximus drove Hannibal out of Italy with guerrilla strategies. Vikings launched commando-style raids from rivers and seas. Spaniards coined the word "guerrilla" during their fight against Napoleon, a term that means "little war." Lawrence of Arabia employed unconventional warriors.

Most armies have recruited guerrillas in some form to patrol, reconnoiter, and skirmish for their main forces. They were particularly significant in the settling of the New World.

The New World was a vast, dangerous, almost trackless wilderness populated by often-hostile natives who avoided the "stand-up" fight. Settlers constructed defensive forts and blockhouses on the frontier, to which they fled during Indian uprisings, while buckskin-clad Colonists called "Rangers" patrolled between the strongholds and operated behind lines to demoralize and defeat hostiles.

Robert Rogers, a backwoodsman from New Hampshire, took command of four companies of Rangers in 1756 during the French and Indian War. His use of "Indian tactics" on long-range patrols against French positions made him the most feared and respected man in the territories.

Following the "shot heard 'round the world" that initiated the American Revolution, British Army planners employed Loyalist partisans in an effort to suppress the uprising. As a counterstrategy, American General Horatio Gates ordered Colonel Francis Marion to form Rangers and disrupt British supply lines in the Williamsburg region. Using classic guerrilla tactics, Marion, known as "the Swamp Fox," conducted lightning raids against the Brits while depending upon local settlers for intelligence, supplies, cover, and reinforcements.

The Swamp Fox harassed the British and their Tory allies until the end of the war, keeping "the whole country in continued alarm," as British Colonel Banastre Tarleton put it, "so that regular troops were everywhere necessary."

So-called "Indian tactics" also prevailed as America's "Manifest Destiny" pushed west and bumped up against guerrilla fighters like the Navajo, Apache, Sioux, and Cheyenne. Kit Carson took on the Navajo and Apache by using their own machinations against them. In the late 1830s, Captain Jack Hays and fifteen Texas Rangers in a "special operations force" routed more than eighty Comanche by utilizing specialized training and special equipment like the revolver.

Some 428 units during the American Civil War were irregulars officially or unofficially known as Rangers. Mosby's Rangers, a battalion of Confederate partisan cavalry, disrupted Union communications and supply lines in Virginia. John Mosby's mission statement well applied to guerrillas operating in the twentieth century: "Harassing their rear . . . to destroy supply trains, to break up the means of conveying intelligence, and thus isolating an army from its base. . . . It is just as legitimate to fight an enemy in the rear as in the front."

Although the Union considered Confederate raiders "unsoldierly guerrillas hiding among civilians," General Ulysses Grant nonetheless countered with unconventional forces of his own. In preparing to move against Vicksburg, he dispatched Colonel Benjamin Grierson into Mississippi to destroy whatever he could, much as Merrill's Marauders were to do in Burma during World War II.

Even in the static trenches of World War I, France had their special operators. "Trench raiders" on both sides stripped down to basics and went over the side in forays against opposing trenches to gather intelligence, capture prisoners, and terrorize the enemy.

The twentieth century from World War I on was an era of almost continuous conflict. Guerrilla warfare scorched the earth in Europe, Asia, and Africa. British experience fighting unconventional forces in its colonies led to the birth of special operations units such as SOE (Special Operation Executive) and SAS (Special Air Services), which in turn influenced the emergence of such units as UDTs, OSS, and the various other guerrilla-type outfits of World War II.

History supplied the basis upon which to continue building.

One night I was on the floor wrestling with Linda Jean. That girl was going to be a tomboy. Elinor answered the phone.

"It's for you, Bill. It's Commander Doug Fane."

CHAPTER ELEVEN

I ACCEPTED COMMANDER FANE'S OFFER to return to Naval Amphibious Base Coronado as his operations officer for COMUDU-One. My duties included coordinating all UDT operations in the Pacific, whether in training or in real-world situations. Elinor, baby Linda Jean, and I packed up the Ford station wagon and headed west. Elinor was happy to be returning to California; at least she would be near her folks.

Red Dog Fane, now forty-five years old and one of the elders of UDT, was crusty, stubborn, and hard to get along with. He knew only one way: "*My* way. So follow or get the hell out of the way."

Truth be known, I was sometimes as obstinate as he. We were bound to butt heads like two rowdy walruses on an ice floe, as we tested theories and ideas and slammed them off each other.

Fane's determination had saved UDT from the military drawdowns following both World War II and Korea, while he struggled to expand the naval special warfare mission, but he and I frequently disagreed over how far that mission should go. He held that although ops on sea, land, and air were viable for our Frogs, such activities should be confined to within sight and smell of salt air in the way our true amphibious counterparts on ponds kept to their lily pads and murky banks. We should restrict our commando work to within the high water mark that was the UDT boundary in World War II.

"It's all right to go landward to blow up something or assassinate some asshole," Fane argued in our continued ongoing discussions on the future of Navy counterinsurgency. "But then get your butt out of there and back to water. That's where we originated and that's where we're most effective. It's not our business to engage in shooting wars. We got the Marines and the dogfaces for that. Let them get their asses shot off. We got bigger fish to fry."

I was just as adamant that the Navy should be more than about boats and planes and blasting landing sites for jarheads.

"UW will become the major instrument of warfare in the nuclear age," I offered. "If we expect to get our piece of it, we have to do more than paddle around in the surf like tadpoles. Army Special Forces is not confined to land. They're training in diving and boats while at the same time developing techniques to work and train guerrillas inside the enemy's own territory. I don't want the Navy to have just a piece of the pie—"

"You want the whole pie—"

"At least the biggest part of it."

We knew we were bucking the system. High-ranking brass of the "old military," both Army and Navy, harbored a stiff aversion to the use of underhanded, clandestine methods that had little in common with tried-and-true ideas of chivalry and the military code of honor. "Snake eaters," in their opinion, were somehow not quite respectable.

Although Commander Fane and I might disagree, not so much on methodology as on goals, I retained great respect and awe for the legendary Frogman and his reputation. His life had been one hell of an adventure. Other sailors accused him of sometimes being more guts than sense.

Born in Scotland in 1909, which made him eighteen years older than me and a generation ahead, he went to sea in his mid-twenties and quickly rose to command merchant ships. He emigrated to the United States and enlisted in the U.S. Navy shortly before Pearl Harbor.

I heard a tale of how he served aboard an ammo supply ship in the Pacific that was transferring cans of powder to the USS *Pennington*, a battle wagon. Friction ignited a can of powder being rolled across the deck. Crewmen panicked and ran for their lives before the powder exploded, some of them even jumping overboard.

Fane turned a fire hose on the can and washed it over the side. It hung up in rigging on the ship's outer hull where it smoldered on the brink of exploding, which might have chain-detonated the magazines and sunk the ship. Fane was unwilling to abandon the vessel to its fate. He jumped and climbed down to the smoking canister and kicked it into the sea. Just in time.

Fane and I might have differed on how far to take UDTs from the seashore, but we were in unison on the nature and makeup of men and officers who served on the teams.

"UDTs are the despair of most conventional Navy officers," Fane preached. "There is no place for epaulets on a wet, sunburned shoulder, but there is plenty of room for mutual confidence and genuine discipline when officer and enlisted alike know that the other will get every man back—or drown trying."

Fane and I worked tirelessly to prove wrong the higher brass who thought the concept of naval special forces had outlived its usefulness after the war and should therefore be abandoned. Our teams were constantly on the move, training, staying ready and edged.

Frogs conducted underwater surveys for the construction of Distant Early Warning (DEW) lines across the northern reaches of Alaska and Canada, in water so cold it would have frozen solid if not for its salt content. UDT swimmers accompanied the first nuclear submarines to dive in the Arctic Sea. Lieutenant Commander Robert Terry swam over a quarter mile underneath the Arctic ice cap.

"It was like a cathedral under there, sun shining through the ice in rays of blue like through a diamond," he reported.

A pair of UDT buddies in Arctic training spotted an Eskimo village on the shoreline and decided to make an impromptu visit. In insulated dry suits, face masks, caps, fins and gloves, all in black, they surface-swam through water and slid belly-down across ice floes in order to reach it. A problem developed when Eskimos saw the black-skinned monsters with huge webbed feet approaching in what they interpreted to be a hostile manner. They opened fire in self-defense while shrieking women and children fled. Bullets zipped past. The demon-beasts sprang to their webbed feet and began shouting and waving their arms.

"No! No! Stop shooting. We're *people* too!"

China had splintered into two nations at the end of World War II. Mao Tse-tung's communists retained the mainland; Nationalist China led by Chiang Kai-shek fled to several small islands off the coast. In 1955, the Nationalists, under repeated threats from the mainland, abandoned their Tachen Islands to fortify the islands of Quemoy and Matsu. The U.S. Seventh Fleet escorted the evacuation.

Commander Fane remained aboard a gunship in the harbor with a UDT detachment to provide overwatch while I went ashore with another team and a boatload of explosives to blow up fortifications and munition stockpiles on the islands to prevent their falling into communist hands. Mao must have felt the concussion in Beijing.

Fane and I logged our share of hours in the water as we pressed on with techniques and scientific experiments to test swimmer limits in mixed-gas deep-diving systems and the use of underwater propulsion vehicles. Even when I wasn't gallivanting off to China or the Arctic or some other remote or godforsaken nook of the world, my days started as early as 0400 and sometimes went over until midnight or after. I kissed my wife and daughter good morning while they were still in bed and I was on my way out the door.

"Sorry, honey. Don't have time for breakfast. Lots of work to do. Don't wait up for me tonight. Red Dog and I have a meeting with COMPHIBPAC to go over some ops—"

"Bill, you never seem to have time for us—"

"Ah, now, baby, give me some slack—"

"Will you think about getting out of the Navy and taking the other job?"

A large San Diego corporation had offered me "the other job," an executive position, if I resigned my commission in the Navy and entered "real life" in the civilian sector. A hefty raise came with the job, plus a lot of other perks the Navy could never provide. We'd also be living near Elinor's folks, could actually buy a house and settle down.

I had thirty days to think it over and make a decision. I promised Elinor I would. And I did. I thought about it a lot during my daily runs on the beach to keep in shape, while diving to re-qualify with all the new equipment coming in, or while having a quick sandwich for lunch at my desk in time to attend a meeting with team leaders or some Pentagon puke from the Joint Chiefs of Staff who wanted to know what Frogmen did anyhow.

What with the secret exercises and commando training Fane and I sponsored for our guys with the regular Navy, the Army, the Marines, anywhere we could obtain it anywhere in the world, we were not surprised when the Chief of Naval Operations called.

"My God!" Admiral Arleigh Burke exclaimed. "How long has this been going on?"

"Several years now, sir."

"Keep at it," he replied to our surprise. "Any problems, you call me."

Admiral Burke was a key supporter of unconventional warfare. But even the CNO could not block peacetime cutbacks and defunding. UDT-22 was decommissioned on the East Coast due to personnel shortages and its men reassigned to UDT-21. The West Coast decommissioned UDT-13 and split the men between its two remaining West Coast teams. That left three teams in Navy SpecOps while Army Special Forces continued to expand.

Commander Fane went to the CNO while I listened in on an extension phone. "Sir, it takes time to train specialized men like UDTs. If we have another war, we won't have the capacity to handle our mission."

"My hands are tied, Doug. The White House is gearing everything toward a mech face-off in Europe with the Soviets and a possible nuclear showdown. We start exchanging nukes, and it won't last a week before the world is blown to hell. We won't need special forces for that."

"That's why the nation needs us now more than ever. To stop the nuking before it begins."

"I understand, Doug. They'll come crying to us to do something when the shit hits the proverbial fan in some rat hole like Korea or Indochina. In the meantime—"

"—we sit on the pot and wait."

The conversation ended. Red-faced, Fane barged into my office.

"You heard that shit, Bone?"

I nodded somberly.

"Damned pencil-dicked paper pushers in Washington!" he raved. "Bone, get your ass up. It's Friday. I could use a night in Tijuana."

Tijuana, Mexico, across the border from San Diego, was Red Dog's favorite watering hole. We occasionally drove down to the crazy little city after work to unwind at a joint on the drag called Feliz Sombrero that featured brown-skinned strippers and quart mugs of even browner beer. Usually, the atmosphere of female skin and suds lifted our spirits higher than a rapture of the deep. Tonight, however, Fane was in such a bad mood that he kept getting louder and more obnoxious. I dragged him out of the bar before he kidnapped one of the girls or got us into a fight with a tough-looking Mex with a knife scar down the side of his face. I tossed him into the car for the drive home.

"I could have kicked that greaser's butt, Bone. Now, I should kick your butt instead."

Commander Fane was my superior and my mentor. I held him in high regard as both a man and an officer. He was just having a bad night.

"Bone, you're a fucking candy ass. I don't care how big you are, you're a 'yes man' with no guts."

Tijuana beer was doing the talking through leftover rage from his conversation with the CNO. I saw him to his front door and turned to leave. He grabbed my arm.

"I'm not finished with you yet, Lieutenant."

A man had his breaking point, his pride. I slowly turned to face him. As I did I unleashed a straight right to his jaw. Definitely the Tijuana beer talking or I wouldn't have done it. The legendary Frogman sat down hard on his top doorstep, dazed.

"Good night, sir," I said.

Striking a superior officer, no matter the provocation, was a serious offense. Friend or not, he would surely have me court-martialed. That meant the end of my UDT career, if I weren't kicked out of the Navy altogether. My long-nurtured dream of helping create a true Navy special operations outfit was about to go up in smoke.

Elinor seemed less than disappointed about developments. "It's not the end of the world, Bill," she exulted. "You have a good job waiting for you. All you have to do is take it. We can have a real family life. Your daughter is growing up and hardly knows what you look like."

Perhaps she was right. Maybe it was fate that I get out of the Navy and settle down like ordinary people. The strain my career placed on her and our marriage had approached the breaking point more than once. Over half the men I knew in UDT were divorced at least once; Fane was working on his third marriage. Elinor often bitched that she was my *second* wife; my *first* wife was Navy UDT.

Maybe it wasn't the end of the world to Elinor, but to me it seemed like it. To complicate things further, we learned that Elinor was pregnant again.

I fretted the entire weekend, keeping to myself and barely responding to Elinor. I finally decided maybe it was best to resign and save the Navy the trouble of kicking me out.

On Monday I knocked on Fane's office door. "Commander Fane, I need—"

He rubbed the bruise on his jaw. "I been shot at, nearly drowned, cursed by a witch doctor, pissed on and pissed off—and now, can you believe I slipped and fell off my own porch?"

He grinned. "Don't just stand there, Bone. We have work to do. By the way, I was wrong. If you're a candy ass, I've never seen one can punch harder."

CHAPTER TWELVE

A NATION'S MILITARY IS INEXTRICABLY tied to its history and geography and guided by current events, all of which mold the character of both the institution and the soldiers who populate it. Ocean borders on either side of the United States necessitated a strong Navy, while the early frontier-settler mentality produced tough, self-reliant soldiers with a strong sense of freedom and the capability to meet events head-on.

From childhood, I possessed an appreciation of that history and tradition that lent itself to the discipline and honor code of the military. Part of it I inherited from my Navy father, part of it from a strong-willed mother, and the rest came from happenstance, perhaps, and from being born at the right time when the nation's military was being shaped in new directions.

The unfolding Cold War directly encouraged the development and deployment of special operations forces in both the U.S. Navy and U.S. Army. In many aspects, Army Special Forces and UDTs were sprouts from a common root. Both owed their modern genesis to World War II, each taking a slightly different path toward a common goal.

Some initial developments in special operations techniques took place in an unexpected corner of the world, even before Hitler appeared on the scene in Europe.

During the 1930s, violent criminal gangs ruled the densely-packed Shanghai International Community in China. Well-equipped with military weapons and employing terrorist tactics, the gangs kidnapped for ransom, smuggled drugs, extorted businesses, assassinated rivals, and murdered law enforcement officers.

A tough English musketry instructor named William Fairbairn came along to "take back the streets" by utilizing street cop methods and employing counterterrorism tactics. He established heavily-armed military-type squads whose principle aim was to kill terrorists. Riot squads busted heads while undercover officers infiltrated the gangs to provide intelligence to counteract the violence. Within a few years, Fairbairn the "town tamer" had tamed Shanghai.

He returned to England in 1940 to instruct British SOE (Special Operations Executive) and the SAS (Special Air Services) in underground battle techniques he had developed in China. A couple of years later the United States relied upon his success and upon the examples of the SOE and SAS to help flesh out its OSS (Office of Strategic Services).

In July 1941, with Nazism on the march and war looming, President Franklin Roosevelt created a service responsible for gathering and preserving secret intelligence and conducting special operations. He tapped William Joseph "Wild Bill" Donovan, fifty-eight, a wealthy Wall Street banker, to direct his newly formed office of Coordinator of Information (COI). Donovan's stout, white-haired appearance belied his background as a cavalry troop commander who pursued Poncho Villa in 1916, and as commander of the "Fighting 69th" Infantry Division in World War I, where he won the Medal of Honor.

Six months after Pearl Harbor, Roosevelt placed COI under the military authority of the Joint Chiefs of Staff with Donovan still in command and renamed it the Office of Strategic Services. Formed along the lines of England's SOE and SAS, the OSS had the primary function of obtaining information about enemy nations and sabotaging their war potential and morale.

OSS volunteers trained at "Area F" on the grounds of the former Congressional Country Club outside Washington, D.C. Emphasis was on espionage, sabotage, "black" propaganda, guerrilla warfare, and other "un-American" subversive techniques that set a precedent for clandestine tradecraft. Columnist Stewart Alsop tallied this new breed as "missionaries and bartenders, polo players and baseball pitchers, millionaires and union organizers, a human fly and a former Russian general, a big game hunter, a history professor . . ."

"They were a rough-and-tumble gang," concluded OSS instructor Roger Hall. "They didn't know the exact nature of their future assignments and they couldn't care less."

"Their appetite for the unconventional and spectacular was far beyond the ordinary," added an OSS captain.

OSS operators joined with British SOE in three-man "Jedburgh" teams to work with the resistance in German-occupied France, Holland, and Belgium. Teams parachuted in to train partisans and lead them in conducting guerrilla operations in the rear to open up second fronts against Nazi occupiers. By the end of September 1944, more than a hundred Jedburgh teams dropped behind enemy lines tied down thousands of Hitler's troops on D-Day and in the months afterward.

OSS operated in two primary configurations—Jedburghs and larger bands called OGs (Operational Groups). Donovan also created a Special Operations Branch (SO) to liaison with underground movements and a Secret Intelligence Branch (SI) to oversee the generation of intelligence.

OGs performed direct-action combat roles such as sabotage and attacks on key targets. They linked up with partisans to blow bridges, blast trains and rail lines, to provide reconnaissance and intelligence, and to exfiltrate downed pilots and other Allied personnel. "The OGs undertook and carried out more different types of enterprises calling for more varied skills than any other single organization of its size in the history of the country," noted a member of the OSS psychological staff.

OG Detachment 101, led by Captain Ray Peers, equipped and organized several thousand Kachin tribesmen to take on the Japanese in northern Burma. Peers and his Kachin slaughtered an estimated 10,000 Japanese while losing only 206 of their own. Theater commander General "Vinegar Joe" Stilwell questioned Peers and a Kachin Ranger leader on how they could be so sure of the exact number of

Japanese killed during one engagement. The Kachin dumped a pile of dried human ears on the table.

"Divide by two," he suggested.

"To unorthodox, traditional soldiers," said former Jedburgh Aaron Bank, unconventional warfare "was something slimy, underhanded, illegal and ungentlemanly."

OSS operated for less than four years before being disbanded in September 1945, one month after the end of World War II. It was one root of several that eventually grew into Army Special Forces. Darby's Rangers, Alamo Scouts, the Devil's Brigade, and Merrill's Marauders provided other roots of the special forces lineage.

In June 1942 when Army Chief of Staff General George C. Marshall decided to train and utilize commandos, he appointed thirty-one-year-old Lieutenant Colonel William O. Darby to establish Ranger units and command the 1st Ranger Battalion, which became known as "Darby's Rangers." They were called "Rangers" because the term was used in early American history to designate units displaying "high standards of individual courage, determination, ruggedness, fighting ability and achievement." Darby's Rangers and subsequent Ranger units became known for their rallying cry "Rangers lead the way!" They were involved throughout Europe and the Pacific in direct action spearheads and assaults and made beach landings at Tunisia and Salerno. Darby was killed in action in Italy in April 1945, only days before Germany surrendered.

The Alamo Scouts were South Pacific commandos brought into existence in November 1943 by General Walter Krueger, commander of Sixth Army. Officially named the Sixth Army Special Reconnaissance Unit, the Alamos were "selected volunteers trained in reconnaissance and raider work." Lieutenant Colonel Frederick W. Bradshaw assumed the task of producing well-trained, highly motivated six- to seven-man teams to infiltrate enemy lines, gather intelligence, and return undetected.

"This little unit has never failed the U.S. Army," declared General Kreuger when the Alamo Scouts disbanded in November 1945.

The "Devil's Brigade," the 1st Special Service Force (FSF), contributed major genes to the "bastard children" that grew into military special operations. It was originally conceived as an elite joint airborne assault force of Canadians and Americans trained to operate in mountains and snow to destroy German hydroelectric plants in Norway and the Italian Alps and target Romanian oil production.

Instead, the FSF found itself attached to Amphibious Task Force 9 to run the Japanese out of the Aleutian Islands off the tip of Alaska. Later, events unfolded that made the Devil's Brigade the only Allied combat outfit to take part in a "two-ocean war" when it was assigned to scale an "unscalable" mountain wall in Italy to take the Difensa enemy stronghold and hold it.

The Devil's Brigade was deactivated on November 22, 1944. Cut loose, its commandos along with former Jedburghs and Rangers moved east and south into the Asian theater to operate with OSS OGs or Merrill's Marauders. Much of the brigade's organization, equipment, training, tactics, and missions would later become standard procedure for U.S. Army Special Forces.

"Merrill's Marauders" sprang out of the Quebec Conference of August 1943 between President Roosevelt and Prime Minister Winston Churchill, during which they forged a joint U.S.-British Southeast Asian Command (SEAC) to open a first Allied offensive, code-named "Galahad," against the Japanese on the Asian mainland. General Frank D. Merrill, thirty-nine, was appointed to command the regiment-sized 5307 Composite Unit (Provisional) on January 1, 1944.

Merrill's Marauders inserted into Northern Burma to begin what *Time* magazine described as "a twenty-three-day mountain march that was one of the epic infantry advances of the war. The Marauders swept east to cut Japanese supply lines, block trails and enemy movements, and destroy whatever got in their way. It was difficult terrain. High mountains, deep valleys, jungle, and numerous rivers. Men suffered from dysentery, disease, fatigue and constant hunger. Their only means of supply was through periodic air drops, which often ended up in enemy hands."

The Marauders marched more than six hundred miles through seemingly impassable terrain while fighting five major and seventeen minor engagements that drove the Japanese from an area the size of

Connecticut. Only a thousand men of the original three thousand remained when replacements arrived.

"In the next war," predicted Major Samuel Vaughn Wilson, a recon platoon leader, "we are going to have to rely on Galahad-type forces—small, free-ranging units unhampered by fixed ties to their bases. The massing of armies is out in an era of atomic weapons."

"It is time to realize that most modern war is guerrilla in nature," asserted Major General Orde Wingate, originator of the long-range penetration concept.

Wingate was to be proved profoundly prophetic as America, Britain, and France became increasingly entangled in Indochina with communists led by Ho Chi Minh.

"The next war after Korea," I predicted while working with Lieutenant Reynolds in Japan, "will be in Vietnam. I can already see it coming. We'd better start preparing."

"So," Reynolds teased, "Planning and Research now includes prophesying?"

The United States readily abandoned its capability for unconventional warfare with the end of World War II and the disbanding or drawdown of its SpecOps units. A number of foresighted men—Commander Fane, Draper Kauffman, Phil Bucklew, and, I liked to think, myself—saw red clouds on the horizon and realized what was coming. Third World nations were beginning to fall like dominos to the Soviet and Sino spheres.

Brigadier General Robert McClure realized the only way for unconventional warfare to be successful was to prepare *beforehand*. He had been Eisenhower's officer-in-charge of psychological warfare in Europe, where he often worked with OSS. He was now in charge of the Psychological Warfare Center located at Fort Bragg, North Carolina. He incorporated in his command a special warfare detachment and began gathering veterans experienced in guerrilla warfare. Among them were Colonel Aaron Bank, famous for his exploits with the OSS, including one operation intended to capture Adolf Hitler; Lieutenant Colonel Russell Volckmann, the former guerrilla leader on Luzon; Wendell Fertig, Volckmann's counterpart on Mindanao; Joe Waters, who had served with Merrill's Marauders; and Robert McDowell, a former OSS operative with Tito in Yugoslavia. Their mission was to develop a concept for guerrilla warfare in a world threatened by communism.

Bank and Volckmann were the most influential of the group in convincing the Army that it needed permanent special forces. Initially, they thought such elements would be deployed behind the Iron Curtain in Eastern European nations dominated by the Soviet Union following a nuclear war. They would assemble survivors in the wastelands of enemy territory and develop partisan bands capable of resistance and disruption in rear areas.

In March 1952, the Department of Army approved a Special Warfare Center at Fort Bragg. Three months later, on June 19, the U.S. Army Special Forces came online with the activation of the 10th Special Forces Group and an allocation of 2,500 men under Colonel Bank's command. Although it was the first group, it was designated the 10th in order to confound the Soviets with the possibility of nine more groups.

"Present for duty," Bank noted that first day, "were seven enlisted men, one warrant officer, and me, making for a slim morning report."

Volunteers rapidly filled up 10th Group ranks, a number of them from the armies of Poland, Finland, even Russia and Germany. A change in law called the Lodge Act permitted foreign recruitment for special operations purposes. The unit adopted as its patch an arrowhead similar to that worn by Devil's Brigade. Three lightning bolts slashing across the arrowhead signaled Special Forces' ability to arrive against the enemy by land, sea, or air. Its motto was *De Oppresso Liber*: "Liberate the Oppressed."

Colonel Bank turned to the OGs for the Group's structure. This produced the twelve-man Special Forces A-team consisting of two teams of six sergeants cross-trained in five specialties—light weapons, heavy weapons, combat medicine, demolition-engineer, and intelligence. A captain or first lieutenant and an operations sergeant were the leaders. The A-team was the basic on-the-ground operational element and must be capable of teaching and leading other warriors.

A B-detachment, like an infantry company, controlled and supported three A-teams. A C-detachment (battalion) commanded three B-teams. Three C-detachments formed an Operational Group, commanded by a colonel.

The restlessness I observed in Vietnam, from afar at the present time, resulted from the Geneva Conference of 1954 following the French defeat at Dien Bien Phu. The conference pressured Vietnamese communists to accept the partitioning of Vietnam into a North and South, much as Korea had been partitioned following World War II. China, however, encouraged Ho Chi Minh to keep fighting to reunite the country under communism.

Within two years of its coming online, 10th Group began preparing to send teams into Vietnam. Commander Fane and I anticipated claiming a part of the war for UDTs when it broke out, as we felt it inevitably must.

Chapter Thirteen

Fate, it seemed, selected my destiny for me. A man couldn't go against his fate. Military career counselors had warned me that a UDT path led to delayed promotions and a stunted career, that if I proceeded on this course I would never make admiral as my father had. But wasn't vision more vital to the nation than gold braid on my cap and stars on my shoulder boards?

After mandatory rotation out of Red Dog Fane's COMUDU-One, I pulled another "shore duty" at the General Line Course in Monterrey, a sort of graduate school for naval officers. I might have been a good student except my instructors bitched how I lacked commitment. Being thrust into a classroom environment or behind a desk too long took something out of me. I had graduated Annapolis in the middle of my 1949 class because I refused to sit and study more than the minimum I required to pass. Although I was an avid reader of history, especially military history, I didn't do much better in the Line Course.

Elinor naturally liked our being there. It was *real* shore duty and I was home every night.

My old roommate Warren Parr stopped by Monterrey for a visit on his way to another WestPac tour. He was up for promotion to full commander, two jumps ahead of me. His old man and mine had both made it to admiral rank. It appeared Parr Jr. was on his way there as well.

"Bone, you big lug," he chided. "When are you going to wise up and get out of this pond playing with frogs? You've been in the water so long your brain has shrunk."

"I'm not taking a desk job."

Red Dog Fane would have understood.

Stubbornly, I selected my own course through the shoals as I volunteered and applied for duty that advanced me toward the goal I had designed for myself out of the Naval Academy and which by now had become hardwired into my being. I was determined to become versed in every aspect of the undersea world—diving and swimming, EOD, amphibious vessels.

Elinor seemed ready to accept that she could never be a *real* Navy wife. Settling in one place barely long enough to memorize the street address, then uprooting the family to trek to the opposite coast. Then back again.

I was pulling sea duty aboard the USS *PCE* off the East Coast when Linda Jean was born a few months before the Korean War ended. The little girl was barely walking when I attended UDTR School at Coronado, followed by another Korean tour and then a year or so with Fane bouncing around with the teams everywhere from the Arctic to South America to China. I was even gone on a mission when Elinor gave birth to our son William Henry Jr. on June 8, 1956. She glared at me when I finally showed up.

"Maybe the kids and I should go stay with Mama until you get this . . . this *whatever* out of your system," she suggested.

But she didn't. Not this time.

The kid was still in diapers when I bundled newborn, three-year-old daughter, and unhappy wife into our old Ford station wagon and set out for the East Coast again. Frigid conditions diving off Alaska and around the DEW line in the Arctic were nothing compared to the temperature inside the Ford as I wended our way across the continent to my next duty station with the Navy Diving School in Washington D.C. "Hard-hat" diving was used primarily for salvaging; I considered it another step on the course I had set for myself.

Most roads in the Southwest were narrow and rough and air conditioning was a luxury not available in many vehicles. I was afraid

Elinor was ready to give up on me by the time the four of us reached the Atlantic.

"Honey—?"

"Bill, don't you think we've been gypsies long enough? We need a home, Bill, a *real* home."

She was right, I knew she was right. I loved her, I adored the babies. Still, something in me just wouldn't, *couldn't*, give up. I flourished on physical and mental challenges that led me relentlessly back to the sea and its promises.

I completed hard-hat dive school in Washington, then dragged the family to the Navy's Explosive Ordnance School at Indian Head, Maryland, on the Potomac River near the Patuxent River Naval Air Warfare Center Test Facility. Having previously attended EOD training, and afterward gained experience in demolitions, I was assigned as training officer over students from every military service, the CIA, and other government types. It was precise and dangerous duty involving correctly and safely disposing of, disarming, and utilizing explosives in various situations on land and sea. UDTs were required to handle dynamite, nitro, plastic, and other materials in blowing obstacles for amphibious landings, as well as destroying enemy targets ashore, such as bridges, railroad tracks, and even friendly arms and supply dumps to keep the enemy from getting them.

One of my students was an old Navy friend named Rudy Enders, whose position in EOD School I secured for him and whose path continued to cross mine well into our future. Another was a senior CIA agent up-training for clandestine assignments to Vietnam, where Army Special Forces was involved in training South Vietnamese troops. A Special Forces officer, Captain Harry G. Cramer, had already become the first SF soldier killed in Vietnam, on October 20, 1957. Both students would later influence my course in special operations.

Next stop was Underwater Swimmers School at Naval Air Station, Key West, Florida, where I was the school's executive officer and Rudy Enders was training officer. I requested the assignment, thinking I needed advanced exposure to management techniques in the world of military diving. Our trainees were Navy, Marines, and Army Special Forces personnel, there to receive underwater experience in everything from submerged hand-to-hand combat to escaping from various situations to avoid drowning.

Enders and I made a good team. He was a year or so younger than I, shorter, since nearly everyone was shorter, stockier, with slightly bowed legs and buzz-cut hair bleached almost white by the sun. His passion was spearfishing.

One afternoon I arranged to use a Navy torpedo boat for the two of us to dive and spearfish on the sunken *Luckenbach* ship north of Key West in about seventy feet of water. Enders shot a 150-pound Jew-fish with a powerhead. He missed his mark and the big fish fled, trailing blood in the water. We chased it until a shark suddenly appeared that looked about the size of a small submarine. It took the two of us about two seconds to scoot into the wreck and hide until the shark lost interest.

Shore duty meant home cooking and evenings with the family watching TV. It seemed as our family grew, Elinor's dissatisfaction with Navy life became more clearly focused on me. Our third child, daughter Jana Lee, was born on May 20, 1958, as fresh as ocean breezes and as lovely as a sunrise. Elinor now had three powerful and beautiful weapons in Linda Jean, Bill Jr., and Jana Lee with which to try to knock some sense into my head.

"Honey, things are getting better," I pleaded. "Bear with me. The kids will go places and see things most others will never experience. It's a good life for them."

"What about for wives? Bill, the Navy Wives Club and the little social cliques are no substitute for family life."

At unexpected times, often prompted by the sound of a jet engine or the sight of an aircraft flying over, I experienced a flashback to that morning in Korea when I played my terrifying game of cat-and-mouse with the MiG that shot up my unarmed F9F. Nightmares were made of such memories—of going down with my plane, being trapped in the cockpit and regaining consciousness while underwater and sinking.

Rear Admiral Emerson E. Fawkes, head of the Design Branch in Bureau of Aeronautics, led pioneering efforts to devise a cockpit system that permitted underwater escape. It involved mechanical ejection in which a charge blew off the canopy and propelled the pilot free of the sinking aircraft, much the same as the procedure in an air exit, except underwater. I volunteered to be the first human subject to test the system for the Pilot Underwater Escape Program. I figured it might save pilot lives if I proved it could be done.

Tests included a series of simulated aircraft crashes in twenty-two fathoms of water in the Atlantic off the coast of Key West. We used a fully-instrumented aircraft in order to obtain water impact, deceleration and sink rate, entry attitude, and canopy implosion for a variety of crash conditions. We began with anthropometric dummies and reduced catapult charges and moved up to the first live test dummy—*me*.

"A *live* dummy," Enders ribbed me. "Maybe you're not as tightly wound as I thought you were."

It was a serious undertaking, which meant conceivably I could die. Physical trauma was a possibility once I activated the explosive seat, followed by shock, air embolism, and drowning at one hundred feet below the surface. I was, however, the ideal subject to give it a go—former naval aviator, superb physical condition, experienced in diving and in the use of explosives.

I donned pilot gear in the morning sun with salt air blowing against the AD-1 cockpit hoisted onto the fantail of a transport LSD (landing ship, dock). I climbed in and sealed the canopy. Someone once commented on how parachuting from an aircraft "feels like committing suicide." What about doing it underwater?

A member of the support personnel tapped on the canopy. "God look over you," he mouthed.

Minutes later, the cockpit with me inside was hurled over the side. I felt it sinking like a stone. Rays of sunlight shafting from above faded. Saltwater filled the canopy.

I yanked the curtain to initiate the ejection charge. Immediately, I experienced a sensation of crashing into a stone wall. The seat, with me buckled into it, tumbled through the sea. I thought I was going to pass out. My lungs burned from lack of air.

Finally, I broke free of the seat and stroked toward the surface while UDT safety divers and a curious dolphin kept pace. Busting out into Florida sunlight, alive and uninjured, I gave a whoop of triumph, having successfully proved a pilot could eject underwater and live.

Eventually, the president of the United States awarded me the Legion of Merit for my "deliberate and heroic" contribution to naval aviation safety.

I never told Elinor what I had done. She would have thought the words "deliberate and heroic" should have included "foolish" as well.

After I received my promotion to lieutenant commander, now only one step behind my old Academy buddy Parr, I became eligible to command a UDT. I had my eye on UDT-21, the only team remaining on the East Coast following RIF (reduction in force) at the end of the Korean War. COMUDU-One in California retained two teams.

But first I wanted to complete my UW bona fides by qualifying in amphibious vessels to learn the duties and responsibilities in supporting underwater commandos. In November 1958, I reported aboard the USS *Shadwell*, an LSD ported at Little Creek, Virginia. LSDs were large ships designed to haul huge amounts of equipment, landing craft, and personnel to a combat beachhead. Beach assaults in the Pacific during World War II might have been unsuccessful but for the support of these big mother ships.

Assigned as the *Shadwell's* operations officer, I set sail for deployment with Sixth Fleet while Elinor and the kids returned to California to stay with her parents. While I was away, Mom received letters from Elinor and her mother begging her to convince her hardheaded son to leave the Navy and accept "the other job" in California.

"Please, Marjorie, I don't know how much longer the children and I can take it," Elinor wrote. "For everyone's sake, you have to make him quit."

Mom admonished Elinor to suck it up and stop whining. "Billy is who Billy is," she responded. "You should be proud of him, as I am proud of him and his father. He is accomplishing important things."

These were exciting and dangerous times. I would have felt like a traitor and a coward to desert my country now. History was playing out right in front of me; I was a part of it.

The Soviets won the Space Race in 1957 by being the first to launch a satellite, *Sputnik*, into orbit. Fidel Castro was about to take over Cuba to add it to the communist win column. U.S. Army Special Forces were in Vietnam training guerrillas to resist Ho Chi Minh. The USSR built a wall around East Berlin, adding to tensions rising throughout Europe. New Soviet prime minister Nikita Khrushchev threatened that communism would bury the United States and Western capitalism.

Having completed my year's sea tour aboard the *Shadwell*, I prepared to take command of UDT-21, based at Little Creek, Virginia. A hard-muscled mustang lieutenant named Roy Boehm was sitting propped up at my desk in the skipper's office when I reported aboard. In faded dungarees and unshined boots, he looked as salty as the former bos'n mate he had been in the South Pacific and on the *Big Woo* in Korea before he volunteered for UDTs and won an officer's commission.

He looked me up and down, one amused brow cocked. I was bright as shit and Shinola polish for my first day back in the teams.

"Damn, skipper," Boehm rumbled with a chuckle. "This ain't no country club. You know that, right?"

This rough-talking sonofabitch bowed to no one. As a former bos'n coxswain, he knew how to get things done. Neither of us knew it at the time, but we were about to make history together.

CHAPTER FOURTEEN

AT AGE THIRTY-ONE, Bos'n Mate First Class Roy Boehm had been the oldest of approximately 140 who began UDTR Class 13—"Lucky 13"—at NAVPHIBSCOL, Little Creek, Virginia, in July 1954 at the end of the Korean War. George Walsh was the next oldest at twenty-eight. Because of Boehm's age, he was one of only two left standing at the end of selections when partners teamed up, like a kid unchosen in sandlot baseball. The other was a scrawny kid with a tendency to be a smartass.

"Looks like me and you," Boehm growled. "What's your name?"

"Digger."

"You got a fucking *real* name?"

"Eddie O'Toole."

Boehm did everything the other Frogmen did during training, it just sometimes took longer. Black Hats ragged his ass.

"You're too fucking old, Boehm. You're an old man. Old and crippled. A useless piece of shit and the stupidest trainee in the whole U.S. Navy. Come on, Boehm. Why don't you quit? Quit before you kill yourself. You don't have to do this shit anymore. You're not going to make it anyhow."

"I ain't never giving up."

At Guadalcanal during the Battle of Cape Esperance, the Japanese sank his destroyer, USS *Duncan*, out from underneath him. It blazed like a Viking funeral pyre when he leaped overboard.

For the rest of that interminable night he swam towing a badly injured shipmate, Seaman Dubiel, toward a distant ink blot that had to be tiny Savo Island. Dubiel lapsed in and out of consciousness.

As daybreak approached in a hard blue sky, he became aware he and Dubiel were no longer alone in the bright sea. Dorsals cut the surface like knife blades. He had never before experienced such near-mindless horror. Merely sighting a shark was enough to strike panic into the bravest heart. But to be in the water *with* them!

The casual detached way the sharks approached set his heart pounding and ignited every nerve ending. Dark dorsal fins slicing the water, snake eyes glinting, teeth-filled jaws drooping. Boehm held on to his comatose friend, unwilling to abandon him even though to do so might distract the sharks and save his own life.

Dubiel screamed. He must have had some awareness at the last instant before his body exploded out of the water like an insect sucked in by a bass. He twisted violently in the white froth and then, gripped in the shark's jaw, he was wrenched from Boehm's grasp and was gone, his scream broken off to linger in Boehm's nightmares. Although Boehm managed to reach Savo Island ahead of the sharks, he vowed never to go into the water again.

Having survived sharks and the sinking of one ship, Boehm was aboard another destroyer, USS *Bennett*, when the ship took Frogmen aboard prior to the invasion of Saipan, and he received his first astonished look at the special men he had heard so much about. They were chiseled, hard-muscled young specimens who carried themselves with a reckless, *special* air. Each was flagged with blue-green paint as camouflage and then marked with black stripes from toes to chin and down each arm in order to use their bodies to measure the depth of water near shore. UDT—*Underwater Demolition Teams*. It was said a man had to be "half fish and half nuts" in order to join up.

"Look at them, Boats," one of the gunners chided Boehm. "Why don't you go with them? Get your ass shot off. I'll take care of your girlfriend for you."

Dropped from rubber boats, Frogmen swam and waded ashore, where they planted and detonated underwater explosives to knock out man-made obstacles, and mapped enemy minefields by swimming among the mines and counting them. All this was accomplished under fierce defensive fire from the Japanese shore while they were armed only with knives and explosive packs and wearing no more than sneakers, fins, swim trunks, and dive masks. *Frogmen*—a term coined by a comic book writer because of the UDTs' fins and blue-green camouflage—porpoised the surface of the water, grabbing a breath of air when they could between mortar rounds and machine-gun fire.

The encounter with them and the UDTs' legendary exploits had more of an impact on Boehm than he at first realized. At the time, however, he was too war-weary to pursue it. All he wanted was to get out of the Navy when the war ended and go home to New York and marry his girlfriend. Besides, after the loss of Dubiel to sharks, he associated diving and the undersea world with death. He couldn't help but look warily about for sharks every time he went over the side to clean the ship's screws or props.

He returned to New York after V-J Day to discover his girlfriend pregnant by a draft evader. She gave his engagement ring back and he left, needing a stiff drink and a good fight.

He decided the Navy *was* his home after all. What was so *special* anyhow about a little ticky-tacky house in the suburbs and a houseful of snotty-nosed brats? Had he survived the sinking of the *Duncan* and the sharks only to end up bullshitting with other veterans at the VFW?

He went down, reenlisted, and ended up on the USS *Furse*, a battered radar patrol destroyer heading out on a Far East cruise to China. The ship put in at Tsingtao, then held by Nationalist President Chiang Kai-shek in his struggle against the communists of Mao Tse-tung. The United States backed Chiang. Boehm was assigned to help train a platoon of Chiang's Nationalist troops. That was where he met and befriended a Nationalist Chinese army officer named Colonel Kang and a holy man named Li.

Li was a very quiet, peaceful man with a wispy gray beard and a dirty black robe to cover his birdlike body. Colonel Kang was tall for an Asian, with shined boots and a thin mustache. He insisted that Cold War conflicts from now on were more apt to be uprisings of "the people" against oppressors rather than full-blown, set-piece wars with nuclear missiles flying everywhere. Future war, he predicted, lay in cloak-and-dagger, behind-the-lines night fighting guerrillas using unconventional tactics, as per Mao's writings. The Orient would show the way to the rest of the world.

Boehm visited Li for the last time when the *Furse* pulled out of port and the United States withdrew from China to permit Mao and Chiang Kai-shek to work out the nation's destiny between them.

"You are a warrior who has a mind willing to learn," Li said to Boehm in farewell. "As a warrior, you will be involved in much and have many things upon which to think. Guerrilla wars, both nationalist and revolutionary, will by their very nature flare up in many countries. Outbreaks may be initiated on many grounds, but all will be supported by commandos and all will be anti-Western."

Boehm carried with him Li's and Kang's comments on guerrilla warfare. He studied Mao and Sun Tzu, picking up everything he could find on unconventional doctrine, tactics, and strategy. Although UW had been practiced in America since its earliest days on the frontier, it remained alien to much of the American mind. The Navy especially was not ready for "new" concepts. It remained steeped in the doctrines of large-scale global conflict. It often seemed stuck in preparing for the last war rather than for the next one.

Early in 1954 after Boehm returned from Korea, he and Chief Warrant Officer Tom Moss, his supervisor, were spearfishing from a whale boat in the Virgin Islands when Boehm spotted an eight-foot blacktip shark basking on the sandy bottom. A chill trickled down his spine as he flashed back to Cape Esperance and the shark snatching Dubiel. It occurred to him that he had not extracted revenge for that long-ago day of terror. He suddenly wanted to kill this shark more than he had ever wanted anything.

He ripped his combat knife from its sheath, dove into the water, and flew swiftly through the clear seawater, coming down on top of the big fish from slightly behind, surprising it. His knife flashed. Blood spilled.

The fish exploded. With his legs and arms wrapped around the blacktip, Boehm stuck to its sandpaper hide like wool to a rasp. As though fused together, he and the fish thrashed across the bottom, boiling up sand and silt and blood. He continued stabbing the fish. Thirty, forty times, until in its death throes it slowly sank to the bottom.

Boehm and Chief Moss lashed the conquered fish to the side of the whaleboat, like Hemingway's character did in *The Old Man and the Sea*. Boehm grinned happily, the curse lifted.

"Will you approve my transfer chit to UDT school?" he asked Moss.

"Roy, you're on the borderline, age-wise."

Boehm slapped the dead shark. "After this, you call me *old*?"

In November 1954, the twenty-one surviving members of UDTR Lucky 13 assembled in the auditorium at the Amphib School Building to graduate. Boehm limped in with them on the bad leg he brought back from World War II, limped back out, grinning. He was UDT, assigned to UDT-21.

A few weeks later, Captain Don Gaither, commander, Underwater Demolition Unit Two (COMUDU-Two), stopped Boehm at UDT-21 headquarters. The bos'n was on his way to New London, Connecticut, to test a two-man submersible called the Mine Hunter.

"Where do you think you're going, Boats?"

"I have to be in New London in the morning, sir."

"Negative. You're staying here tonight. You *are* taking the exam tomorrow for Limited Duty Officer."

Boehm stared. "Me, sir? An officer? I'm no gentleman, sir. I don't know a salad fork from a chopstick. I don't want a commission. I don't have time for it."

"The hell you say, Boats. What's this I've heard about your sea warriors? There's talk the Navy may implement and build up naval special operations. *Unconventional warfare*. You have a chance to become a part of it—especially if you're an officer."

Unconventional warfare? Boehm snapped a crisp salute. "Yes, sir. Get my ass in and take the exam."

When I took over as skipper of UDT-21, Boehm was a UDT trainer with a field commission as a lieutenant. He was rough around the edges, foulmouthed as only a sailor could be, but a better man I couldn't have selected for my second-in-command.

CHAPTER FIFTEEN

E ARLY IN 1960, ON the outskirts of Washington, D.C.'s government district, a cold winter's rain at daybreak slashed against the weathered square-block buildings of what was formerly known as Quarters Eye, the largest Navy WAVE (Women Accepted for Volunteer Emergency Service) base in the U.S. Some of the three- and four-story buildings had been converted to high-end apartments. Others were now either government buildings or private offices. Men dressed unobtrusively in overcoats and raincoats over slacks or jeans parked their cars at a plain, unmarked building and drifted through the back door to an office on the third floor. Windows whose shades were partially drawn oversaw wide expanses of drenched lawns, the grass withered and brown and as severe looking as the men called to the meeting by Richard Bissell, the CIA's chief of clandestine services.

Bissell, President Eisenhower's go-to man when he needed a dirty job done competently, was referred to as the "spook's spook." No minutes were kept of the meeting. The assembled men were all adept in establishing "plausible deniability" for intervention in hot spots around the globe. This was the same team Bissell had called up six years ago in 1954 for a covert operations known as PB Success to depose Guatemala's president Jacobo Arbenz Guzman. Some used their actual names, others used aliases: David Atlee Phillips, "Rip" Robertson, Frank Bender, E. Howard Hunt, Grayston Lynch, and Troy Barnes.

Tonight, the spooks had a new target. It was called the "Cuban Project." Boehm and I, along with UDT-21, would soon find ourselves tossed headfirst into the mix.

Bissell stood up. He was a lank, hawkish man, all business and to the point. He surveyed the room full of veteran CIA operatives.

"We've been given the go-ahead to get rid of the Castro regime and replace it," he said, "but it has to be done without any appearance of U.S. intervention."

Previous proposals for getting rid of Fidel Castro and his communist regime ranged from assassinating him clandestinely to dropping bombs on his ass. Bissell's new plan had been approved and settled from the highest levels of government.

"What we'll consider tonight is the feasibility of training and organizing a Cubans-in-exile invasion force. If it is able to establish a beachhead on Cuban soil, it could broadcast to the world as a government-in-arms. Under international law, the United States could then supply and reinforce the invaders and get rid of that communist bastard."

The Cold War had fully bloomed, and in the prevailing "domino theory" one country after another would fall to communism, as Cuba had, until finally the United States stood alone and isolated in a hostile world. Castro's overthrow of Cuban dictator Fulgencio Batista in 1959 provided another crisis to bring America closer to accepting the concept of limited unconventional warfare. It would also prove to be the United States' first test of will against communism in the Western Hemisphere.

Born on August 13, 1926, Castro became radicalized by the writings of Karl Marx, Friedrich Engels, and Vladimir Lenin while studying at the University of Havana, where he obtained a law degree in 1950. On July 26, 1953, he and an "army" of 163 anti-Batista revolutionaries attacked Moncada Barracks outside Santiago de Cuba, his intent being to capture weapons and spark revolution among Oriente Province's impoverished cane cutters. The attack turned into a rout, with six of his "soldiers" killed, fifteen wounded, and the rest rounded up to be tortured, imprisoned, or executed. His first venture into revolution ended with his being sentenced to fifteen years in prison.

While imprisoned with twenty-five of his comrades, Castro renamed his gang the 26th of July Movement, or MR-26-7, in memory of the date of the Moncada attack. He was released on May 15, 1955, as part of an amnesty agreement. He and his brother Raul fled to Mexico, where they met and befriended a Marxist Argentine doctor named Ernesto "Che" Guevara, who, as Fidel admitted, was "a more advanced revolutionary than I."

On November 15, 1956, Fidel, brother Raul, Che Guevara, and eighty-one armed revolutionaries set sail from Veracruz to Cuba in a corroded old yacht named *Granma*. Other MR-26-7 fighters led by Frank País planned an uprising in Santiago and Manzanilla to correspond with *Granma's* arrival.

Granma came in two days late and ran aground in a mangrove swamp at Playa Los Coloradas. By this time Batista had dispersed País and his rabble. The Castros, Guevara, and their raiders joined País in desperate flight into the Sierra Maestra Mountains of Oriente Province. Only nineteen made it; the rest were either killed or captured.

The survivors hid out in the mountains and bonded with local peasants. Like fish in the sea, as Mao Tse-tung put it in his *Little Red Book*. Little by little, the revolutionaries overran Batista's outposts. Their success attracted more and more recruits.

During the summer and fall of 1958, using classical guerrilla strategies, the relatively small band of determined irregulars pushed Batista's government forces all the way back to Havana. Batista capitulated on December 31 and fled into exile with an amassed fortune estimated at more than $300 million. The Castros and Guevara marched their ragtag column into Havana on January 2, 1959. Fidel swore himself in as Cuba's prime minster the following month.

Castro soon acknowledged to the world that he was a communist and in bed with the Soviet Union. Recognizing the strategic value of the little island nation, Soviet premier Nikita Khrushchev declared dead the Monroe Doctrine that proclaimed United States hegemony in the Western Hemisphere.

As a developing dictator, Fidel proved more aggressive than the ruler he overthrew. Guevara led the way in executing thousands of resisters and imprisoning thousands more. Many escaped by fleeing to

Florida, where Miami became a hotbed of counterrevolutionary activity. Dissidents funded by the CIA and various foreign sources plotted and planned, bided their time, and lobbied for support.

Relations between the U.S. and Cuba deteriorated to the point that the two nations dissolved diplomatic relations. At a meeting of the Organization of American States held in Costa Rica, U.S. secretary of state Christian Herter publically asserted that Cuba was being used as an operational base for the spread of international communism into the Western Hemisphere.

Now, as Richard Bissell and the other CIA attendees at the Cuba Project meeting left Quarters Eye, Bissell paused outside in the cold sprinkle of diminishing rain and lifted his eyes to the disappearing cloud masses. A ray of morning sunshine broke through. He took it as a good sign. A balding man built like a whippet, with a long thin face and nose, stopped next to him.

"Will the new president be with us or against us?" E. Howard Hunt wondered.

John F. Kennedy had won the 1960 election and would be inaugurated in January.

CHAPTER SIXTEEN

WHEN I ASSUMED COMMAND of UDT-21 at Little Creek, Virginia, in early 1961, with Lieutenant Roy Boehm as my operations officer, I found the outfit studded with Boehm's old shipmates, who followed him over to UDT from the fleet. They were hard-muscled, tough bastards like Harry "Lump-Lump" Williams; Clements and Holloran, always referred to as "Heckle and Jeckle"; Eddie "Digger" O'Toole, with whom Boehm attended UDTR; "Hoss" Kacinsky; "Legs" Martin; Rudy Boesch; Lenny Waugh; and others. My first impression of them was of a gang of blackguard Caribbean pirates who would as soon slit your throat as shake hands.

"What did you expect, sir?" Boehm growled. He was the crustiest of the bunch. "You want men who can kick ass—or kiss ass?"

By the time I returned with them from winter training in the Virgin Islands, I knew I had raw material for the saltiest outfit in the Naval Amphibian command. Not only had these Frogs pissed off and embarrassed ship skippers by seizing or sabotaging their vessels right from underneath their noses, they had also kidnapped two fleet admirals and one cute WAVE administrative assistant and held a member of COMPHIBLANT's staff for ransom. It was one hell of a war game; I was so proud of these ugly bastards I could have kissed them right on their butts.

"Don't turn them loose on the citizens of this country unless they're chained and have a zookeeper with them," cautioned Vice Admiral G. C. Towner, Amphibious Commander of the Atlantic Fleet (COMPHIBLANT). I wasn't sure if he was kidding or not.

Admiral Towner apparently placed great stock in me. He had personally selected me to command UDT-21 by noting on my fitness report that I was "undoubtedly the foremost expert on UDT matters in the U.S. Navy." I found myself also wearing other hats he assigned to me: commander of UDU-2 (Underwater Demolitions Unit-2), which didn't mean squat until I had more than one UDT assigned to my UDU; and as one of his Amphibious staff members.

Boehm and I were looking to Cuba as a proving ground for turning UDT into genuine behind-the-lines commandos. I approached Admiral Towner about the possibility of converting them. My overtures remained dry-docked, but I had sown seed into the Navy's higher echelons.

"Skipper," Boehm said, "all you gotta do is get them weenie-necks in the Pentagon to use us. Turn us loose on Castro and we'll soon have that cocksucker begging to suck your dick."

Something as big as the Cuban Project discussed by Richard Bissell and his CIA spooks at Quarters Eye last winter was bound to leak out sooner or later. Rumors spread as CIA procurement teams scouted the United States and Europe for airplanes, tanks, ships, and other weapons with which to arm an exile army while not implicating the United States. A CIA reception and debriefing center at Key West directed arriving Cuban refugees to Miami's Dinner Key, where the Frente Revolucionari Democratico (FRD) had established a Cuban government-in-exile and a recruiting office. News soon broke in American and Mexican newspapers that a Cuban attack force known as Brigade 2506 was training at various sites in the hemisphere.

I knew where most of these sites were located, since the CIA expected to use Frogs from my UDT-21 as trainers and prospective guerrilla leaders. I coordinated with the CIA station chief in Miami to distribute my best trainers everywhere from a coffee plantation and refurbished airstrip in southern Guatemala to Fort Gulick in Panama and Vieques Island off Puerto Rico, and from Homestead Air Force Base in south Florida to Fort Benning's Infantry School in Georgia.

CIA operatives were in charge of the entire operation, good men like Grayston Lynch and Rip Robertson, who I learned would personally accompany any invasion force, and Theodore Shackley and Rudy Enders, who had by now gone over to the CIA from the Navy.

Robertson had attended the Quarters Eye meeting and was close-mouthed and secretive. Lynch said the man didn't trust his own mother or wife, who still thought he was a traveling salesman. Lynch was the same, except a bit more talkative. He had been severely wounded at the Battle of the Bulge during World War II, with a wound that kept him hospitalized for five years.

Shackley was hard to get to know, a cold, calculating character, deliberate—the living epitome of *Mad* magazine's *Spy vs. Spy* agent in white. Rudy Enders was charged with infiltrating commando teams into Cuba to carry out highly secret ops against Castro's government—attacking military outposts, sabotaging critical superstructure like factories and railroads, and, in general, creating chaos.

I often traveled with spooks to inspect various sites or check in on my UDT trainers. One week I might be shuttling into Guatemala to observe aircraft bombing maneuvers, the next to a U.S. bombing range or diving grounds on the uninhabited island of Vieques. As operations officer, Boehm was even more on the move and heavily involved in day-to-day training matters.

While training continued, Bissell and E. Howard Hunt arranged with Eduardo Garcia of the Garcia Line Corporation, the only Cuban freighter line still running rice and sugar off Castro's island, to lease six small freighters to transport an invasion force. The freighters were old, slow, and run-down and would never be suspected as a military armada.

But then I thought of Castro's *Granma* and wasn't so sure *el Jefe* might not remember what he had learned about UW and the advantage of going unnoticed.

I watched the sun setting over Vieques one afternoon from the quarter-deck of an LSD as it motored toward a number of figures that, from a distance, appeared to be frolicking tourists on a beach. The LSD anchored offshore, and I rode the rest of the way in on the ship's launch. Boehm, in charge of training ashore, recognized me as soon as I got off the ship. He turned his class over to a former UDT-trained spook, Smarty Marty Martinez, and waded out toward me in the surf in his swim trunks.

"Are they ready?" I asked as Boehm approached and shook hands. His Cubans were working with SCUBA in the use of demolitions.

Boehm turned to look at his students. A practice detonation went off near mangroves in the shallows, erupting a geyser of water. I heard someone laugh.

"When do you need 'em, skipper?"

"Yesterday. I've spoken to Admiral Towner and with Bissell and Howard Hunt. The invasion's not far off. They want us to insert more saboteurs to keep Castro off balance."

Boehm shrugged and slung seawater from his hair. "That's why we get paid the big bucks."

"Maybe as early as next week," I said.

I passed out cigarettes as the Cubans congregated among their camping tents on the beach to ask questions and be reassured that all their hard training was not in vain. Some of them seemed anxious. They were always asking *when*. *When* would the invasion be?

Eduardo Bazan, a slender, dark-haired man in his mid-twenties, nodded thanks when I handed him what was left of a pack of Camels. He tapped out a cig and offered the pack back to me.

"Keep it."

"*Gracias, jefe.*"

When Castro took over, he confiscated Eduardo's father's farm, two houses, and a pair of shrimp boats. Eduardo joined the anti-Castro underground until he escaped to Miami in September 1960. There he met Tony de Varona, who told him Brigade 2506 needed swimmers. Eduardo was good in the water and immediately volunteered.

He had cut his dark hair short, military style. Water dropped from his mustache. I lit his cigarette for him. He inhaled smoke deep into his lungs. He looked worried.

"*Caramba!*" he exclaimed. "How can we win with one thousand men? Fidel he has thirty thousand, maybe more."

A recruit named Parada spoke up. He had supported Castro at first and was captured with him at the Moncada Army post and imprisoned.

He turned against Fidel afterward and fled to Florida with the help of a CIA operative who coerced him into either joining the brigade or being deported back to Cuba.

"I am being told by Colonel Frank," he said, meaning Frank Bender, "that our undertaking cannot fail in any case. I ask him, I ask, 'How do we know this is so?' Upon that, he answer me, 'If the landing in Cuba should happen to fail, we will in all event intervene directly. And immediately too, no matter that the OAS might object.' Is that for true?"

I had asked the same questions of Shackley and Bissell. I didn't particularly trust the State Department.

"President Jack Kennedy said he will protect the invasion with an air umbrella," Bissell told me. "The skies will belong to us."

A lot of good Cubans were going to die if they went in trusting us and we failed to follow through.

"The president promises air cover by American combat aircraft and by U.S. Navy destroyers," Bissell said. "An American Navy ship will bring landing boats to the Cuban invasion freighters to haul troops ashore. We have the president's word that he will support."

"*Cuando?*" the recruits kept asking. When?

Signs indicated it would be soon. Just yesterday, April 2, 1961, the State Department at JFK's instructions issued a white paper declaring Cuba a Soviet satellite and warning Castro to either break all ties with Khrushchev or be considered "a clear and present danger to the authentic and autonomous revolution of the Americas."

In Miami, CIA-created Radio SWAN had become especially active within past weeks. Propaganda twenty-four-seven urged the Cuban people to rise up and overthrow their corrupt and aggressive government.

"The bullshit is about over," Boehm predicted. "We're getting down to the nut cutting."

CHAPTER SEVENTEEN

From the air, the forty-five square miles of land and water that made up the U.S. naval base at Guantanamo Bay seemed to sparkle back the sunlight. Arranged like a thumb and forefinger around the bay, it was America's oldest overseas base, having been acquired in the Cuban-American treaty of 1903. It was also the only American base inside a communist country—and a sharp stick poked in Castro's eye.

Aboard the C-54 military transport as it turned upwind on final were, in addition to Boehm and me and Frog-turned-spook Smarty Marty Martinez, fourteen Cuban patriots trained in demolitions, communications, escape-and-evasion, and survival. Our Cubans, along with other teams of saboteurs and spies, had been inserting onto the island for the past several weeks to prepare the way for a landing, their mission to blow up roads, bridges, and railroads when the invasion began.

"Listen to your radios," spooks instructed during a team briefing held at Naval Station Little Creek the night before. "You will hear the codes that tell you where and when to go into action."

Boehm, Marty, and I had strict orders not to accompany the Cuban teams when they infiltrated. Roy was pissed off about the prohibition, grousing his usual "fucks" and "cocksuckers," but there was little we could do about it. There'd be hell to pay internationally if Castro captured an American inside the country blowing up something.

The C-54 rolled off the runway and immediately into a hangar. The door closed against possible spies. The base commander met us to ensure everything went smoothly. Boehm and I hootched up at the BOQ with Smarty Marty and other CIA operatives while a covered deuce-and-a-half truck transported our Cubans to a barracks isolated on a corner of the base. Boehm and I weren't essential to the mission, but we had insisted on going along to Guantanamo in moral support of "our" Cubans.

There was little to do for the next couple of days except cool our pipes and stay out of sight. Finally, we got a go for that night. A Jeep drove Boehm and me to the Cuban barracks as soon as the sun went down. Smarty Marty and another agent had arrived for last-minute briefings. The Cubans seemed in high spirits as they made final preparations, having been issued C-rations, weapons, radios, maps, and other gear. The plan called for them to split into two seven-man teams for insertion at two separate locations.

Teams assembled dockside where a Navy landing craft and an eighty-five-foot open-sea rescue "crash boat," an AVR, waited. The crash boat bristled with twin 50-caliber machine guns and a 20mm anti-aircraft gun. Nothing said we couldn't fight back if attacked while in international waters.

It was a moonless night so far. Dark settled around the two boats as though all light in the world was shut off. We had to feel our way up the gangplank and onto the landing craft; not a single light penetrated the darkness, not even the pinprick glow of a cigarette. No one spoke.

The boat low-throttled to sea followed by the crash boat running overwatch. I rode the bow with the salt air in my nostrils and the warm breeze off the tropic island brushing across my cheeks. Boehm and I spoke in low tones. Smarty Marty took the bridge with the captain. The Cubans waited silently on deck gripping M-14 rifles and huddled around backpacks full of dynamite and C-4 plastic explosives, radios, ammo, rations, and survival gear. Once deposited, they must hide out in swamps and in the mountains until they received word to sweep into action.

I wondered if they felt as nervous as I had the night I ran my first mission with UDT-5 in Korea.

The Sierra Maestra Mountains, Fidel Castro's old refuge in Oriente Province, rose dark and irregular off to starboard. So far so good. Even fishermen avoided these seas after dark in fear of being fired upon by Soviet patrol boats.

Our boats pulled alongside each other and pulled throttle. Infiltrators along with Marty and Boehm silently transferred to the crash boat with its shallower draft in order to pull nearer the shoreline. Rubber rafts, ready to go on the crash boat, provided the last leg into wooded coves and hidden swamps. My duty was to remain aboard the first craft and use it as a command ship until Boehm and the spook returned. I solemnly shook hands with my Cubans as they departed the ship.

"When we meet again, Commander Bone," Eduardo said, "it will be in a free Cuba."

"*Ojalá que es verdad,*" I replied.

I gripped Boehm's arm as he prepared to drop over the side of the landing craft into the crash boat. I felt it necessary to issue a final warning.

"Roy, stay on the boat and keep your sorry ass off Cuban soil. All Khrushchev needs to start an international incident and fuck up the landing is capture a U.S. personnel."

We dropped the first team of seven near the mountains about forty miles east of Gitmo. The other seven infiltrators went into an inlet called the Bay of Pigs.

"Remember the story I told about killing the shark?" Boehm reminded his guerrillas before they vanished into the darkness. "Don't give yourself away until you have the element of surprise. Then—"

A soft Spanish chuckle. "And then—*fuck* them over. Right, *jefe?*"

"Fuck 'em good. Fierce and deadly."

Aboard the command boat we waited out a time interval listening for gunfire or some other indication the infiltrators may have been compromised. Smarty Marty finally sighed with relief. Nothing out there but waves washing against shoreline and the occasional night bird.

"They're in," he said. "Let's get out of here before daylight and we're spotted."

The next day Boehm and I hopped the C-54 back to UDT-21 at Little Creek. I couldn't help feeling that we had deserted our guerrillas in not accompanying them ashore. I knew Roy felt the same way.

"I wonder if we'll ever see those poor bastards again," he said.

CHAPTER EIGHTEEN

THE BREAKUP WAS A long time coming. I couldn't say I was surprised.

"I'm tired, Bill," Elinor said before she packed up and took the three kids back to Mama's in California. "I'm tired of you being gone all the time and leaving me and the kids behind to wait for you, not knowing where you are, what you're doing, or when and *if* you'll be back. We're not going to live like that anymore."

"Elinor . . . Elinor, I'm sorry—"

"Sorry's not enough, Bill. You don't need *anybody*. Better you go take care of your Navy and we'll go home. Maybe I'll never have to see the Navy again."

Now they were gone. Linda Jean was in the third grade already, Bill Jr. would start kindergarten in the fall, and little Jana Lee was toddling about the house chanting "DaDa." Gone where I would rarely see them and be an influence in their lives. Too often I saw families breaking up like this: Daddy gone so much, returning home after a WestPac or Far East tour, disembarking to a lonely and troubled wife and children bawling in terror at the sight of some big stranger trying to hug them.

Elinor was right. I wasn't around all the time and I should have been.

I drove Elinor and the kids to the airport and saw them off in a flood of largely unspoken recriminations and tears. Then, having been informed that the Cuban invasion was on, I caught the next military flight to Guantanamo to be near the action when the excrement hit the prop. I didn't wait long. At dawn on August 17, 1961, radio traffic in the Gitmo Operations Center began to crackle with excitement as brass from all over the military arrived for the show.

At the other end of the island, about four hundred miles away, Fidel Castro awoke when two B-26 bombers flew rooftop-low over "Point One," the national military headquarters in suburban Havana.

"What are those planes?" he demanded of his staff.

No one could tell him. He bolted to the window and watched in helpless rage as the American-made, World War II–type bombers began diving on Campo Libertad Airport nearby. He heard the crump of exploding bombs and the stutter of anti-aircraft fire.

He was sure the long-dreaded invasion had begun.

* * *

While CIA personnel promised Cubans that America would assure the invasion's success, JFK was saying something else. On April 12, three days before the B-26 strikes on Castro's air force, Kennedy announced to the Alliance for Progress for Latin America that "there will not be, under any circumstances, an intervention in Cuba by the U.S. armed forces or American civilians."

Bissell, Hunt, Enders, and other CIA operatives assumed JFK's statement to be one of misdirection to lull Castro into a false sense of security. They continued with their plans to attack.

"These men are ready," I assured E. Howard Hunt after one of my jaunts to the main training base in Guatemala. "They're trained and overtrained, and from now on they can only go downhill. How soon do they get to fight?"

"I haven't been told," Hunt replied.

President Kennedy still vacillated. He couldn't seem to make up his mind. To give himself more time, he established an invasion date of April 11, then changed it to April 17. He still had time to call off operations, even though the first troop ships had left the staging area at Puerto Cabezas, Nicaragua, on April 11, six days before the scheduled landing. The last ships would start across the Caribbean on Thursday, April 13.

Two events were scheduled on April 15, two days before troops landed. First, B-26 air strikes against Castro's air force; and, second, Nino Diaz would lead a diversionary force ashore in Oriente Province.

JFK telephoned Richard Bissell to ask how many aircraft would fly against Castro's airfield. Bissell told him sixteen.

"I don't want it on that scale," the president said. "I want it minimal."

On the morning of Saturday, April 15, a bomber force sharply reduced to six airplanes took off from CIA base Happy Valley in Nicaragua. President Luis Somoza bade the pilots farewell, with an admonishment to bring back Castro's beard. Two planes would strike each of three Cuban airfields—Campo Libertad on the outskirts of Havana, Antonio Maceo airport at Santiago de Cuba 450 miles southeast of Havana, and San Antonio de los Baños. The planes would strike simultaneously at dawn with bombs, rockets, and machine guns.

Gustavo Ponzoa and his wingman, Gonzalo Herrera, were the first to take off from Nicaragua. The two B-26s skimmed the Caribbean at an altitude of fifty feet to avoid radar detection, then climbed over the seashore cliffs in Cuba and roared down the runway at Santiago de Cuba at 1,200 feet. Ponzoa released both his 500-pound demolition bombs. Heavy red-and-black smoke billowed up from underneath his right wing as he throttled and pulled out of his bombing glide. Anti-aircraft fire and tracers from machine guns arched skyward.

Herrera, Ponzoa's wingman, followed with his run. In the meantime, the two other teams of two attacked their own targets at Antonio Maceo and at Campo Libertad, where an alarmed Castro watched from his window.

Each team was supposed to make two runs. Ponzoa and Herrera made five, thundering in at fifty feet above the runway to slam rockets and machine gun bullets into hangars and aircraft. Ponzoa's bomber took a hit in the nose on his fifth run. Herrera was also hit.

"Gus!" Herrera yelled over the radio to Ponzoa, "I can see holes in both wings."

Ponzoa radioed back, "Let's get out of here and go home!"

All six bombers managed to return safely to Nicaragua, although Herrera busted all three tires when he landed. Jubilation that Castro's air force was wiped out soon turned to gloom when U-2 reconnaissance photos revealed that only five of his aircraft had been destroyed on the ground. Anticipating attack, wily Fidel had dispersed his planes and used several broken-down ones as decoys. He still possessed a formidable force to use against an invasion.

On Sunday at Quarters Eye in Washington, the Air Operations Officer was ordering ordnance for a cleanup strike against the airfields when General Charles Cabell arrived. Cabell was acting director of the CIA in Allen Dulles's absence. Dulles was in Puerto Rico.

"What are you doing?" Cabell asked.

"Readying the follow-up strikes, sir. We have to finish them off."

"Seems to me we were only authorized one strike at the airfields," replied Cabell.

"Oh, no, sir. There are no restrictions on the number of strikes. The authorization was to knock out the Cuban Air Force."

Cabell's jaw jutted. "I don't know about that. So to be on the safe side, I'm going to ask Dean Rusk about it." Dean Rusk was secretary of state. "Cancel that strike order until I get someone to approve it."

JFK, who had given the go-ahead for the invasion, now scrubbed the cleanup air strikes. Rebel pilots in Happy Valley were revving up B-26 engines for the follow-up when they received orders to cancel. Major General George "Poppa" Doster, the American commander of brigade pilot training, slammed his hat on the ground and yelled, "There goes the whole fucking war!"

The chairman of the Joint Chiefs of Staff referred to the cancellation as "pulling out the rug . . . absolutely reprehensible, almost criminal."

The other elements of the invasion were experiencing their own difficulties. During the final days of preparations, the CIA decided to change the landing site from the Trinidad sandy beaches to the Bay of Pigs, more than 100 miles farther east along the southern coast. CIA intelligence showed the area to be a sparsely populated stretch of territory isolated from the rest of the island by the treacherous Zapata

Swamps, crossed only by two narrow-gauge railroads and tricky paths known to local villagers alone. The small 108-man government militia detachment at the village of Giron was not considered a real threat to the invasion. Bissell decided that since there were no rapid communications between the Bay of Pigs and Havana, the invaders could land, capture the airfield at Giron, and begin flying in war supplies before Castro realized what was happening.

What the Americans did not realize was that Fidel knew the region well from having fished for trout in nearby Laguna del Tesoro. Three hard-topped roads now crossed the swamp. A resort facility and another 180 concrete houses were under construction. Changing the invasion site was simply another planning snafu in a long line of mistakes and poor judgments leading up to the night of April 16, when a U.S. naval task force consisting of the aircraft carrier *Essex* and seven destroyers secretly rendezvoused off the coast with Eduardo Garcia's seven ragged freighters of the invasion fleet.

This U.S. task force had orders to merely escort the insurgent craft to the coast, nothing more. It was to remain strictly uncommitted when the invasion began.

Shortly before midnight on Sunday, April 16, six Cuban Frogmen led by Andy Pruna and the stocky and balding CIA agent Grayston Lynch slipped toward shore at Playa Giron to mark the beach for landing. Their rubber boat was still fifty yards from land, grounded by a reef that planners thought was a stretch of subsurface seaweed, when a jeep swung along the beach and bathed the landing party in its headlights.

An American fired the first shots at the Bay of Pigs. Grayston Lynch opened up with one twenty-round magazine from his Browning automatic rifle. The Cuban Frogmen joined in, riddling the jeep and two militiamen with gunfire. The headlights went out.

Knowing the element of surprise was blown, the Frogmen scurried up and down the beach, placing landing lights. About twenty-five Castro militiamen pulled up in a truck; Lynch radioed an urgent request that the landing craft (LSVPs) from his freighter, the *Blager*, be quickly loaded with troops and rushed ashore.

Gunfire rattled as the two LCVPs roared in for the invasion's first troop landing. One of the landing craft struck the reef and soon sank.

Wet but uninjured, the first fighters at the Bay of Pigs waded onto sand. They took off for Giron, firing wildly into the pastel-colored bungalows of Castro's new recreation colony. The militia retreated to the woods and swamps beyond.

Grayston Lynch returned to the *Blager* after Pepe San Roman and the other brigade commanders waded onto Cuban soil. An urgent message from Washington awaited him: "Castro still has operational aircraft. Expect you to be hit at dawn. Unload all troops and supplies and take ships to sea as soon as possible."

In spite of the reef, the brigade's 1,453 soldiers began pouring onto "Blue Beach" at Playa Giron in the predawn hours of April 17. The other half of the landing under the command of Hugo Sueiro disembarked at "Red Beach" at Playa Largo deep in the mouth of the bay, twenty miles away. It received light machine-gun fire but landed without casualties to find a microwave radio station still warm from use. So much for the CIA's intelligence that the Bay of Pigs was without communications.

In New York, E. Howard Hunt dictated a press release in the name of the Frente Revolucionari Democratica: "Before dawn, Cuban patriots in the cities and in the hills began the battle to liberate our homeland from the despotic rule of Fidel Castro."

And in Havana, Fidel Castro was awakened at 1:15 a.m. and told that the land invasion had begun. He took immediate personal command.

By 6:00 a.m., even while the invasion fleet was still offloading infantry and equipment, Castro's troops and his nine surviving aircraft were in full counterattack against Brigade 2506. Garcia's freighters in the bay were being pounded by Castro's Sea Fury aircraft and B-26s. Grayston Lynch and Rip Robertson on the freighter *Blager* fired 50-caliber machine guns so steadily at the attacking planes that the barrels turned white hot.

The freighter *Houston* was sinking, still laden with ammunition. The *Rio Escondido* exploded in a massive eruption of fire, struck by rockets from a Sea Fury. The ship contained the bulk of the invasion's ammunition, fuel, and medical supplies. The planes also knocked out

Marsopa, from which the invasion was being coordinated, as well as several smaller vessels used to ferry troops ashore. Garcia, the ships' owner, must have been crying his eyes out.

Lynch, in command on-site, was assaulted by messages from headquarters: "To sea!" The ships would have to return after dark to offload supplies. The agent radioed San Roman ashore: "Pepe, we're going to have to go."

"Okay, but don't desert us," Pepe responded.

"We're not going to desert you," Lynch promised.

JFK's ill-advised decision not to provide U.S. air cover, coupled with his unwillingness to permit the knockout blow against Castro's air force, took a toll on the rebel air operations that day.

Shortly before sunup, Captain Eddie Ferrer, pilot of the first of six lumbering C-46s en route to drop 177 paratroopers northeast of Blue Beach to cut off and defend the invasion site, passed over the aircraft carrier *Essex* and two destroyers plowing toward the beaches. He was certain they were joining the battle.

"Hell, we can't lose!" he exclaimed to his copilot.

The C-46s were slow and unarmed and without a fighter escort. Rebels were still under the impression that the United States was providing an "umbrella." Ferrer was thus all the more surprised after he dropped his paratroopers on the San Blas Road to find Castro's T-33s attacking the brigade flight. Machine gun bursts puffed smoke from attackers' wings. Ferrer saw one of the C-46s plummet to earth streaking smoke. He managed to escape to sea by skimming the waves and slow-flying with full flaps.

As the battle progressed, T-33 jets picked five of the Brigade's twelve remaining aircraft out of the air, including the B-26 flown by Americans Pete Ray and Leo Francis Baker, who were killed on the ground when they tried to escape their crashed bomber amid the fighting. Their bodies would be kept frozen in a Havana morgue for the next eighteen years.

American A-4D pilots from the carrier *Essex* watched helplessly as Castro's bombers and fighters made sorties against the beaches, the freighters in the bay, and the hapless C-46 transports. A Cuban T-33 made a run at pilot Tim Lanahan, who was cruising his jet at twenty-five thousand feet. Within seconds, both jets were diving, with the A-4D close on the Cuban's tail.

"Don't fire! Don't fire!" came the air controller's frantic cry from the *Essex.* "Rules of engagement have been changed."

Lanahan had no choice but to drop his pursuit of the T-33 and return to the carrier.

Pilot Jim Forgy came upon a Cuban Sea Fury riding the tail of a Brigade B-26. The bomber's starboard engine erupted in flames. The Sea Fury closed in for the kill.

"I have a Sea Fury shooting this B-26 down," Forgy radioed. "Request permission to take positive action."

"Negative," came back the reply.

On the ground, Erneido Oliva's Second Battalion requested two Brigade B-26s to attack an enemy column of nine hundred approaching the battle zone in sixty vehicles, including buses. The bombers routed the battalion, but a Castro T-33 and a Sea Fury shot down one of the bombers.

By midnight of the first day, Fidel and twenty thousand soldiers had arrived to trap the invaders against the beaches, squeezing them into tighter and tighter perimeters. Castro's tanks and infantry battered the Brigade with artillery fire for forty-eight straight hours. At the traffic circle on the northern outskirts of Playa Larga, Oliva and his men endured more than two thousand shells falling on them in less than four hours. Stalin tanks rumbled against Oliva's dug-in defenders until midnight.

A little former barber called Barberito ran around and around one of the advancing tanks, peppering it with fire from his recoilless rifle until the frightened crew surrendered. Barberito was killed later by a machine gun burst.

A Brigade tank driver named Jorge Alvarez knocked out an enemy tank with his last shell, then deliberately crashed his tank into another Stalin. The two monsters rammed each other in a remarkable nose-to-nose battle until the Stalin's gun barrel split and it retreated.

Of Oliva's 370 men, twenty had been killed and another fifty were wounded by the time they beat back the enemy's initial attacks.

Weakened and bleeding, knowing another attack at dawn was inevitable, the Red Beach invaders retreated to Giron to link up with Blue Beach invaders. They arrived at 8:45 a.m. on Tuesday, April 18.

Castro closed in on Blue Beach.

Oliva organized the last battle of the Bay of Pigs, which came to be known as "the last stand at Giron."

Armed with seven bazookas and three tanks, Oliva's battalion destroyed three Castro tanks and an armored truck during the first fighting. The Brigade's 81mm mortars fired so fast the tubes started to melt. When Castro's troops pulled back to regroup, Oliva found he could no longer raise Pepe San Roman on the radio.

San Roman had pulled back to within twenty feet of the water. Crouching on the sand with artillery fire bursting around him, the Brigade commander issued his last radio message, shouting across the air to Grayston Lynch aboard *Blager*: "Am destroying all equipment and communications. I have nothing left to fight with. Am taking to the woods. I can't wait for you."

Abandoned by the United States, surrounded by a force ten times larger, pounded by artillery and fighter bombers, pushed back to the beaches and swamps, unable to escape, out of ammunition, Pepe San Roman ordered his command to break into groups and escape however they could. Grayston Lynch later told me it was the first time he was ever ashamed of his country.

I knew how he felt. At Guantanamo, I lowered my head and bit my lip to keep from bawling like an abandoned baby seal as news of the failure streamed in across the operation center's commo. I wanted to go home—except Elinor was gone and I no longer had a home.

CHAPTER NINETEEN

I N MY ASSESSMENT, THE Bay of Pigs defeat and our reneging on aid to the rebels led to the communist presumption that the United States might no longer possess the moral courage to honor its commitments to the Free World. Communist foreign policy was like a pig in a gunnysack—a push here, a push there, withdraw at one point, then kick a leg out over there—a missile-rattling strategy that kept the rest of the world on the edge of paranoid schizophrenia.

MAD—Mutual Assured Destruction—seemed an appropriate term to describe the nuclear protocol whereby if you attacked me I struck back and we destroyed each other. Vaporize humanity, if necessary, in the pursuit of victory. American culture developed an apocalyptic side. Nuclear air-raid drills conditioned schoolchildren to cringe underneath their desks. Suburbanites dug air-raid shelters in their backyards.

Brigade 2506 lost 120 men killed during the Bay of Pigs landing. Pepe San Roman and about fifty of his followers hid out in the Zapata Swamps for two weeks before hunger and thirst forced them to surrender. Castro announced the capture of 1,800 invaders, many of whom Che Guevara executed.

"We abandoned those poor fuckers to die when they depended on us," Boehm protested.

The fiasco in Cuba was still in the headlines, along with a new crisis developing in partitioned Berlin, when I received orders to report to the Chief of Naval Operations at the Pentagon as soon as possible. More than twenty thousand military and civilian employees worked in the U.S. Department of Defense. I had been to the Pentagon a few times and always before found the massive five-sided structure active with energy. This time, however, it seemed somber and bleak, under a dark cloud. Or perhaps I was merely transferring to it my own state of mind about Cuba.

I passed through Marine security at the main entrance and wended my way down the corridors to the office of the CNO, the most senior-ranking officer in the Department of Navy, where a sour-faced civilian receptionist showed me to Admiral Arleigh Burke's office. His cluttered desk looked the size of my entire office at Little Creek.

Admiral Burke was sixty years old, fit looking, with a long Nordic face and a Marine Corps haircut with wide sidewalls. "Sit down, Commander," he invited, gesturing. "I received your proposal outlining your plan to create a naval special forces unit."

I submitted that proposal months ago. I thought it must have either been discarded or lost in the bureaucracy.

"Commander Hamilton, I hear scuttlebutt that you've already been training your UDT-21 men."

"Yes, sir," I admitted. "It seems needed. The Army has already done it."

The admiral nodded and pressed his lips together. He lifted one eyebrow. "It appears a lot of other people may agree with you. Your proposal has been widely circulated. Commander, I may have a job for you."

He handed me a copy of a letter that had not yet been signed or distributed. The subject line read, "Development of improved naval guerrilla/counter-guerrilla warfare capability."

I looked up, not quite willing to believe it. Admiral Burke nodded and motioned for me to keep reading.

". . . augment present naval capabilities in restricted waters and rivers with particular reference to the conduct and support of paramilitary operations. It is desirable to establish Special Operations Teams as separate components within Underwater Demolition Units One and Two. . . ."

I read it twice to make sure I understood. I felt dizzy with disbelief. Apparently, more military people than I imagined shared my vision. While I was occupied with training and preparing for the Cuban invasion, ideas expressed in my letter were secretly floating around within the Defense and Navy Departments. My proposals, I discovered, were the impetus needed to invigorate movements already under way.

The Unconventional Activities Working Group had been established back on September 13, 1960, in response to increasing insurgency challenges in Laos, South Vietnam, and Cuba. It was directed to investigate "naval unconventional activity methods, techniques and concepts, which may be employed effectively against Sino-Soviet interests under conditions of Cold War."

Deputy CNO William Beakley suggested: "[T]he Underwater Demolition Teams and the Marine reconnaissance units are organizations capable of expansion into unconventional warfare."

At the National Security Council meeting of February 1, 1961, less than a month after John Kennedy assumed the presidency, McGeorge Bundy, special assistant to the president for national security affairs, noted in a top secret memorandum that President Kennedy "requested the Secretary of Defense, in consultation with other interested agencies, examine means of placing more emphasis on the development of counter-guerrilla forces. Accordingly, it is requested that the Department of Defense take action . . . and inform this office promptly of the measures which it proposes to take."

A month before the Bay of Pigs disaster, Rear Admiral William Gentner, director of the CNO's Strategic Plans Division, approved a concept for "additional unconventional warfare capabilities within, or as an extension of, our amphibious forces."

This latest concept by Admiral Gentner was based on the one I submitted. It was the reason I now sat across the desk from Admiral Burke. The admiral pushed back in his chair.

"While the United States concentrated on conventional warfare and nuclear global deterrence," he said, "the unconventional has slowly outflanked the conventional. As Cuba proves, we have failed to deter low-intensity conflict while strategists tell us this is the most likely form of conflict for at least the rest of the century. That makes us well prepared for the least likely conflict and poorly prepared for the most likely. Now we're playing catch-up."

He paused to study me. I was literally on the edge of my chair.

"Commander, I want you to be instrumental in building a naval special warfare unit using the UDTs as the base. You will work with Captains Mort Prince and Sandy Warren in OP-343E until we find a relief for you at COMUDU-Two. In the meantime . . ."

I would continue to also occupy my other slots as skipper of UDT-21 and COMUDU-Two. My additional new title would be CNO Assistant Head of Special Support Operations, Strike Warfare Division, which also included membership in the Unconventional Activities Working Group.

"It's a lot to ask of you, Commander."

"I'll take it," I responded before the CNO changed his mind.

Burke smiled. "That's why I picked you, Bone."

The CNO promised me wide leeway in training and bringing the new unit online. Roy Boehm was waiting for me when I returned to Little Creek. I gave him a mysterious smile.

"Lieutenant Boehm, you and I have shared a vision."

"Yes, sir. Go back and kick Castro's butt."

"Better than that, Roy. You're my ops and training officer. Can you make commandos out of our people?"

"We're almost there already, sir."

"We've just received the Pentagon's approval."

Boehm stared. A grin slowly crossed his rugged face. "I'll coordinate with the staff right away."

"No. This is classified top secret. You will report directly to me. I want you to select and train men as a nucleus for a special operations force to be incorporated into Underwater Demolition Units. You will discuss the creation of this unit with no one except me. You will volunteer information on the purpose of training to no one, not even the men undergoing it. Is that clear?"

"Aye, aye, sir. I will build a team within a team and tell no one. What kind of mission do you have in mind?"

I leaned across the desk on my elbows. I felt excitement welling through the both of us.

"Roy, do you know what this means? We've been granted carte blanche to create the finest bunch of unconventional warriors in the world. President Kennedy has taken a lot of flak for the Bay of Pigs. He's not going to let it happen again. Now, let's get to work. We want night fighters who can successfully complete any mission anywhere in the world. Provide me your concept of operations, a mission profile, and a profile of the men we need. Get cracking."

On May 25, 1961, President John F. Kennedy delivered a "Special Message to the Congress on Urgent National Needs." He enunciated his goal to land an American on the moon within the decade and to expand U.S. special operations forces.

"The great battleground for the defense and expansion of freedom today is the whole southern half of the globe—Asia, Latin America, Africa, and the Middle East," he said. "[Communist aggressors] have fired no missiles, and their troops are seldom seen. They send arms, agitators, aid, technicians, and propaganda to every trouble area. Where fighting is done, it is usually done by others—by guerrillas striking at night, by assassins striking alone—assassins who have taken the lives of thousands of civil officers in the last twelve months in Vietnam alone. . . .

"I am directing the Secretary of Defense to expand rapidly and substantially, in cooperation with our allies, the orientation of existing forces for the conduct of non-nuclear war, paramilitary operations and sub-limited or unconventional wars. In addition, our special forces and unconventional warfare units will be increased and reoriented."

CHAPTER TWENTY

WITH MY DUTIES SPLIT between the Pentagon and UDT-21, I made Boehm my XO and put him in charge under my supervision for the largest share of training our new special warfare unit. I ran interference to keep the brass off his ass while he got the job done.

He was a rough sonofabitch, like most bos'n mates, and never played the political game of CYA—*Cover Your Ass*. By the time we finished he would have four courts-martial pending against him for various crimes and misdemeanors involving acquiring equipment and training outside the normal military channels. Sometimes it was all I could do to keep his ugly butt out of the brig and working on our warriors.

JFK wanted sea warriors; Boehm and I would give them to him. Commies were spreading like lice throughout Latin America and you could whiff Vietnam on the wind. It was up to us to stop the cocksuckers. We knew what we wanted for our unit. Swift, deadly, like the shark. Capable of infiltrating or striking from the air by parachute or helicopter, from overland, from the surface of the sea, or from underneath the sea.

They had to be more than killers, all muscle and neck and attack-dog mentality. I wanted—*demanded*—creative men who operated with their brains as well as with their muscles. Men of courage, dedication to duty, sacrifice, personal dexterity, and intelligence. Team and mission must come first. At the same time, they must be individuals, near rogues in fact. Rough men, tough men who could kick ass and operate outside protocol.

Boehm liked to tell the story of a man he knocked down during a fistfight. "You're not going to kick him while he's down, are you, Roysi?" asked Lump-Lump, his old shipmate, with a sly grin.

"What the fuck you think I've got him down for?"

I gave the lieutenant a complement of ten officers and fifty enlisted and asked him to report back to me with the names he selected. The officers he chose were all young junior officers, like Lieutenant (JG) Dante Stephenson, who had a hair-trigger temper but whom we could use if he controlled it. Also, "Tex" Hager, George Doran, Dave Graveson, Jose Taylor, John Callahan. Most were LDOs (limited duty officers) like Boehm, mustangs who had worked their way up through the enlisted ranks and weren't preoccupied with their careers as officers.

From the enlisted ranks came tried warriors. Harry Dick "Lump-Lump" Williams, "Hoss" Kucinski, "Legs" Martin, James Tipton, Rudy Boesch.

I went down the list when Boehm submitted it to me.

"Rogues," I commented.

"These are the caliber people we need for what we're asking them to do, skipper. We don't want Jack Armstrong all-American types who'll say, 'Yessir, nosir, two bags full, anything you say, sir.' We need sonsofbitches who can and will think for themselves and will get a job done no matter what. We might not win popularity contests—but we'll be capable."

I agreed. "Make it happen. Start training."

I had the CNO's green light to go anywhere, do anything to provide the right training. Boehm went even farther than that sometimes. We laid on Ranger training, jungle warfare, martial arts. One group went to Annapolis to learn how to sail boats. I figured we'd be in Vietnam sooner or later—and the Vietnamese junks had sails. We sent men to prison to learn safecracking from experts. Our people became automobile hot-wire artists and lock pickers. They went to learn trick shooting, photography, and intelligence gathering and analysis. At Ops and

Intel Training at Fort Bragg, Hoss Kacinski creatively photographed his naked penis and balls with a pair of sunglasses to show hairy heavy jowls and a long nose, which circulated around as "Bos'n Hose Nose."

Everyone became parachute qualified, including Boehm and me. Not merely conventional hop-and-pop, but also HAHO (High-Altitude, High-Opening) and HALO (High-Altitude Low-Opening). I wanted our commandos capable of jumping from an airplane at twenty-seven thousand feet and *flying* from over international waters into enemy territory.

An article appeared in the *Bayonet* post newspaper at Fort Benning, Georgia:

AIRBORNE NAVY: PARA-FROGMEN GRADUATE

A new breed of American fighting man—the para-frogman—is being created through the joint efforts of the infantry school's airborne air mobility department and the navy's Underwater Demolition Team 21 at Little Creek, Virginia. Lt. Commander W. H. Hamilton Jr., one of 21 officers and enlisted men from UDT-21 who will complete airborne training May 13, said that the jump training will give the frogmen added mobility and another way to get to the objective.

I established liaison with General "Jumping Joe" Stillwell, commander of all Army Special Forces, while Boehm buddied with Captain Rudy Kaiser to exchange training between UDT and elements of the 5th and 7th Special Forces Groups. With a handshake, we linked two competent groups of professional men of war.

"I'll set you up with a diving allowance list and increase your training," Boehm promised Kaiser while I made a similar offer to General Stillwell. "We'll teach you everything we know about water training and demo. In exchange, I want our men to know everything you know about parachute ops, foreign weapons, kitchen table demolitions, small-unit tactics, and Ranger-type ops. We both have beneficial training and can increase the operating and killing potential for both."

Officers and men, again including Boehm and me, attended the Special Forces "Q" (Qualification) course, while Army SF guys went through UDT training.

It was a period of excitement, watching the birth of modern naval unconventional warfare. The men Boehm selected out of UDT-21 often became conspicuously absent from the naval base at Little Creek. They were always coming and going. As soon as they returned from one course, Boehm hustled them off to another, to train in everything from political assassination to waging covert nuclear war. Still, so far, we had barely tapped the surface of what commandos might be called upon to do in the name of national security and defense.

"They believe in what we're doing so much," Ensign Gordie Ablitt commented, "that the guys volunteer to pay their own way to schools just to get the qualifications."

The men knew something was coming down, that they were being drawn into an orphaned twilight between UDT and something else, but we couldn't tell them what it was. Only Boehm and I knew the true nature of our intended mission, but I assured our guys it would all become clear at the appropriate time.

Lieutenant Mo Lynch, UDT-21's executive officer and second-in-command to me now that Boehm was full-time training with our SpecOps group, was furious at having been excluded from the secret. He cornered Boehm.

"Damn it, Roy," he fussed, about to bust from curiosity. "What's going on here? I've got guys scheduled for things—and you're always snatching them up and sending them off on boondoggles. What's all this training about? The least you can do is consult me."

"Sorry, Mo. I'm not at liberty to say."

Mo attempted every way he could to weasel the secret out of Boehm. He finally came to me.

"Skipper, Boehm has just destroyed my Med Cruise by taking all the men. Whatever he's doing is not good for morale. The men don't know where they're going from day to day, nor even *why* you're doing this to them."

I winked at Roy. "What do you feel about that, Boehm?"

"Mo's a good man, skipper. I agree with him."

I nodded. "Look, Mo, you have no need to know. Boehm is instructed to carry out my orders."

Lynch pouted. "Without informing me?"

"That'll be all, gentlemen."

Boehm was thirty-eight years old, I was thirty-four. The grind sometimes had our asses dragging. But any officer who couldn't hack it, who couldn't or wouldn't endure the same training as his men, didn't belong in *any* unit in the military, much less a special outfit like UDT or Army Special Forces. Anytime one of my men took a step, an officer's footprint had better be there before his.

I was at the Pentagon on a task when the CNO called me into his office to inform me that the men we had been training for much of 1961 were being chopped from UDT to become a separate special warfare unit. At the same time I received orders transferring me full-time to the Pentagon.

"I know it doesn't seem fair to jerk you out now that you've got the unit going," the new CNO, Admiral George W. Anderson Jr., apologized. "But you're up for promotion and you're needed here to oversee naval special warfare. Who do you recommend to take your place?"

I didn't have to think about it. "Lieutenant Roy Boehm, sir."

Before I had the opportunity to pass the news to Roy, an old friend of his at BUPERS—Bureau of Personnel—telephoned him.

"Hey," the yeoman greeted. "What in hell is a SEAL?"

"Fury little critter lives in the ocean?"

"You'd damned well better find out for sure, ol' buddy. 'Cause you are now one with a license to steal."

On January 7, 1962, Department of Navy made its decision. Backdated to January 1, Navy SEALs were commissioned into service as the Navy's answer to guerrilla warfare and Army Special Forces in the Cold War. I didn't know where the acronym SEAL came from, but I knew *how* it originated: SEA AIR LAND. SEALs were authorized black berets and a gold unit crest that featured an eagle clutching a U.S. Navy anchor, trident, and pistol.

Lieutenant Boehm received East Coast SEAL Team Two's first orders, which meant the salty old sailor, WWII and Korean war vet, and former bos'n mate, was now *acting commander* and the very first

SEAL to be commissioned in the United States Navy, with ten officers and fifty enlisted. SEAL Team One under the command of Lieutenant Dave Del Guidice was activated on the West Coast.

"Damn, sir," Boehm exclaimed when I arrived at Little Creek to congratulate the men. "*You* got this going. *You* should have received the first orders."

"Roy, you deserve it. You worked harder and longer at it than any of us. Now, shut your fat mouth and go out there and kick ass. I'm at the Pentagon now, but I'm still over Navy special warfare, which still makes me your skipper."

"Aye, aye, sir. Keep my fat mouth shut. But, damn," he added. "Damn, sir—*we did it!*"

CHAPTER TWENTY-ONE

I WAS NOW A DEFENSE-ESTABLISHMENT beltway insider riding a desk. Long meetings and discussions in the morning with the Joint Chiefs or the president's advisors, a quick lunch, then more conferences with National Security or the CIA and the other intelligence services. It reminded me of my early hectic days with Doug Fane on the West Coast—except with Fane we were as often out with the teams some- where in the world as stuck in an office. There was no such relief in Washington, D.C., where everything, it seemed, was paperwork and bullshit.

Fane had retired from the navy two years earlier, before Cuba and all that. He telephoned me the day he left. "Bone, I still say you're a candy ass. By the way, do you know where I can find a new wife?"

"You can have my ex-wife."

"Elinor? She's gone?"

"I might have had something, but I guess I kicked it around and lost it."

"Ex-wives come with the territory."

I hadn't seen Elinor since she and the kids left me for California. Divorce papers came in the mail in August 1961 while I was deeply involved in getting the SEALs going. I couldn't show up for the hear- ing, so the court awarded her a generous portion of my income and future pension and everything else we owned. Which wasn't much, actually. Most Navy men gathered less moss than a rolling stone.

I didn't begrudge her; what she received from me would support Linda Jean, Bill Jr., and little Jana Lee. I signed the papers, put them back in the mail, and then went out and got drunk with a Navy wife I met at the Officers Club at Little Creek.

Lonely wives were a fixture around most Navy shore bases. Mary was thirty-three years old, tall, attractive, and lonely because her naval aviator husband spent more time on deployment than he did at home. While he was off flying, his wife stayed home and tested her own wings.

She and I had a lot in common. Misery loves company and all that. My wife left me because of the Navy; Mary was ready to leave her husband because of the Navy. She was an unconfessed alcoholic; I was on the verge of becoming a heavy drinker, not to the point that it affected my life and career, but I could still toss 'em down. We were both drifting in our personal lives, flotsam passing in the night that got hung up on the same snag.

One evening we were together in a Virginia Beach night club when her husband walked in on us. I heard Mary gasp above the sounds of Elvis on the jukebox, the clinking of glasses, and the melodious flirting mixture of male and female voices. I followed the direction of her gaze and saw the tall man in a flight jacket standing in the doorway looking over the crowd.

"Oh, my God!" Mary cried in a muffled voice. "Bill wasn't supposed to be back tonight."

That was another thing we had in common: her husband was also named Bill. He spotted us and, wearing a stricken look, walked slowly over to our table. He stood silently looking down on his errant wife and me. Poor bastard. None of the three of us spoke. We tried not to look at each other for what seemed about ten years.

"You're welcome to the lush," the other Bill said to me and walked away.

I resisted the urge to jump up and shout after him, "But I don't want the lush!" Instead, I just sat there feeling about as low-down as a man could get.

I felt responsible for breaking up Mary's marriage. Maybe that and rebound was the reason I married her. I tried to talk her out of it, give her a way out. I tried to talk myself out of it.

"Look, girl. I'm not much of a catch. Shore duty won't last and I'll be deploying again."

"What's with you men and the sea?" she said. "It's like you all keep trying to escape from the land."

Mary was pretty, but not very smart. I always figured she would have been a good and faithful wife if she had found herself some ordinary nine-to-five Joe with a new car and a little house in the suburbs. Certainly, she should never have ended up with another sailor who couldn't stand the thought of barnacles on his hull.

She and her preteen daughter moved into my apartment with me in D.C. I figured she'd be straying again as soon as I left the Pentagon and went back to the fleet. In the meantime, I tried to settle in and make a proper husband and military paper-pushing bureaucrat.

Out at SEAL Team Two, Lieutenant John Callahan took over as the new skipper. Limited Duty Officers like Roy Boehm were generally not eligible for most command slots. I explained it to Roy, who accepted it willingly and returned happily to his old position in operations. He was, after all, unpolished and two-fisted, more at home in a sleazy waterfront bar than in an officer's stateroom. He kissed no ass in kicking ass. He was never going to make captain or admiral anyhow.

The day Callahan showed up to take over, Roy gave him a briefing on the team's status.

"I'm damned glad the ball is in your court now," he concluded.

At the Pentagon, the unresolved "Cuba problem," as it was being called, was not going away and showed every sign of escalating into something unintended. I had worked with a number of the Quarters Eye bunch during the lead-up to the Bay of Pigs—Richard Bissell, E. Howard Hunt, David Atlee Phillips, and Ted Shackley. It was difficult to keep up with who's who in the CIA, as they were a secretive organization. I sometimes met one or the other of them over a drink to discuss growing concerns in the Caribbean over Nikita Khrushchev's ICBMs.

"If Americans knew what was about to happen down there," Shackley remarked, "they'd crawl into their cellars and not come up again until after the fallout cleared."

CHAPTER TWENTY-TWO

AIR FORCE GENERAL EDWARD Lansdale, former OSS in World War II and now JFK's deputy assistant secretary for special operations, was a square-jawed officer with a dark, penetrating gaze that gave him an intense, almost fanatical appearance. Outside the door to the larger conference room on the Pentagon's fourth floor stood a Marine for security and, inside, a pot of coffee for alertness. Lansdale rose to his feet from the massive oaken table around which congregated grave-looking CIA operatives, top-level government officials, military Special Ops representatives, and various other advisors and consultants. I leaned back in my chair as he began speaking.

"The president has to do something, and quick," he asserted. "I've provided him a timetable for action to overthrow Castro. I'm suggesting guerrilla operations begin in-country by September for open revolt and overthrow of the communist regime—or the missiles will be there and we'll be too late."

U-2 spy planes discovered surface-to-air anti-aircraft missiles in Cuba a month ago, in August 1962. CIA Director John McCone concluded their presence made sense "only if Moscow intends to use them to shield a base for nuclear ballistic missiles aimed at the U.S."

Meetings like this one had been ongoing in Washington from shortly after New Year's as various departments of the Defense establishment debated a response to possible Soviet nuclear missiles in Cuba.

Suggestions on what to do about it bounced around like Ping-Pong balls at a championship tournament. Options presented included: do nothing; diplomacy; give Castro the choice to eject the Russians or be invaded; an immediate full-force invasion to overthrow the dictator; guerrilla insurgency; blockade to prevent Russian ships from entering or leaving Cuban harbors.

The Joint Chiefs of Staff opted for invasion. JFK and Secretary of State Dean Rusk opposed it.

"The Soviets won't let an invasion proceed without doing something," the president said. "They can't permit us to take out their missiles, kill a bunch of Russians, and do nothing."

General Lansdale paced the edges of the room, tapping his teeth with the point of a pen, deep in thought. He stopped and wheeled to confront the table.

"Damn it, I'm not talking invasion," he said. "Why did we build Special Ops if we don't intend to use them for that purpose?"

His dark gaze fell on me. "Commander Hamilton, are your SEALs prepared to train and lead an insurgency inside Cuba?"

I slowly stood up.

"Sir, I think it's a bad plan. Let me tell you why. First, an internal insurgency takes time to organize, arm, and coordinate. If Director McCone is right, we don't have that kind of time. Besides, you're talking about a job for Army Special Forces. Their primary mission is infiltration behind enemy lines to build up and train insurgents. SEALs prepare for direct action—quick insertions to take out an enemy leader, an ammo depot—"

General Lansdale interrupted. "—or an ICBM site?"

"Yes, sir. You give us the mission and we'll pull it off better than anyone else in the world. That's a money-back guarantee."

Lansdale nodded after a moment, and I sat down.

I refrained from saying what was really on my mind. We had had our chance at the Bay of Pigs, and the president blew it by behaving like the Cowardly Lion in *The Wizard of Oz*. That one incident, I believed, left Khrushchev with the impression that Kennedy was indecisive and further emboldened the Soviets to do what they might not otherwise do.

Six weeks after the Bay of Pigs failure, President Kennedy had attended the Vienna Summit, during which Premier Khrushchev threatened to close off American, British, and French access to West Berlin and actively halt the masses of Eastern Europeans seeking asylum through the Free Berlin corridor. Twenty percent of the entire East German population of 4.5 million people had already escaped.

On August 13, East German troops and workers began to tear up streets in order to build a ninety-six-mile wall to isolate West Berlin in the middle of East Germany and thereby prevent further escapes. It was all part of Khrushchev's campaign to destabilize the West. Introducing ICBMs into Cuba was another part of the campaign. What he was counting on, in my opinion, was that Kennedy would avoid confrontation and accept the missiles and other Soviet encroachments around the world as a fait accompli.

Chapter Twenty-Three

I WAS TEMPTED TO CALL Dad and Mom on the telephone and warn them: "Dad, you and Mom get the hell out of Florida and head north. Go as far as you can get in Canada."

Mary made us drinks. It was late, nearly midnight. The night was hot and humid, like no air stirred for fear of bringing a wind that bore no good. Mary came out onto our apartment patio carrying cocktails—*Make mine a double; hell, make it a triple.* She wore a sheer nightgown, nothing underneath. I barely noticed. I was so exhausted from another day in the giant beehive that Washington had become for me.

One time when I was a kid, I watched a beekeeper down the road from us in Virginia rob honey from his hives using smoke from a torch. The bees went crazy when smoke penetrated their little Fort Knox of honey, buzzing and frantically diving and banging about in mindless, frenetic activity. I felt like one of those bees now, as mad and insane as the very important people who were in and out of the Pentagon and the Defense Department at all hours, meeting each other in conference rooms, speaking in harried whispers in corridors, sometimes raising their voices to stress particular points.

Mary and I sat not speaking, with a night view of the Capitol Building dome in the distance. I remembered—I would always remember—the story of Toshiko Saeki of Hiroshima.

This was no way for humans to have to live, under constant fear of destruction.

"Is there going to be a nuclear war?" Mary asked flatly.

Newspapers and TV were full of speculation, in spite of all the secrecy. Enough facts had leaked into the reporting to make Americans ask questions.

"Bill, is there?"

Dad would understand why I couldn't talk about it.

"Bill?"

"Why would you even ask that question?"

"You're a shithead, Bill."

The crisis dragged on from day to day, hour to hour. On television, JFK looked almost too young to be president. Now, I was shocked to glimpse him one afternoon leaving SecDef Robert McNamara's office. Lines of stress and worry seemed freshly carved into his face. General Lansdale said he was on the phone almost hourly with Khrushchev.

"We've let the genie out of the box," he said, "and if we don't put the sonofabitch back in the box, we'll end the next war fighting each other with sticks and stones. At least those of us unfortunate enough to be left alive will."

One little mistake, one misunderstanding, a minor error of judgment, might be the spark to blow up the whole damned world.

On August 24, a former Brigade 2506 member named Jose Basulto ratcheted up international tensions when he borrowed a thirty-one-foot power cruiser and pooled enough cash to buy a 20mm semiautomatic cannon with one hundred rounds of ammunition. Arms like that could be purchased off the streets in Miami in 1962.

Basulto and a half dozen other exiles sailed from Miami into Havana Harbor and staged a raid on the waterfront Hotel Rosita de Hornado where a large number of Soviet advisors billeted. They shelled the front of the hotel with their cannon, raked it with small arms fire, and returned to Miami.

McNamara called such quixotic ventures "insane."

In the meantime, U-2 flights revealed Soviet ships slipping out of Black Sea harbors on their way to Cuba with greater and greater numbers of "advisors." And, quite probably, nuclear missiles. JFK doubled the frequency of spy plane overflights of Castroland. So far, there was no substantial proof to convince the world of the presence of Soviet ICBMs.

Intelligence briefings kept those of us with a need-to-know informed of findings in Cuba by the CIA's deep-cover network of spies and informants in-country.

A former employee of the Hilton Hotel in Havana told an operative he believed a missile installation was under construction near San Cristóbal. Another overheard Castro's personal pilot drunk in a bar boasting about missiles. An operative reporting out of CIA headquarters located on the University of Miami's campus maintained regular contact with a farm owner in Oriente Province. The farmer escaped to Florida, where he relayed an unusual story to Felix Rodriguez, one of the CIA's most successful agents.

"The Russians are going crazy," he said. "They're trucking big loads of ice to their base. Every day they drive truck after truck of ice, and the Russians take over at the gate and drive it into tunnels they've built."

Missile fuel had to be kept at a constant temperature. Apparently, cooling systems in the tunnels had broken down and ice served as a substitute.

Even such random sources as these slowly dried up as the Castros and Guevara put a clamp on the island. Since the Bay of Pigs, Castro's security forces had used the invasion as an excuse to continue imprisoning hundreds of political opponents. Secret police prowled the shadows, while organized government watch groups spying on neighborhoods intimidated most Cubans.

In September, during a State Department brainstorming session, John McCone, the director of Central Intelligence (DCI), settled his eyes on me.

"It is imperative," he said, his eyes holding mine, "that we obtain reliable *proof* that the Soviets have placed ICBMs on Cuban soil."

I knew what he was getting at. This was a job for Navy SEALs.

CHAPTER TWENTY-FOUR

T HE EVENTS OF THAT summer and autumn of 1962, as Secretary of Defense Robert McNamara put it, forced the world to confront its "greatest danger of a catastrophic war since the advent of the nuclear age."

On John McCone's request, I left Washington, D.C., to link up with SEALs and one of his spooks named "John" in Key West, almost within spitting distance of Cuba. SEAL Team Two's commander, John Callahan, and I drove Lieutenant Roy Boehm and Chief Petty Officer Lump Williams to a sheltered cove at Naval Station Key West, where the submarine *Sea Lion* waited for them dockside in the failing light of approaching darkness. The "John" spook and a State Department goon whom I didn't know and who refused to supply even a cover name were waiting.

Mr. State Department, dressed in Ivy League shirt, sweater, slacks and deck shoes, was a pencil dick with an Errol Flynn mustache and a Bud Abbott face. John was a photographer, a fragile Cuban twig upon which hung a pair of thick glasses. Next to John and Mr. State, Lump-Lump looked like a walking man mountain with his broad shoulders, cliff-like jaw, long swimmer's legs, and short quills of hair driven like nails into his scalp.

"They'll complete your briefing aboard the submarine," I told Roy and Lump, motioning to their two mission companions.

Boehm was . . . Boehm was *Boehm*. He regarded John and the State Department weenie with some amusement. "Little fuckers ain't going to *grope* me, are they?"

"They wanna suck my dick," Lump-Lump added, glaring, "they'd better bring extra teeth 'cause they'll be needing 'em to eat with from now on."

Callahan and I saw the team off. "I should be with you, not cooling my ass here on safe land while you're risking yours," I said to Boehm.

"That's not the way it works, skipper," Boehm replied. "The higher up you go, the more valuable your ass becomes. We'll pay your regards to Papa Fidel."

Callahan and I waited out the tense hours at the Naval Station, swigging coffee and catching naps on a sofa in the Ops Center.

* * *

Once *Sea Lion* dove in the Florida Straits, John, Lump, and Boehm crowded into the captain's wardroom along with Mr. State, who launched his briefing with the subdued relish of a neighborhood gossip.

"Gentlemen, you are about to embark on the most significant mission of your military careers. The forces of communism and the forces of the Free World are being cornered into a standoff the outcome of which only God knows—"

"Get down to it," Boehm growled. "SEALs don't need motivation speeches."

Mr. State looked offended. He sourly produced from his travel bag a series of high-altitude U-2 photos of Bahia del Mariel, code-named Pinlon. He spread the photos on a table for the SEALs to study while he continued his briefing.

The photos showed a deep-water harbor a few kilometers west of Havana. It bulged into land like a lopsided condom with one narrow opening to the sea. Ships were tied up to piers inside the harbor. Trucks with large flatbed trailers appeared to be hauling away long cylindrical objects covered with tarps.

"We must obtain irrefutable proof that these are ICBM missiles," Mr. State Department said. "The president will broadcast it to the world as soon as we confirm it. This time President Kennedy will not back down, not even if we verge on the threshold of a nuclear war."

It was Boehm's and Lump-Lump's job to insert into Pinlon with John the spook photographer and protect his scrawny nerd ass while he sneaked up and took snapshots of the missiles. In a real war, they would have swum in, attached limpet explosives to the freighters, and blown them up with the missiles still aboard. *Sayonara, motherfuckers.* In the Cold War, however, it wasn't done that way.

The three of them left the State Department goon behind the following night and locked out of the sub off the Cuban coast, using a rubber raft as transport to shore. The *Sea Lion* slid off as silent as a shark to wait in the black-running Gulf Stream for the team's signal to return.

John rode the raft with two waterproof bags while Lump and Boehm swam on either side, pushing him. The gear bags contained dry clothing, rations and water, John's cameras, binoculars, and two .38 Combat Masterpiece revolvers. The State Department had ordered them not to go in armed, as it would create an international incident if they were caught and provide Guevara an excuse to execute them. But just before they locked out, the submarine's chief petty officer secretly passed them the pistols.

As they drew near land, the mouth of the harbor turned into a narrow black vagina. Deep inside, yellow lights reflected off the water where two Russian freighters rode, tied off to long concrete-and-wood piers. Lights draped over the freighters' sides and shining into the water were supposed to discourage underwater saboteurs and spies. Two chunky Komar patrol boats rode at anchor farther inside the harbor, their machine guns unmanned.

A flashlight dotted the darkness twice from dead ahead on Punto Barlovento, the harbor's outer lip.

"The contact," John whispered.

John and the contact, an elderly Cuban, embraced each other like long-lost cousins. Quickly, the team gathered up equipment, wiped out tracks, and followed the contact up a short, steep bank to the dead end of a narrow street. Dilapidated warehouses and other run-down buildings lined it. They appeared abandoned. The only illumination came from the freighters nearly a thousand yards farther along.

They came to a weathered building attached to the water by a tiny wharf on pilings. It smelled of wood rot and fish guts and hemp and seaweed. There were two doors. A tiny window in the door that opened toward the wharf let in the weak, distant light from the enemy ships and the growing wedge of approaching dawn.

John and the Cuban prepared to leave.

"Where the fuck you going, Charlie?" Lump-Lump rumbled. He called everyone "Charlie."

"You've done your job. Now I'll do mine."

Dry land seemed to have restored his confidence. He packed his cameras into a worn satchel.

"Don't be seen while I'm gone," he cautioned, then left with the old Cuban.

For all Lump and Boehm knew, either John or the old man could have been double agents. Boehm visualized himself and Lump-Lump lashed to the nose of missiles as they descended onto Washington, D.C.

Sent on a mission to protect the future of the Free World—and there they sat, hiding in a smelly fisherman's shack, armed with pistols against nuclear missiles and Castro's machine guns.

Suffocating heat seeped into the shack as the sun rose out of Havana and climbed above them. Still no activity among the warehouses. Cubans and their Soviet cohorts must have evacuated the waterfront to help protect the secret of the arriving ICBMs.

Lump stepped outside just as two teenaged boys swung chattering and grabassing into the end of the street. They spotted Lump immediately and waved. Lump kept his cool. He waved back and laughed as he tossed the boys a colorful fisherman's net float. They caught it and played catch with it as they ran out of sight. Lump looked grim as he retreated and closed the door. The two SEALs hissed at each other.

"Roy, they seemed to think I belonged . . ."

"All they have to do is to let slip one word . . ."

"Jesus! I don't think they thought anything . . ."

"You want to bet your life on what two kids did or didn't think?"

Boehm kept watch while Lump erased obvious signs of their presence. Then they crawled underneath the shack with their gear to hide out during the day. The crawlspace was a tight fit. Sand crabs edged up sideways and eyed them speculatively with their stilted exclamation-point eyes.

"Lieutenant, I ain't going to one of them Cuban gulags," Lump whispered.

"We won't have to. They'll execute us."

"We fight then?"

"Lump, do you have a better suggestion?"

They huddled together in the dark mud with the crabs watching them like hangmen and the strong odor of the incoming tide in their nostrils. Boehm chuckled at the thought of the fate of the world riding on their shoulders.

"Roysi," Lump murmured sardonically, "tell me again how much glamour there is in this job."

* * *

Nightfall was a long time coming. Lump-Lump and Boehm, driven from underneath the dock shack by the incoming tide, finally felt secure enough to venture back inside. The two kids had probably forgotten all about seeing Lump by this time. Sounds of activity drifted to them from the direction of the docked Russian freighters. Truck engines. Winches sounded like chalk against the blackboard of the night. Incredible that security was so lax. The Reds were moving around ICBMs as casually as though they were unloading a grain elevator. Boldness, perhaps the utter unbelievability of shipping nuclear warheads into America's own backyard, substituted for subterfuge.

"*Someone's coming!*" Lump-Lump drew his weapon and spun away from the door window where he kept vigil. Roy took the other side of the door.

The door creaked open. A dark figure. Boehm yanked the man inside and thrust the muzzle of his revolver against his temple.

"*Por Díos, Señor!* It is only I coming for you."

It was the old man, their guide. In broken but passable English, he explained. "They move one missile only each night. They hide from—how you say?—aircraft surveillance." He pointed skyward and flashed a quick grin. "But this night they are seen from more near, *si*? Come. We have work to do."

He led Lump and Boehm to a three-floored warehouse set in the dark along the waterfront. Missile-moving sounds came from beyond it. They hid in the shadows and watched the building for a full quarter hour. The complete lack of enemy security unnerved Boehm. This was *too* easy.

Presently, guns in hand, Lump-Lump and the lieutenant fast-trailed the old man across the open street and into the warehouse. The unpartitioned bottom floor appeared littered with old empty packing crates and rusted machinery of some sort. Squeaky wooden stairs immediately to the left led up to the third floor. Their stealthy footfalls on the stairs released mold and dust. They entered a room at the end of a musky hallway on the third floor and closed the door behind them.

Pale moonlight through the open shutters of a single window illuminated chairs, a table, and a bed with the bare mattress rolled back. "We are to wait here for our *amigo*," explained the old Cuban, who called himself Carlito.

A quick but thorough scouting of the entire building pinpointed escape routes and defensive points. A window at the end of the third-floor hallway opened onto a neighboring rooftop. Satisfied that they were safe for the time being, the three of them returned to the hideout room and waited in the darkness while they listened to the sobering grind of machinery moving ICBMs in preparation for possible nuclear strikes against the United States.

John was in a hurry when he returned. He wore old sneakers and work clothing and carried his cameras. He jabbed a finger toward the roof. Lump-Lump remained behind to check John's back trail before joining the others where they sprawled on their bellies at the roof's peak, glassing the harbor below with binoculars.

Water lay still and black in its protected land cup. Komar patrol boats with their running lights extinguished inscribed slow, vigilant rounds at the vagina's opening. Illumination came from lights strung over the sides of the Russian freighters. Stevedores rigged lines and cables around a long canvas-covered cylinder aboard one of the ships. A tractor truck had trouble maneuvering a long trailer around the sharp corner where the street turned toward the piers. Its engine moaned and groaned in granny gear until a little crane arrived to pick up the end of the trailer and move it around on line.

The truck trailer was specifically designed with chocks and blocks to receive the missile, which was still concealed beneath tarps. John used a light-grabbing telephoto lens to shoot several rolls of film as laborers transferred the Soviet freighter's load to the Cuban truck.

"Not good enough," John fretted, although none of us required an imagination to know what lay hidden underneath the canvas. "I must get closer."

Boehm was cautious. Certainly the Russians would have posted security.

"It's something I have to chance," John decided. "There's nothing you can do if I'm caught. Just get the hell back to sea before they trap you too. Here. Take these with you."

He handed Boehm the film he had already shot. Boehm extended a hand to shake John's.

"You've got balls," he acknowledged.

John flashed a pleased grin and said, "I don't intend to lose them in Cuba."

Then he was gone. Back into the building, taking only a camera the size of his palm.

Boehm nodded at Lump. "Cover his ass. Shadow him from a distance."

Boehm waited with Carlito, both tense and silent as they scanned the piers through binoculars and watched John shadowed by Lump approach the docks. That was one awesome piece of ordnance down there. It harnessed more destructive power than the entire U.S. fleet expended against the Japanese during all of WWII, including atomic bombs dropped on Hiroshima and Nagasaki. Unleashed against Washington, D.C., it would turn the nation's capital and surrounding Virginia and Maryland into a vast smoldering wasteland incapable of supporting life for thousands of years. Four or five of them would render uninhabitable the eastern seaboard from New York to Miami.

Lump-Lump returned alone, sweating, admiration in his voice. "The little bastard's crazy. I had to drop back. He's right in there *with* the workmen."

Lump called off the passing of each quarter hour while they waited.

Sighs of relief escaped the three of them on the roof when John reappeared. He crawled toward them, grinning broadly, clearly on a high.

"I could have *touched* it!" he exclaimed and patted his tiny camera. "We've got it now. Let that bearded sonofabitch try to deny *this* evidence. Gentlemen, let's get the hell out of Cuba. In two or three more days, there may not be enough left on this island to support a goat."

CHAPTER TWENTY-FIVE

S AILORS WERE ALWAYS VISITING exotic ports. Amsterdam occupied a category all its own. I strolled De Wallen, the city's largest red light district, in what I hoped was a casual tourist manner and not that of some tall, shifty-eyed perv seeking a quick tryst in one of the "kamers." Turned out the DCI (Director of Central Intelligence), John McCone, had a mission for me when I got back from Key West. With a sly double-entendre smile, Ted Shackley called the mission a "quick in-and-out." I figured McCone was testing me for some future purpose, since Shackley seemed much more suitable for playing the perv than I.

I flew into Amsterdam that morning and held a return ticket for the evening. This was my first foray into the "secret war" of the spy game. Seemed simple enough.

"It's not cloak-and-dagger," Shackley agreed. "Do exactly what you're supposed to do, then hop the next plane home. Anybody can do it. Rather, anybody we *trust* can do it."

"So you needed a dummy, is that what you're saying?"

Shackley grinned in that twisted-lip smirk of his. "Call it a *decoy*."

He said the contact in Holland was apprehensive about rendez-vousing with his customary handlers and demanded a new face. I was nothing, I supposed, if not a new face. I wondered if I might not actually be a decoy used to confuse Soviet counterintelligence while the real mission took place elsewhere. I didn't know whether to be offended or not.

I wore unpressed slacks and a short leather jacket and carried a box underneath my arm containing a pair of souvenir wooden shoes I'd purchased from a specific shop in Dam Square. The shoe box was a signal to my unknown contact that I was who I was supposed to be.

I checked my watch. Two thirty-five p.m. I paused in the street, inconspicuously, I hoped, to light a cigarette. I glanced casually about for anyone who looked more suspicious than I felt. Which was probably impossible.

I felt as though someone were *watching* me. Perhaps with a silenced weapon and a license to kill.

Christ! I had been reading too many James Bond thrillers.

The park bench was exactly where it was supposed to be: next to the sidewalk between the flat fronts of fourteenth-century Dutch architecture and the green-brown water canal where used condoms floated. Two bicycles, one red and the other blue, were chained together to a lamppost next to the canal, also exactly where they were supposed to be.

Other bicycles up and down the street were double-chained to fixtures to keep potheads from stealing them. The street was beginning to crowd up with single men, mostly sex tourists, I assumed, pervs like me frequenting the sex shops and girly shows that operated between coffee shops that openly sold marijuana. Prostitutes, even this early in the day, displayed their wares behind plate glass windows—"kamers"— where red lights glimmered in highlights on their near-naked bodies. I wondered what twisted sense of humor prompted Shackley, and perhaps the DCI, to send a "newby" to this part of Amsterdam.

Two elderly men occupied my designated bench nibbling pastries from a common bag while pigeons pecked up crumbs dropped at their feet. They weren't supposed to be here. They weren't part of my prescribed scenario.

Between two thirty and three local time, I was told.

I dared not stand there on the street with my face hanging out. I eased into the nearest coffee shop, where I ordered a coffee and found a table near the window where I could keep an eye on the park bench while I sipped my drink with forced nonchalance.

What happened if those old farts caused me to miss my contact time? Perspiration erupted through my skin. Maybe this wasn't cloak-and-dagger, but it was close enough for me. I was an amateur at this stuff.

At two fifty I had to make my move before it was too late. I called the waitress over. After determining that she spoke English, I pointed at the two old men on my park bench and offered her a handful of guilders.

"Will you please give this to those old guys and tell them some-one's buying them a dinner?" I said. "There's also something in it for you. Tell them there are tickets for the show down at *The Pink Pussy* if they'll come on in here and eat right now."

I peeled off some more guilders and left them on the table.

The waitress went out to the bench and bent over the two old men. The geriatrics sprang up like they'd been hot-wired. A pigeon fluttered down to search for crumbs. I picked up my coffee and made for the bench in an unhurried hurry before someone else claimed it.

The whole thing appeared rather sloppy. But maybe that was the way this game was played.

I sat down and placed the wooden shoes in their box next to me. A watery sun broke through cloud cover. I sipped coffee and smoked another cigarette as the long and harrowing minutes dragged by. People walked past; no one paid attention to me. Even the pigeons flew off for more productive territory.

Presently, a shortish man in an overcoat and mustache walked up and sat down on the bench next to me. He carried a box of wooden shoes identical to mine. He placed it on the bench between us, next to my box.

The stranger smoked a cigarette. He gazed out over the canal. Then, without saying a word, without so much as looking in my direc-tion—and I dared not look at him—he got up and left, leaving his box behind and taking mine with him.

It was that simple and undramatic. I got out of town as fast as I could get to the airport. I relaxed only when my airliner touched down on U.S. soil.

Over a year would pass before I learned the full story of Soviet Colonel Oleg Vladimirovich Penkovsky and the role I may have played with him in the Cuban affair.

Penkovsky was a colonel with Soviet military intelligence who fought in World War II and became disillusioned with communism afterward. His CIA defector's account revealed how he approached American students on the Moskvoretsky Bridge in Moscow in July 1960 and surreptitiously handed them a package without revealing his identity. The package contained contact information along with secret Soviet military data that only a Soviet insider could have accessed.

The CIA delayed contacting him since they suspected their agents were under constant surveillance and that this Penkovsky, whoever he was, might be setting a trap. Discouraged, Penkovsky arranged a meeting with British spy Grenville Wynne during an authorized visit he made to London in 1961. Wynne subsequently became one of Penkovsky's couriers—and it was likely Wynne who arranged the secret assignation in Amsterdam in which I participated.

Penkovsky supplied a tremendous amount of intel to his handlers during the eighteen months in which he was active. Most significant was recent information about Soviet plans, descriptions of nuclear missile launch sites, and data on the Soviet nuclear arsenal. It seemed this arsenal was much smaller than previously assumed and that the fueling and guidance systems for their ICBMs might not be fully functional.

Premier Khrushchev stood on weaker ground than most of the world knew. Information supplied by the Russian colonel may have reduced pressure on Kennedy to launch an invasion of Castro's island and instead select an alternative and saner method of confronting Khrushchev. I never learned whether the box of wooden shoes I brought back from the Netherlands, obtained from whomever I encountered that day, was crucial to all this or not. And, naturally, I never asked; I had no need to know. I was the spy who stayed out in the cold.

Colonel Oleg Penkovsky, the mole planted deep inside the Kremlin, was exposed and apprehended by the KGB in October 1962, the same day John F. Kennedy addressed the nation about the presence of Russian missiles off American shores.

Although I had never met Penkovsky that I knew of, I was deeply saddened when I learned later of his execution. Another old Cold Warrior bit the dust.

CHAPTER TWENTY-SIX

Lights in the massive Pentagon building finally dimmed in the predawn. My eyes burned from lack of sleep as I stood only half-seeing at a window at the end of the corridor. Below in the circle drive a group of high-ranking military officers climbed into a staff car to be driven off. Two armed Marines watched from a respectful distance. To my surprise, my lips began moving in rote memory of "The Hollow Men," a poem by T. S. Eliot, which concluded with: "This is the way the world ends / Not with a bang but a whimper."

I hadn't been home at all for the last three nights, since I had to be available to answer questions about the Navy's unconventional capabilities through its amphibious force SEALs and UDTs. I snatched quick naps now and then on the sofa in my office with my legs dangling over the end arm. My dress blues were wrinkled and beginning to smell as I went about in a haze of disbelief, of near-shock at how rapidly things were unfolding.

Days and nights ran together into weary footfalls echoing along the corridors underneath the rotunda. Members of the Joint Chiefs of Staff, heads of the various military departments and intelligence services, presidential advisors, national security representatives—CNO Admiral George Anderson, National Security Advisor McGeorge Bundy, General Maxwell Taylor, Attorney General Robert Kennedy,

Defense Secretary Robert McNamara, once or twice even the president himself—all wore stunned looks on their faces.

Uniformed Marines stood guard at locked doors behind which meetings buzzed day and night like green flies around a carcass.

Mary called me on the phone. "I'm frightened," she said. I imagined her and her poor little teenaged daughter huddling pale and bug-eyed on our sofa. "Is it true what I'm hearing on the TV? Do you think God is going to destroy us?"

I was tired, so damned tired. "I think we'll destroy ourselves first."

Great consolation, Hamilton!

Day by day I watched as the world hung on the brink and two headstrong, contentious, and powerful leaders butted heads with the lives of millions at stake.

On October 15, 1962, DCI John McCone notified National Security Advisor McGeorge Bundy that U-2 intelligence and photos supplied by the Pinlon penetration of the bay at Havana had confirmed missile presence and construction to accommodate as many as forty Soviet ICBMs, each with a range of over a thousand miles. They could be expected to annihilate eighty million Americans within the first few minutes if released against the United States.

Bundy briefed Defense Secretary McNamara at midnight. Together, they briefed the president at daybreak. The time had come for Kennedy to make good his promise that he would act "if Cuba should possess a capacity to carry out offensive actions against the United States."

At 6:30 p.m. on October 16, the president began formulating a response to Khrushchev's blatant aggression by convening the nine members of the National Security Council and other key advisors. At the same time, he and his brother Robert established personal contact with Premier Khrushchev and Andrei Gromyko, Soviet minister of foreign affairs, in efforts to stem the tide of an impending clash.

Four days later, after it became clear that diplomacy would not work, Kennedy placed U.S. armed forces around the world on full alert. Missile crews stood with fingers inches away from nuclear buttons. Troops moved into Florida and the southern United States. The Navy deployed 180 warships into the Caribbean. SAC—Strategic Air

Command—dispersed its aircraft onto civilian airports around the nation to reduce their vulnerability. B-52 bombers loaded with nuclear weapons patrolled the skies; as soon as one plane landed for refueling, another immediately took its place. Air Defense Command redeployed nuclear-armed interceptors and B-52s within striking distance of the Soviet Union while nuclear submarines prowled coastal oceans within missile range of Moscow. The crisis was so real, the threat so imminent, that many minor political types in D.C. loaded up their families, abandoned ship, and fled north to Canada.

Naval special warfare was assigned a major role to help put an end to this nasty business once and for all in the event the U.S. decided to invade Cuba. I received secret orders through the CNO for SEAL Teams One and Two to muster their combined 120 men in Key West. Their mission once "go" came down was to capture and hold Bahia del Mariel at Havana, keep it open in advance of an anticipated U.S. invasion.

I offered to lead the operation, but CNO Anderson quashed it: "You're more useful here." As an alternative, I put Boehm in charge of the Key West mission. After all, he knew the lay of the land, having already sneaked into the bay area with John the Spook to take pictures of missiles arriving. Boehm and I, along with team commanders Callahan and Del Guidice, devised a two-pronged attack to seize the port if it became necessary. Part of the SEAL force would parachute onto the heights above the seaport near the Cuban military barracks, secure the surrounding terrain and the harbor, and seize any ships at the piers to prevent their being sunk at the mouth of the harbor to block it.

At the same time, the rest of the SEALs would launch sixteen-foot gunboats from Florida, each armed with machine guns and 3.5-inch rocket launchers, to take up positions off the coast to defend the harbor against Soviet Komar patrol boats and waterborne security forces.

On October 21, U.S. top advisors scrapped invasion plans and determined they had two options remaining: either air strikes against the Cuban missile bases or a naval blockade. Kennedy selected the blockade as the least risky and announced to the world that all shipping as of this date would be blocked from Cuban ports.

Khrushchev received an "Armageddon" dispatch from Castro urging the use of nuclear force, no matter how "hard and terrible the solution." Cuba, he noted, was willing to sacrifice itself in the cause of an international communist future. I always knew commies were nuts.

Cuban defense minister Che Guevara took a more optimistic tack. While predicting that "direct aggression against Cuba would mean nuclear war," he concluded with, "I have no doubt (America) would lose such a war."

President Kennedy took to the airwaves on October 22 to inform people of the crisis:

"Let no one doubt that this is a difficult and dangerous effort on which we have set out," he announced. "No one can foresee what course it will take or what costs and casualties will be incurred. Many months of sacrifice and self-discipline lie ahead, months in which both our patience and our will *will* be tried, months in which many threats and denunciations will keep us aware of our dangers. But the greatest danger of all would be to do nothing. . . . The cost of freedom is always high—but Americans have always paid it. And one path we shall never choose, and that is the path of surrender or submission."

The countdown to Armageddon continued. I still napped nights in the Pentagon, if I slept at all.

On October 24, Pope John XXIII sent a public message to the Soviet embassy in Rome: "We beg all governments not to remain deaf to this cry of humanity. That they do all that is in their power to save peace."

That same evening, Khrushchev sent a telegram to Kennedy warning that "outright piracy" by the U.S. would lead to war.

On October 25, the Chinese People's Army promised that "650,000 Chinese men and women are standing by the Cuban people."

The situation intensified through events that seemed random and unplanned. On October 27, a Soviet surface-to-air (SAM) missile fired in Cuba took down an American U-2 piloted by Air Force Major Rudolf Anderson, killing him. Shortly thereafter, several U.S. Navy RF-8A Crusaders on a low-level photo-recon mission over Cuba took anti-aircraft fire.

Patrolling off Russia's east coast, a U.S. U-2 spy plane ventured over Soviet airspace in an unauthorized ninety-minute overflight. The Soviets responded by scrambling MiG fighters from Wrangell

Island. Americans countered with F-102 fighters armed with air-to-air missiles.

"What hope there is," Robert Kennedy declared at an ongoing session in the Chiefs of Staff conference room, "rests on whether Khrushchev retains his course for the next few days."

His tie was loose and he was in his shirtsleeves. Sweat dropped from his forehead in beads.

"We don't have much hope," he said. "We expect a military confrontation by as early as tomorrow."

The Russian tanker *Grozny* was about six hundred miles out and steaming toward Havana. Earlier, fourteen Soviet ships presumably carrying offensive weapons turned back rather than test the blockade. SecDef McNamara thought *Grozny* was approaching in order to challenge America's resolve.

"It has to be intercepted," McNamara said. "We can't back down now."

"Black Saturday" continued to unfold into an even blacker Sunday. A Soviet submarine at depth approached the blockade line armed with a nuclear-tipped torpedo and orders to use it if attacked. U.S. Navy destroyers dropped signaling depth charges on it; the very small hand-grenade-sized explosions were used only as warning shots.

The sub rested underwater, surrounded by American warships and running out of air. Captain Valentin Savitsky ordered his boat's torpedo be made combat ready. That set off a heated debate between Savitsky and his two junior officers. The captain finally relented and saw the wisdom of backing down and pulling back.

The Caribbean remained only minutes away from ignition as the Kennedys and McNamara on one side and Khrushchev and Gromyko on the other pursued discussions throughout the night to resolve the crisis. I finally called Mary.

"Look," I said. "Don't ask any questions. Pack your bags, and you and your daughter get ready to leave when I give you the word."

I owed her that much.

"Bill—?" She sounded frightened.

"That's all I can tell you. Just do as I say."

By this time I knew that one careless move was enough to set off the shot heard 'round the world. Only it wouldn't be just a ball from a musket this time. I was beginning to lose hope for a solution outside nuclear war.

I spoke with Lieutenant Boehm in Key West. His SEAL force was prepared to go in the event it was needed. Airplanes and gunboats stood by.

"What's happening in Washington, skipper?" he asked.

An information blackout kept most units in the dark while still on alert.

"I can't tell you anything yet, Roy."

"Our SEALs have signed and initialized their last wills and testaments," he said.

"Roger that, Roy. Uh—"

"I understand, sir."

The countdown was into the hours now instead of days. Shortly after midnight that fateful Sunday, the U.S. informed NATO that "the situation is growing shorter. . . . The United States may find it necessary within a very short time in its interest and that of its fellow nations in the Western Hemisphere to take whatever military action that may be necessary."

I swigged coffee and waited for the showdown. Silence hung over the Pentagon now like that of a wake at a funeral home. The important men were silent as well. They strode the corridors like ghosts and whispered together in shadows. Waiting. Like me.

At 9:00 a.m., President Kennedy received a message broadcast first from Radio Moscow. The word spread quickly from the White House to the State Department to the CIA in Langley to the Pentagon.

"The Soviet Government . . . has issued a new order on the dismantling of the weapons which you describe as 'offensive' and their crating and return to the Soviet Union."

Khrushchev had blinked. *Grozny* and other ships bound for Cuba turned and headed back to the Soviet Union. JFK had partially redeemed himself for turning yellow at the Bay of Pigs.

CHAPTER TWENTY-SEVEN

ONE THING I LEARNED about the CIA during my involvement with spooks at the Bay of Pigs and the Cuban Missile Crisis: the Agency was an important element in an increasingly complex panorama of "night fighters" operating largely unseen in an ongoing battle dedicated to victory without laying waste to the world in the process. DCI John McCone approached me several times about my switching over from the Navy to work for the CIA. I suspected my little mission to Amsterdam might actually have been a test and his doing.

By this time I had been in the Navy for thirteen years, not counting Annapolis, and was up for promotion to full commander, with a captaincy virtually assured. I had an ex-wife and three kids I rarely saw, and a new wife and stepdaughter who liked the fact that I was mostly tied to a desk near home. We had even bought a house in the suburbs and moved out of the apartment. Could a poodle on a leash and PTA membership be far off?

Mary was happy. I was miserable, dragging my briefcase to the office mornings during the eight o'clock rush like every other commuter. My SEALs were *doing* things; my ass was getting broad sitting at a desk.

A month after the Cuban Crisis ended, on November 30, 1962, I signed off active naval duty without consulting my wife, reverted to the

Navy Reserve, and signed on with the Central Intelligence Agency. I should have predicted Mary's reaction.

"You did *what?*"

CIA headquarters at Langley, Virginia, was located about eight miles from downtown Washington, D.C. Its 258 secluded acres surrounded by residential streets resembled more a university campus than the brain center for U.S. worldwide intelligence services. Savillian Chapman, number two in the Maritime Division of the Special Operations Division, picked me up at home in a plain, unmarked Chevy sedan. He pulled off the George Washington Parkway and along a two-lane road that led to Spook Campus.

Chapman was an ordinary-looking fella in his late forties, early fifties maybe, with a thatch of salt-and-pepper hair and a broad, open face that seemed inappropriate on a man in his line of business, snooping through other people's secrets. He could have been a small businessman or owner/proprietor of a mom-and-pop grocery.

As we drove he related a bit of CIA lore from the beginning days. Seemed President Harry Truman had a sense of humor. He convened a small, secret ceremony at the White House in 1946 to swear in Admiral Sidney Souers as the first DCI, presenting Souers with a black cloak, black hat, a wooden dagger, and dubbing him "Commander, The Cloak and Dagger Group of Snoopers."

The enormous main building of CIA headquarters rose almost unexpectedly out of the trees. Nearby in a separate building sat the Headquarters Auditorium, a free-standing, dome-shaped structure connected to the main building by an underground passage.

Any resemblance Langley CIA might have had with the University of Virginia or even the Naval Academy ended at the guard shack. There were no students on campus beyond the entrance. Only undistinguished-looking men hurrying from place to place like automatons in a self-imposed hush.

"It's not as grim as it appears," Chapman said with a smile, as though reading my mind. He stopped at the guard shack and rolled down his window to have our credentials checked. "You'll get used to it, Bill."

The plainclothes security man bent down and looked through Chapman's window at me on the passenger's seat.

"You're new, sir?"

"That's right."

He studied my ID. "You never really get used to it, sir," he said, having apparently overheard Chapman's remark as we drove up.

We parked in front of the main building and entered. The atmosphere of this strange place seemed to settle around us like still air, beginning with our echoing footfalls across the open lobby. A huge CIA seal was inlaid in the floor and a Biblical verse etched into the wall: *And ye shall know the truth and the truth shall make you free. John VIII–XXXII.*

Chapman chuckled at the look on my face. "You already feel free, right? Come on. The director wants to see you."

We took the elevator.

"The cold fact, Bill, is what the guard said. You never really get used to it. You learn never to fully trust anyone."

I had met DCI John McCone on several occasions in consultation on the use of naval special forces. It was after one of these meetings at the Pentagon that he tempted me with a serious offer of a position in the Agency. We got together several other times after that to further explore the offer.

Most members of the CIA were either station-bound intelligence analysts or Foreign Intelligence (FI) officers who worked overseas, generally out of American embassies recruiting and handling local operatives. Spies. A smaller bunch with the CIA known as the Special Operations Division (SOD), the Agency's least-known covert section, was responsible for taking care of most of the dirty work.

SOD was composed of three sections: Ground Branch; Air Branch; and Maritime Branch. Maritime consisted primarily of former SEALs and UDTs. Its primary emphasis centered on amphibious or water-borne ops along hostile shorelines. Various other divisions within the Agency could draw trained personnel from the SOD to form Special Operations Groups (SOGs) to carry out paramilitary operations such as sabotage, personnel or materiel recovery, prisoner snatches, raids, hostage rescues, and other low-profile activities. These men were commonly known as "knuckle draggers." Tough, resilient men like Rip Robertson and Grayston Lynch.

Ed Foster, the number one at Maritime, was dying from liver cancer. I had met him before. He looked much older than his years—like a frail old man with thin hair and yellow shoes.

Chapman was Maritime's number two below Foster. Number three was a man I had not yet met. The DCI offered me Maritime number three when Foster died and everyone moved up in the hierarchy.

The DCI rose and extended a handshake when his secretary showed Chap and me into his office. On a wall hung a portrait of President Harry Truman, the man who gave life to the CIA. On the other wall hung a picture of FBI Director J. Edgar Hoover. On his desk perched a family snapshot of the DCI and a pretty, slender woman surrounded by what I took to be adult children and preteen grandchildren.

McCone was a broad-shouldered, trim man with big hands and short, white hair. As always, he appeared businesslike in a dark suit and red power tie. I thought he bore a striking resemblance to former president Woodrow Wilson. Or, rather, to the professor Wilson had once been.

He got right to the point of outlining my duties: *Responsible for concept and development of plans; selection and training of personnel; selection, procurement and readiness of equipment and staff; and direct supervision of worldwide field activities.*

My ass was about to slim down.

"Welcome aboard, Commander," Director McCone concluded. "Chap here will fill you in on the details of what we have going and get you ready to stand on line. Things are happening fast all over the world. The president expects us to be ready. You'll be responsible for three major geographical areas—Cuba; the Belgian Congo; and Vietnam."

CHAPTER TWENTY-EIGHT

T HE UNITED STATES HAD carried out intelligence activities since the days of George Washington, but only since World War II had it been coordinated on a government-wide basis. The unforeseen attack on Pearl Harbor prompted the creation of a clearing house for foreign policy intelligence analysis. It was only later that a requirement for spying and covert action was imposed.

The first public mention of "Central Intelligence Agency" occurred in the U.S. Senate Military Affairs Committee at the end of 1945 in a proposal advocating a National Intelligence Authority. By this time the OSS and other covert and intelligence gathering organizations were abolished. The military, the U.S. State Department, and the FBI all opposed the idea of a central intelligence, for various reasons having to do with self-interest.

Nonetheless, President Harry Truman signed the National Security Act into law on July 26, 1947, to create the National Security Council (NSC) and the Central Intelligence Agency. A subsequent act in 1949, the CIA Act, allowed the agency to function in secrecy with only nominal oversight.

Different demands were placed on the new agency. Truman wanted a centralized entity to organize and supply information to the presidency; the Department of Defense insisted on military intelligence and covert action; the State Department wanted to meddle politically in foreign affairs. That brought about two areas of CIA responsibility—covert action and covert intelligence.

The Agency's early track record proved abysmal. Not only did it fail to foresee important international challenges, such as the Soviet takeover of Romania and Czechoslovakia or the Soviet blockade of Berlin, but foreign double agents made mockery of new and untried operatives.

By the time of the Bay of Pigs, however, the Agency's record had improved along with its covert experience. It recruited Lieutenant Roy Boehm for one of its covert actions. Spies uncovered a plot by an international assassin headquartered in the Dominican Republic to murder a Cuban operative working with the CIA in Havana. Under the Agency's auspices, Boehm flew into Santo Domingo posing as an advisor to Dominican UDTs. His real mission was to kill the would-be assassin, who went by the name "Manuel."

An undercover double agent known as "Raul" told "Manuel" that Boehm was an international arms dealer working out of Saudi Arabia. During a private meeting to discuss arms shipments, Boehm shot the man through the head with a 9mm German Luger. He looked at the dead man, turned, and walked out.

"I realized that spying, dirty tricks, and political killings were all part of the new unconventional warfare scenario," Boehm told me later. "This Cold War shit, skipper, it's getting brutal. It ain't for the weak-hearted. It's fuck 'em all and count the bodies."

CHAPTER TWENTY-NINE

DURING THE SPANISH-AMERICAN WAR of 1898, Secretary of State John Hay wrote to Theodore Roosevelt, "It has been a splendid little war, begun with the highest motives, carried on with magnificent intelligence and spirit, favored by that fortune which loves the brave."

Change the time and location and you had Vietnam, at least in the beginning.

The first thing that struck me about Vietnam, when I grabbed my carry-on and got off the plane at Tan Son Nhut Airport in Saigon, was the incredible heat. Like opening the door of Mom's old kerosene stove oven back when I was a kid and we were stationed in Panama. The second thing that struck me was the sight and stench of a dead water buffalo alongside the tarmac and the cloud of black flies hovering on it.

I wore light tropical worsted slacks and a shirt loose over my belt for air circulation. Sweat rings appeared underneath my arms by the time I walked across the tarmac to the terminal. Most of the other passengers hurrying along with me were a mixture of Asian and European businessmen in hats, shirts, and loosened ties. None appeared especially pleased with their destination—or perhaps it was just the heat.

I found my luggage—I always traveled light—and left the terminal to check on a ride. John "Jocko" Richardson, CIA Chief of Station in Saigon, was supposed to pick me up at the airport. He must have gotten held up. I dropped my bag and fired up a cigarette while I took a look around. This was my first trip to Vietnam.

Not much to see from here. The shimmering of heat and a hint of city beyond the taxi and rickshaw parking area where rowdy operators vied to capture travelers to deliver to their destinations. At this early period, Vietnam was predominately a CIA commitment. Had been, in fact, since as early as 1950 when President Truman resolved to help the French retain their hold over Indochina and prevent the Communist Chinese expansion into Southeast Asia.

Look at this shitbag little country. Divided at the waist, the North a pissant state bordering on China, the southern half struggling to establish democracy while striving to keep communist guerrillas from absorbing the rural countryside.

William Colby served as CIA chief of station in Saigon from 1959 until recently in 1962, when he was promoted to chief of the CIA's Far East Division and head of the Agency's Civil Operations and Rural Development efforts. Now forty-three years old, he was a mild-appearing man, studious-looking, wearing rimmed glasses with his thinning hair swept back from a broad forehead. His nose and lips were narrow and his ears large and seemingly out of place.

"Quite frankly," he had said during an extended session with DCI McCone, SecDef Robert McNamara, and several other military, State, and Agency personnel, of which I was one, "I don't feel there is much chance of generating any real resistance in North Vietnam against Ho Chi Minh, and I'm not sure South Vietnam can survive without substantial involvement of the United States. I don't think the American people are ready for another Korea."

McNamara, a ruddy, broad-faced man wearing spectacles, looked stricken, as though the statement was a traitor's knife stuck into his back. "The president will disagree with you," he snapped.

Since President Kennedy's speech that opened the hatch for the creation of Navy SEALs nearly two years ago, and since his failure to act during the Bay of Pigs, he had become the nation's foremost advocate of counterinsurgency and unconventional warfare. He referred to the Cold War as a "long twilight struggle leading to a new kind of war—revolution, people's wars, subterranean wars, multidimensional

Lieutenant Commander Bill Hamilton (right) at a formal event. His mother, Marjorie, and father, Retired Admiral Bill Hamilton Sr. in background left.

Captain William H. Hamilton Jr., Unconventional Warfare Renaissance Man.

Bill became intrigued by unconventional warfare while flying F95 Panther fighters over Korea during the Korean War.

Hamilton as a UDT operative in the Caribbean prior to the Bay of Pigs.

Lieutenant Roy Boehm shared a vision with Hamilton to build the finest unconventional warfare unit in the world. Together, they trained and commissioned the first U.S. Navy SEAL Teams. (Roy Boehm)

During the Cuban Missile Crisis in 1962, Bill Hamilton and Roy Boehm prepared this team of SEALs to paradrop into Cuba following an expected nuclear missile attack on the United States. (Roy Boehm)

As a CIA agent, Hamilton was in and out of Vietnam, working with OP-34 and SEALs on the South China Sea to interdict communists smuggling arms and personnel to Viet Cong guerrillas in South Vietnam.
(U.S. Defense Department)

Communist VC guerrilla insurgents. Hamilton designed and tested river craft such as the Swift Boat for use by SEALs, Frogmen, and Riverine Forces in interdicting enemy supply lines in the Mekong Delta of Vietnam.
(U.S. Defense Department)

This is the last known photo of Ernesto "Che" Guevara (right). CIA operative Felix Rodriguez (left) headed the CIA team that worked with Bolivian authorities to capture Guevara in 1967. Hamilton had Guevara trapped in the Congo three years previously, but the wily Cuban made a dramatic escape.
(Felix Rodriguez and CIA)

Known as the "Rogue Warrior," Lieutenant Commander Richard Marcinko worked with Hamilton through the Chief of Naval Operations to create Red Cell to test security on naval installations. Later, again together, they built SEAL Team 6, the most effective and respected counterterrorism unit in the world. (U.S. Navy)

The rise of terrorism in the Middle East following the 1974 Iran Hostage Crisis saw the United States increasingly targeted by Islamic terrorists. This truck bombing of the U.S. Marine barracks in Beirut in 1983 killed twenty-four Marines. Hamilton's duties at the Pentagon as a member of the CNO's Counterterrorism Task Force were to devise methods to fight terrorism throughout the world. (U.S. Defense Department)

Hamilton leaps into the brine during a UDT training operation.

Hamilton (left) was a test volunteer in revolutionary methods for use by Navy Unconventional Warfare— including ejecting from downed aircraft underwater; as a test subject for outer space weightlessness; and the training of dolphins for strategic warfare. Here, he tries out a new pressurized diving suit.

Hamilton exiting from a submarine during an infiltration mission.

Bill Hamilton experiments with "cast and recovery" operations from helicopters off the coast of Japan following the Korean War.

Hamilton (foreground) during SEAL cast-and-recovery operations.

Hamilton prepares to "cast" into the Sea of Japan in experiments for inserting guerrilla operatives clandestinely behind enemy lines.

Hamilton as Operations Officer aboard the destroyer USS *Buckley* in the Atlantic.

Bill Hamilton (far right) in a reunion of his 1949 Annapolis U.S. Naval Academy class in the 1980s.

By 1986, Bill had been fighting terrorists and America's enemies as a naval officer and fighter pilot, UDT Frogman, SEAL, guerrilla fighter, and counterterrorism expert for more than thirty-seven years. Even when he and wife Barbara retired and finally settled down to get the dog he always wanted, they lived near the ocean.

Bill and Barbara Hamilton on their wedding day in 1968. Bill met Barbara when he was the CIA's director of Maritime and she was a CIA analyst.

Bill and Barbara at home for Christmas while both still worked for the CIA.

war, slow-burn war, war in the shadows [that required] a new kind of fighting force."

South Vietnam had no chance on its own. Special warfare strategies and tactics in countering the North's continuing guerrilla incursions were the little nation's only hope of becoming a democracy free of communist domination.

"Sir—?" I ventured.

Colby and McNamara looked at me.

"President Kennedy is right," I said. "Special operations forces from the Navy and Army can make the difference—if they're used correctly."

McNamara lifted an eyebrow to offset his lenses. "You think you can use them correctly, commander?"

"They're an answer to Vietnam."

I hoped I wasn't letting my alligator mouth overload my hummingbird ass.

Green Berets were already in country, twelve teams of them training South Vietnamese troops, with another twelve currently preparing for overseas deployment. SEALs worked with the CIA along sea and river fronts, the first SEAL detachment of two officers and ten enlisted from Dave Del Guidice's SEAL Team One having arrived in Da Nang earlier in the year to operate a secret military project called OP-34.

OP-34 was the reason I came to Vietnam. I much preferred getting in on the action and not leaving the hazardous stuff just to the lower ranks.

I spotted Jocko Richardson driving onto the Saigon airport in a blue Toyota with another man. He waved and stopped.

"Hamilton?"

I nodded. "Richardson?"

I tossed my bag and carry-on onto the backseat and scooted in after them. The man in the front passenger's seat turned to shake hands with me and introduce himself as Averell Harriman. I knew the name and position: ambassador-at-large in Vietnam and undersecretary of state for political affairs.

They drove me to the Majestic Hotel. I dropped my luggage off in my room on the fourth floor. It was typical of tropical Asia—high ceiling with a fan to stir up a breeze and disperse mosquitoes, two rattan chairs, monsoon mildew creeping up plastered walls that were no longer whitewashed every dry season. The three of us proceeded to the roof patio, where we had drinks in the shade of a striped awning.

Jocko was an ordinary-looking man of about fifty, medium height and build. I liked his sincere and open manner right away.

Harriman was beginning to age, was in fact around seventy, but his hair had not yet turned completely white and he still walked with a steady gait. His eyes were of a strange hue and piercing, his mouth thin and wide, and his nose like the predatory beak of a raptor bird.

Colby had briefed me on both men before I left Langley. He thought Jocko could be trusted implicitly. He sounded less than certain about Harriman. Two years ago, Anatoliy Golitsyn had defected from the Russian secret police and denounced Harriman as being a spy for the Soviets. The CIA investigated and dismissed the accusation as unfounded.

Drinks on the roof were a pleasant experience after the long, tiring flight across California to Hawaii and Japan and then over Korea to Saigon. Relaxing, I leaned back in the shade of the awning in a new wicker chair and gazed off toward the brown Saigon River swarming with sampans and junks. Apparently, whole families lived on the boats with their chickens, geese, and hogs.

The conversation proceeded light and general. It seemed to me that Jocko was deliberately guiding it that way. That aroused my curiosity. When Harriman got up to go downstairs to check for dispatches, I took advantage of his absence. I offered Jocko a cigarette and lit it for him. I decided blunt was the best approach.

"You don't like that old man," I said.

He looked at me. "*Like* has nothing to do with it."

He tried to shrug it off. But then he turned in his chair to look out and down toward the river.

"President Kennedy," he began thoughtfully, "appointed Averell to Vietnam as ambassador-at-large. Fred Nolting might be ambassador here, but it's Harriman who calls the shots. He makes decisions without consulting the ambassador, the attorney general, or the president."

The station chief's voice harbored a decided undertone.

"You don't *trust* him?" I amended from *like*. Colby didn't trust him either.

Jocko rose and walked to the plaited fence that enclosed the roof patio. "We'll have dinner on the open patio below," he said, with his head turned away and his neck stiffening.

I was discovering that in this business no one trusted anyone else.

We three had dinner together below on the open sidewalk terrace where pretty Vietnamese women in colorful *ao dais* and men in cone hats and loose black trousers mingled with Saigon merchants and armed ARVN (Army of the Republic of Vietnam) soldiers. Pedestrians, rickshaws, pedicabs, and Honda-kazis emitted a mixed cacophony of conversation, laughter, screaking wheels, and roaring Honda engines.

During their colonial stay of less than a century, the French left behind a rich architectural heritage. Colonial buildings possessed a seedy and languid charm, blending Western and Asian elements along tree-lined boulevards and dense, walkable side streets. But architecture wasn't the only thing they left. Many of the women displayed the influence of the French occupation in their features. Eurasian women had to be among the most beautiful in the world.

Jocko demanded a table on the terrace apart from other diners in anticipation of more serious talk.

"I haven't given up on saving Vietnam," he said. "I know Averell disagrees with me, but I think we need to keep working with President Diem and his brother if we're going to realize any progress."

Harriman cut him off with his old man's garrulousness. "What this country needs is new leadership in the palace. That pair of Diems is screwing up the works. While you're up in Da Nang, Hamilton, look and listen and you'll see what I mean."

"Progress will come," Richardson said, digging in. "Look at what the Army is accomplishing with their Green Berets and the Civilian Irregular Defense Groups in Darlac Province. *That's* success. SEALs will do likewise when they're fully operational. Special forces are the key to countering the Viet Cong guerrillas."

"Yes," Harriman agreed, after which he issued an ominous prediction that I was to recall a few months later. "But it's the Saigon leadership that will screw the pooch. In my opinion, that fat asshole Diem should be shot right through the head before he screws up the entire country."

He leaned across the table toward us. "And it will happen, gentlemen. It's coming."

CHAPTER THIRTY

W HEN I FIRST CAME over to the CIA, a movement was under way at the Pentagon, the State Department, and even the CIA itself to withdraw the Agency from the covert business due to its perceived failure in properly managing the Bay of Pigs. However, with DCI John McCone at the helm replacing Allen Dulles, the CIA returned to the point of view that a paramilitary wing was essential as the nation's active focus shifted toward Vietnam.

President Kennedy might have screwed the pooch at the Bay of Pigs, but he had been making up for it ever since. "When I was in Norfolk . . ." he wrote in a letter addressed to the secretary of Navy and the chief of naval operations, "I noted particularly the members of the SEAL teams. I was impressed by them as individuals and with the capability they possess as a group. As missiles assume more and more of the deterrent role and as our limited-war mission grows, the need for special forces in the Navy and Marine Corps will increase."

The CIA attempted to fill a special forces role in Vietnam after the French defeat at Dien Bien Phu. It was mostly a low-level, low-budget covert effort that concentrated on stay-behind programs like the ones set up in Europe to seed resistance should the communists prevail. It was largely ineffective.

Lieutenant Commander Philip Bucklew showed up in Vietnam around 1961. I knew Bucklew from his UDT work from World War

II and Korea. He was a competent, farsighted UW warrior who succeeded in persuading Department of Navy to reactivate WWII navy
tactical cover-and-deception units known as Beach Jumpers. Beach
Jumpers had trained alongside UDTs in support of amphib landings
in the South Pacific.

With Bucklew in command, Jumpers began operating out of Da
Nang using revolutionary new methods in psychological and elec-
tronic warfare, monitoring Soviet signal intelligence (SIGINT), and
jamming hostile radio signals. A U.S. Air Force detachment set up at
Monkey Mountain to work with the Jumpers in intercepting North
Vietnamese HF and VHF communications.

Bucklew subsequently authored a report predicting the communist
Viet Cong, the VC, would make far more use of intercoastal waterways, rivers, and Vietnam's 1,200-mile coastline to smuggle arms, supplies, and personnel into South Vietnam than they would of the Ho
Chi Minh Trail network. To stem this tide and control coastal shipping, the CIA encouraged the South Vietnamese government to build
a three-hundred-vessel coastal patrol consisting of both a regular naval
contingent and a paramilitary junk force. They faced a formidable task
since on any particular day as many as fifty thousand sampans, junks,
and trawlers traveled Vietnam's coastline.

At the same time, in the program known as OP-34, the Agency
transformed low-level espionage operations into paramilitary units
that could be cast behind enemy lines in North Vietnam to stir up
resistance and create such chaos that Ho Chi Minh would call off his
conspiracy with China and Russia to take over South Vietnam. Our
infiltrators into Ho Chi Minh land were essentially *terrorists*. But they
were *our* terrorists.

Things worked well at first. Operatives disguised as North Vietnamese fishermen dropped agents and supplies off north of the DMZ,
then picked them up later for debriefing at Da Nang's China Beach.
It wasn't long, however, before Uncle Ho wised up and his increas-
ingly-sophisticated intelligence apparatus grew more aggressive. Coast
watcher spies and double agents prowling Da Nang and China Beach
kept the North informed of movements. Roughly 250 operatives

dispatched north by the CIA in long-range teams failed to return. They were believed to have been captured or killed.

By this time I was head of the CIA's Maritime Division. I recommended SEALs be placed in charge of OP-34 Maritime and that they be supplied with heavily armed watercraft.

The Joint Chiefs took their time buying off on my plan. Even William Colby, who was in overall charge of OP-34 covert ops due to his position as bureau chief, Far Eastern division, openly expressed reservations.

"I've come to the conclusion that the operation should be called off," he said. "They're not contributing what we hoped to, and they are suffering losses. There's no further point in it."

I went to my boss, DCI McCone. "Sir, Colby has a point, I won't deny that. But it's because we're piecemealing the war, playing patty-cake with Ho Chi Minh while giving him time to build up his strength in the South. We can keep at it the way we're going or we can use Special Ops to make Hanoi pay a price for its aggression. Either way, we *are* going to end up in a real shooting war. Let's make it to our advantage when it happens."

McCone leaned across his desk, hands tented and wearing his professional look. "Bone, what with the commies in China and Moscow backing Hanoi, a wrong move on our part could end in another nuclear confrontation. This time Khrushchev might not chicken out. How do you foresee it playing out?"

"It's going to be a guerrilla war, sir. At least at the beginning. That's the only way it can play out. The battleground is the South. We try to go North, the Chinese and Russians will send in support and troops and we're fighting Korea all over again. What this means is we have to fight unconventional—Army Green Berets, Rangers, SEALs."

McCone nodded. Shortly thereafter, Del Guidice's SEAL detachment arrived on China Beach.

CHAPTER THIRTY-ONE

CHINA BEACH WAS A twenty-mile stretch of white sand northeast of Da Nang extending into the blue waters of the South China Sea, only ninety miles from the DMZ. It was an idyllic setting out of a scene from James Michener's *Hawaii*, certainly from appearances not the site of a secret CIA operation and base for deadly sabotage and espionage overtures against communism. Located at the foot of the dark and bare Monkey Mountain, OP-34's cover name was innocent sounding—Naval Advisory Detachment.

At this point in 1963, Americans were strictly forbidden north of the 17th Parallel. The detachment from Commander Dave Del Guidice's SEAL Team One limited itself to training Viet guerrilla fighters hidden away in secret little camps along a ten-mile stretch of beach between the two commanding promontories of Monkey Mountain on the north and Marble Mountain to the south. Each camp housed forty or fifty men, volunteers from the South Vietnamese Navy. Some were being trained as swimmers and behind-the-lines operators, others as shooters. Their boats, disguised as fishermen junks and trawlers, were harbored at finger piers and floating dry docks at the base of Monkey Mountain.

I was surprised to find the SEAL uniform of the day consisted of shorts, tennis shoes, and suntans. Hair was of varying unkempt length. Some men grew beards. They resembled beach bums from southern California.

"They blend in," Del Guidice said. He was here on a short visit to check on his men. "As far as the local Viet Cong know, we're rag-tag 'advisors' to the South Vietnam Navy and have no connection to spooks or special operators."

SEALs had the beach all to themselves and were living the life of Riley. They didn't bother the local VC, the VC didn't bother them. They seldom found it necessary to go armed when they jogged the beach, swam, or gathered at little beach bars near Da Nang to talk, drink, and watch moonlight sparkling off breakers rolling in from the sea.

"The VC aren't interested in harassing us," Del Guidice further explained. "That way they know where we are and what we're doing. We suspect the boats and men we're losing originate at an NVA naval base at Quang Khe, about thirty miles north of the DMZ. It's a staging base for small boats smuggling arms and infiltrators south. The real danger is that it is also a base for Swatow gunboats."

The Swatow was China-built, based on the Soviet P-6 class torpedo boat. It was steel-hulled and bristling with guns as its main armament rather than torpedoes. Slow, with a maximum speed of about ten knots, it was still faster than the junks and trawlers used by OP-34.

Christ! We were sending out matchboxes to take on warships.

More than two years previously, Admiral Arleigh Burke had pushed for greater efforts from the Navy to prepare for river and restricted water operations, to include the development of shallow-water craft and coastal-patrol craft. Captain Joseph Drachnik, chief of the Naval Sector for MAAG-Vietnam (Military Advisory Assistance Group-Vietnam), devised a concept for a "Riverine Warfare Force" with river craft backed up by helicopters and armed support ships. The CNO rejected both proposals on the ground that "we are required to remain in an advisory role [that prevented] our development of a U.S. force for use in your area."

If I hoped to change minds, I needed the personal experience of conditions along the South Vietnam coast to bolster my argument. There was only one way to acquire it. I informed Del Guidice I would accompany a boat inserting South Vietnamese saboteurs into North Vietnam. He frowned but said nothing.

* * *

The sun sank into the South China Sea, turning the ocean blood-red, as though in premonition of an uncertain future. I boarded a Viet junk at the floating docks to ride north with the crew to insert an espionage team of five Vietnamese north of the DMZ. The five huddled together in the open stern, muttering nervously among themselves and glancing anxiously about as the fishing junk departed and rode the outgoing tide from the bay.

I couldn't blame the poor bastards for being jittery.

Full darkness descended. I wore unmarked dungarees and a black cone hat, as though a disguise made a difference if the VC captured a six-four round-eye. Sails sloughed in a moderate night breeze. We pretended to be a fishing boat as the crew navigated past shadows of other fishing boats off the point of the bay and headed north. The black mound of Monkey Mountain disappeared into the night.

I rode easy at the bow with the captain, who spoke some English but was such a taciturn individual that he uttered few words even in his own language other than to bark orders at his crew. I looked up at the stars, at the sliver of a moon already high, back toward the black-paja-maed "fishermen" shaking out nets and lines for the sake of appearance should we be stopped by enemy patrol boats once we crossed the invisible water line into North Vietnam.

What a hell of a way to make a living.

Still, tonight, this night, with the salt scent in my nostrils, the soft brush of ocean breezes in my face, the gentle billowing huff of sails, the buzz of the small outboard engine, the motion of the boat, and the sing-sing of a foreign language in my ears—I could imagine being no other place in the world. I was born to the sea, I belonged to the sea.

An uneasy feeling stirred in the pit of my stomach as the low black line of landfall unraveled off our port side. The captain navigated not by the stars or moon or even an ordinary compass. He followed the coast and depended on his fishermen's masquerade to protect us. Not a good course of action.

We arrived off the enemy's shore between midnight and dawn. The sea was black and calm. The sliver of moon disappeared, leaving stars reflected in the water. Land and sea seemed to merge.

Low brittle words full of tension were exchanged between crew and swimmers as our infiltrators cautiously checked radios, weapons, and other gear in their waterproof bags. The junk swung in toward shore and cut speed. The silhouettes of men, like little pieces of stirred night, slipped over the gunnels and with barely a splash vanished into the black of night and water.

I had questions: How had this particular site been selected? What about security? How many people knew about it, and about tonight? Could contacts ashore be trusted? What was the point in all these infiltrations if the operatives were betrayed and captured once they reached landfall?

It suddenly occurred to me why our boats were rarely sunk. Swatows weren't going to mess with our boats. Sonsofbitches *wanted* us to keep transporting sacrificial lambs to the slaughter. The only way to stop the slaughter was to bring in armed, fast patrol boats with skilled navigators and operators.

"Wait!" I commanded when the captain ordered full sail for departure.

"No—No. We go now," he insisted.

"We go pick up those men before it's too late," I snapped. "Do you understand?"

I couldn't be sure he did. The other two crewmen stared into the darkness, waiting for further commands.

I latched on to the captain's shirt front and jerked him up on his toes. "Those men are going to die. Do you understand? Go after them. Now!"

The junk lay only a short distance offshore. About now the swimmers should be emerging from water onto sand. Suddenly, a fusillade of rifle shots erupted from the beach. Screams and shouts and more shots. Muzzle flashes sparked, a grenade exploded,

The massacre ended as quickly as it began. Silence returned to the night. I glared in disbelief and horror. We had killed those five men as surely as if we had squeezed the triggers ourselves.

Our captain turned the junk south to return to China Beach. I stood alone on the fantail and watched North Vietnam vanish into darkness. We couldn't keep sending brave men to their deaths like this. There was a better way—bring in fast American patrol boats and skilled special warfare operators.

CHAPTER THIRTY-TWO

A MAJOR DISAGREEMENT WAS BREWING in D.C. over the conduct of a war that was not a war and over whether the U.S. should continue to support it. Powerful and influential officials lined up on each side of the issue. Muttering and grumbling spread throughout the federal government as people jockeyed for position. Backbiting, snitching, struggling to wrest concessions, infighting to press their views. I was fast learning that unconventional warfare encompassed more than SEALs, Green Berets, and foreign intrigue. It also included domestic political intrigue, plotting, and conspiracies in the seats of power. I hadn't realized before just *how* dirty a business politics could be.

"Things are going to hell," DCI McCone said. "Hang on. It's going to be a hairy ride."

Buddhist monks and their dispute with South Vietnam president Ngo Dinh Diem proved to be the catalyst that propelled the issue of "yes we will, no we won't" into crisis. My new friend Jocko Richardson, CIA station chief in Saigon, filled me in on internal politics in South Vietnam. We were lunching on the terrace of the Majestic before I caught my flight back to the United States.

A Catholic, President Diem was growing increasingly unpopular largely because of his discriminatory policies against the country's Buddhist majority. On top of that, Richardson said, Diem was a power-hungry sonofabitch who consolidated his political strength through staged elections and by banning opposition parties and eliminating rivals through jailing or assassinating them. So far, he had survived two major attacks against him—one in 1960 when factions of the military unsuccessfully tried to force him out of office, again in early 1962 when disgruntled air force pilots dropped bombs on the palace.

"South Vietnam is plagued by corruption and political intrigue—and we Americans are contributing to it," Jocko said. "President Kennedy is slipping us into a quagmire."

"From what I understand," I replied, "JFK wants to pull a Bay of Pigs and get out of Dodge."

Richardson sipped hot black tea and rubbed lines in his forehead with his fingertips. He looked up at me across the tiny wrought-iron table.

"Bone, I'm telling you this for what it's worth: Word has it that Henry Cabot Lodge is being appointed new ambassador to Vietnam to replace Fred Nolting. From my point of view, that signals a policy change. I've warned the DCI to use caution. Because if State screws this up, the CIA is going to own this war. We're going to own it, Bone."

He paused. Sweat beaded on his forehead, although it was a cool morning. "Bone, I've also heard talk of a coup against Diem—and talk of assassinating him that may be coming from State and the White House. I don't much care for Diem either, but someone is fucking Kennedy over."

Diem's current imbroglio with Buddhists began on May 8 after he prohibited monks from displaying their flags. South Vietnamese security forces acting on orders from Diem's security advisor Ngo Dinh Nhu, who also happened to be Diem's younger brother, fired into a crowd of Buddhist protestors, killing eight of them.

In the weeks after that, Buddhists wearing their saffron robes conducted almost daily protest marches through the streets of Saigon, burning incense, carrying icons, and chanting.

In June, a monk named Thich Quang Duc burned himself to death in protest at a busy Saigon intersection. Photographs of his self-immolation circulated around the globe.

"No news picture in history has generated so much emotion around the world as that one," President Kennedy publically proclaimed with honest emotion.

Protests escalated in Saigon with other monks aping Quang Duc's example and self-immolating. Diem's brother, Nhu, urged on by his Dragon Lady wife, the de facto First Lady since President Diem was unmarried, launched nationwide raids on Buddhist pagodas. He killed thirty Buddhists. More than two hundred were wounded and 1,400 arrested. The cremated remains of Quang Duc, considered a sacred relic, were confiscated. The raids caught U.S. officials back in Saigon and in Washington flat-footed.

"It's hitting the fan," DCI McCone said. "Bone, I want you to go back over there now. Get with Jocko Richardson to see what the hell is going on."

Richardson, I discovered, was under a load of stress. He looked much older when he picked me up at the airport than when I last saw him. During the days after my arrival we observed events as they played out while I attempted to provide McCone a comprehensible picture of the situation. If things were fucked up in Washington, they were bleeding over tenfold into Saigon.

As Jocko predicted, Henry Cabot Lodge's arrival in June to replace Nolting as U.S. ambassador signaled a dramatic change in policy. A firm believer in the "Domino Theory," Lodge insisted the U.S. had to take a stand somewhere; it might as well be in Vietnam as in Mexico or Central America.

The new ambassador seemed convinced the U.S. could not defeat the communists with Diem in office. Jocko intercepted a dispatch Lodge sent to Washington in which he supported disgruntled Viet officers who were apparently plotting a coup to overthrow Diem.

In response, Secretary of State Dean Rusk advised Lodge not to push the coup plot "pending final decisions which are being formulated now."

"We kill Diem," Jocko said to me, "and it's a point of no return in Asia."

I agreed. "Ho Chi Minh will exploit it to infiltrate NVA into South Vietnam. We'll have no choice but to send in combat troops."

"That's what Lodge is pushing for."

In Washington, the choosing of sides and the plotting continued. Lining up with Lodge were McGeorge Bundy, special assistant to the president for national security affairs and a chief architect of U.S. policy in Southeast Asia; Averell Harriman, undersecretary of state for political affairs; and Secretary of State Dean Rusk.

"A pit of vipers, the bunch," Jocko opined. "They'll bite you when you're not looking."

On the other side were Jocko Richardson, who opposed a coup against Diem and argued for patience; Bureau Chief Far Eastern Division William Colby, who opted against abandoning Diem, although he had become disillusioned with the way the struggle against the communist National Liberation Front was proceeding; DCI John McCone; and Attorney General Robert Kennedy, both of whom feared supporting a coup made the U.S. responsible for South Vietnam and whatever came afterward.

Secretary of Defense Robert McNamara likely stood with Kennedy on whichever side the president finally landed.

So far, JFK remained committed to backing Diem, arguing that Diem had been a U.S. ally for nearly a decade now and that there was no guarantee that whoever replaced him would be any better. Nonetheless, the Buddhist uprising was weakening Kennedy's commitment and forcing him to straddle the fence.

"I think we want to make it our best judgment," he hedged over the question of whether or not to support a coup against Diem, "because I don't think we have to do it."

Ambassador Lodge considered Jocko a symbol of American support for Diem. He attempted to have Richardson fired as Saigon station chief in back-channel letters to the president. McCone warned Kennedy that the ambassador was so eager for a coup that he might act unilaterally.

Dean Rusk's State Department transmitted Cable 243 to Averell Harriman, with a copy to Bundy, stating that—and I only got the gist of it through sources—if "Diem remains obdurate . . . we must face the possibility that Diem cannot be preserved."

I was back in Langley when a dramatic confrontation between Ambassador Lodge and Jocko in Saigon ended with Richardson's recall to Washington and his replacement by a new station chief who took orders from Harriman and Lodge's military assistant, an Army

Special Forces officer named James Michael Dunn. Dunn, I discovered through the DCI, was known to be in touch with Colonel Big Minh and other plotters against Diem.

Sending Jocko home was a public signal that the U.S. had withdrawn support for the South Vietnam regime. I also took it as a sign that Kennedy may have caved and would allow the coup to proceed.

In the predawn of November 1, 1963, Colonel Big Minh made his move. Ambassador Lodge received a frantic phone call from Diem, demanding, "What is the attitude of the U.S. toward this coup attempt?"

The ambassador equivocated: "I'm not well enough informed at this time to be able to tell you," he replied.

Rebel soldiers dragged pudgy little Diem, his brother Nhu, and a Catholic priest out of a church where they were hiding and shoved them into the back of an armored personnel carrier. The APC stopped at a railroad crossing, where all three were executed with bullets to the backs of their heads.

On November 22, 1963, three weeks after Diem's murder, bullets from another assassin felled President John F. Kennedy in Dallas. When I heard the news, I trudged through the underground passageway that connected the CIA headquarters building to the auditorium. The auditorium was unoccupied. It was one of my favorite places when I had some thinking to do. I stood at a window overlooking the grounds outside. I couldn't help considering how the president who became the most fervent supporter of military special operations may have himself become its victim.

DCI John McCone approached quietly from behind and stood next to me looking out the window. He was the first to speak.

"Maybe we were blind," he said. "Maybe we should have anticipated this."

CHAPTER THIRTY-THREE

THE DIEM COUP AND assassination uncorked instability throughout South Vietnam, which the communists immediately exploited. Lyndon Baines Johnson, Kennedy's VP and now the new United States president following JFK's assassination, appeared ready to tackle Vietnam head-on.

"I'm not Jack Kennedy," he declared in a meeting of top Defense officials. "Them little yellow bastards are gonna get their asses kicked so high they'll have to take off their shirts to shit."

"A *real* war," McCone gloomily forecast.

Johnson was a Cold War warrior whose first impulse was victory. He made his new direction clear when he stripped control of all operations in Vietnam from the CIA and transferred authority to a military entity labeled as Military Assistance Command, Vietnam (MACV) under the command of Army Lieutenant General William C. Westmoreland. The military took to the locker room to ramp up for it. The introduction of American combat troops was only a matter of time.

With CIA activities reduced from active control to more or less an advisory status, and with renewed requirements for innovation on the battlefield, CNO McDonald was ready to consider recommendations I submitted from my fact-finding tour of OP-34. He released a study by his office supporting the expanded use of naval special warfare and for the development of watercraft to support it. No more junks and sampans and pretending to be fishermen.

What his report requested was "boats of many kinds and sizes for real fighting. . . . U.S. national policy will permit the use of effective military means short of open warfare to counter communist aggression. . . . The U.S. Navy will be called upon to conduct sublimated warfare in restricted waters, rivers, maritime areas, and on the high seas."

I volunteered the Maritime Office to design and test boats for use by SEALs, UDTs, and Riverine Forces. I took on the task personally.

Doug Fane, who had retired from the Navy in 1960, called me up. "Bone, you're doing a hell of a job."

"I owe it all to your nasty, ill-tempered ass," I retorted, laughing. "How's your, what? *Fourth* wife?"

"How's your *second*?"

He *had* been keeping up with me.

During the following months, I logged more time out at the Little Creek SEAL Base working on new boats than I did at Langley. The DCI simply shook his head whenever I showed up now and then to let him know I was still alive.

My partner-in-crime was a fellow named Perry Pratt, vice president of United Aircraft Corporation (UAC), which built Pratt & Whitney engines for Navy aircraft and hoped to get into the Navy boat business. He was a rather small and frail-looking man in his forties who nonetheless had a big set of balls and the brains to go with them. We were often together offshore on the Atlantic testing boat styles, types, and prospects, returning in the evenings drenched with salt spray and burned by the sun.

Mary complained that I was never home. I shrugged. What else could I do? This was my job.

Pratt trailered in for testing an old WWII PT boat variant like the one JFK commanded in the South Pacific. The inboard ran rough as hell, but we took along a 500hp outboard as a spare and headed for high seas.

"I smell a gas leak," Pratt remarked from the bridge.

I checked the engine compartment. Gas fumes were filling up the cockpit and cabin below.

"Turn it off!" I shouted.

Too late. The explosion tore through the deck, burping out a red-and-black ball of fire and smoke, shooting debris in all directions, and hurling Pratt and me overboard. I surfaced coughing and stunned but otherwise suffering only minor burns. The flaming PT drifted away like a Viking funeral pyre. I looked about for Perry.

His head appeared not far away. I swam to him as he shook water from his hair and eyes. We watched the burning boat disappear beneath the waves.

"Damn!" he exploded, coughing. "Damn! I thought you were a goner. I couldn't see you. Where were you?"

I pointed. "Over there. Weeping like a little girl, as is my custom in dangerous situations."

So there we were in the open ocean, no land in sight. Scorched, soaked, and giggling our fool heads off. Survival is an adrenaline high unlike any other. A civilian boat eventually came by and plucked us out of the brine.

The Navy ultimately awarded Perry's UAC-affiliated company a contract to produce one thousand Swift Boats for use in Vietnam. The Swift was based on boats used by offshore crews in Louisiana. Built of welded aluminum, it was fifty feet long with a shallow five-foot draft. Twin diesels with a range of four hundred miles at more than forty knots powered a deep V-hull. It was designed to accommodate 50-caliber machineguns and rockets. A fast, formidable weapons boat bound to jerk a knot in the drawers of VC along the Vietnam coast.

Wait until the bastards got a load of *this*.

* * *

Rudy Enders was the first man I met when I strolled onto the University of Miami campus, where the CIA kept an office. I spotted him approaching wearing slacks and an open, short-sleeved "Florida" shirt as he wended through a group of students playing grab-ass in front of Admin.

"Bone!" he exhorted. "Haven't seen you since Moses was a pup. What the hell you been doing?"

"Fighting crime and evil and commies."

He looked around at the students. "You've come to the right place."

Rudy was the spook commander for missions still being run out of Florida into Cuba against Castro. We might have Vietnam bubbling, but we still had Cuba. Castro and that scrawny little bastard Che Guevara were busy carrying the water for Khrushchev in exporting communism around the world.

Over coffee in the bustling student cafeteria, where spooks on campus might be easily mistaken for professors on break, Rudy and I caught each other up on which of our old mutual acquaintances had gotten married, gotten divorced or killed, had kids, were in Vietnam or Cuba, the Dominican Republic, or in Nicaragua or Africa or the Far East.

"You heard about Boehm?" Rudy asked.

"Haven't had a chance to talk to him. I've been testing boats."

"Roy gets things done but he's like a rogue elephant in a village of pygmies. He pissed off some high ranker in the Pentagon, and now he's being kicked out of the SEALs to shore duty."

Enders explained. As de facto commander of SEAL Team Two under John Callahan, the crusty old mossback had played every underhanded trick he knew to obtain equipment and training for his sea commandos. Pushed, shoved, raised hell with the bean counters, circumvented the system while tweaking the noses of officialdom. Along the way he collected an impressive list of enemies and contributed his name to some even more impressive shit lists.

"It doesn't make any difference how good you are at your job if you don't play the kiss-ass game," Rudy said. "'Want me to wash your ass, sir? 'Cause I'm gonna kiss it a lot.' Well, they caught Boehm up on a court-martial for obtaining weapons outside the system and replaced him with someone they can control."

I lit a cigarette in commiseration. "Bring out the warriors and dust us off when we're needed, shove us back out of sight when it's over."

"Roysi is assigned to Service Squadron 8 at Norfolk as an engineer in charge of propulsion plants. We have to do something for him, Bone. He'll go stir crazy."

I thought it over. "I may have an idea. In the meantime . . ."

I asked him if he was up for an adventure to test my Swift Boats before I sent them to Vietnam. I thought we might cruise Cuba and outrun Castro's Komars. Rudy did me one better.

A covert Cobra Team led by a CIA operative in the vicinity of Cayo Buenavista may have been compromised. A commo team at Key West noticed in a request for resupply that the sender's "wrist" was different. Each Morse code operator had a distinctive signature in his dots and dashes.

"The Castroites may be trying to lure us into a trap," Rudy concluded.

We couldn't abandon the Cobra Team without knowing for sure.

We arranged with the Key West commo chief to set up a rendezvous with the Cobra Team—or whoever was passing as the Cobra Team—for 2:00 a.m. the following night with the promise of delivering supplies. Before setting out with a crew of trusted Cuban exiles, Rudy and I armed the Swift to its gunnels with machine guns, 40mm grenade launchers, and various personal weapons. The State Department didn't want U.S. nationals getting into open pissing contests with Castro's commies, but I didn't intend us to go into a possible gunfight unarmed.

Usually a resupply boat darted in and out of a Reception Site as quickly as possible. I timed our arrival for midnight, two hours ahead of rendezvous time. Being early to the dance allowed us to look and listen for anything out of the ordinary.

Using binoculars, I scanned the mangrove-shrouded shoreline and glassed a pair of small islands offshore about a half-mile to the southwest. The islands were small dark blights against the sea and thick with tropical vegetation and palms. I listened to the sough of the ocean against the boat's hull. From somewhere a disturbed bird squawked. Nothing unusual, so far.

One of the crew named Pablo and I slipped into black wetsuits and slithered over the side into a rubber raft to go ashore and make contact with the clandestine team. Rudy wanted to go along, but one of us had to remain aboard the Swift to make sure it got back to Florida safely in case something unexpected happened during the rendezvous.

If everything went according to Hoyle and we made the contact, Pablo and I would return to the Swift to begin transporting supplies ashore. Otherwise . . .

We paddled the rubber boat into a line of mangroves extending into the surf and pulled up to look and listen. We were still an hour early. That extra hour saved our butts.

Mosquitoes buzzing our faces turned into a different sort of buzz— that of power boats approaching the two small islands. The commo team in Key West was right. This was a trap. I nudged Pablo with a paddle and motioned back the way we came. It was over. There was nothing we could do for the captured Cobras.

"*Es una trampa,*" Pablo whispered. A trap.

Roy Boehm in this situation would have sped past the islands and opened up with everything he had. Kill the bastards and let God count 'em. I was tempted. But it was that kind of aggressiveness that led him to courts-martial and supervising landlocked power plants.

"Sneaky bastard, Castro," Rudy remarked when we returned.

"He's had practice at it."

The Swift was capable of outrunning anything the Cubans had. By daylight we were back in Key West, boat and crew intact. My boat was indeed swift, long-range, almost silent, and carried a lot of firepower. An excellent war boat for Vietnam waters. CNO McDonald would be pleased with the product.

CHAPTER THIRTY-FOUR

F EW CONVENTIONAL MILITARY AND political leaders understood the extent to which unconventional warfare encompassed literally every component of society—military, political, economic, educational, religious. . . . Anything could be used as a weapon and a tool to further political goals—terrorism, assassination, intrigue, espionage, boycott, propaganda, disinformation, threat. . . . The insurgent *always* had the advantage when it came to tactics. The only way to stop him was by using unconventional *tactics* within a conventional *strategy*.

DCI John McCone gave me my head when it came to expanding CIA Maritime reach and understanding. After all, part of my job description read: "Direct supervision of worldwide field activities." And since the CIA through our SOGs (Special Operation Groups) and intelligence-gathering efforts was still active in Vietnam, I had a legitimate purpose for inviting Roy Boehm into Saigon for dinner and a drink at the Majestic Hotel, where I always stayed when in-country.

Rescued from SERVRON 8, Boehm was operating out of Cat Low, a fortified junk base on the dark, marshy flats along the Mekong Delta in an area known as Rung Sat, or the Forest of Assassins. From that isolated outpost Boehm functioned as an "advisor" to the Vietnamese UDT/SEALs known as Lien Doc Nguoi Nhai (LDNN), along with Commander Jerry Ashcroft, who "advised" a Vietnamese junk force he called Biet Hai. Together, they fought the vicious 514th VC Battalion, taking war for the first time into the Viet Cong's home territory.

From what the Saigon Chief of Station told me, this Ashcroft was a badass, no-holds-barred, get-the-job-done night fighter who turned a ragtag bunch of river pirates, most of whom were former VC, into a formidable band of cutthroats whose exploits were catching the attention of both foe and friend in the Rung Sat and Mekong Delta.

Boehm accomplished the same miracle with his Nguoi Nhai. They were well-trained in UDT/SEAL tactics, motivated, and kick-ass confident. The first of their kind. Together with Ashcroft's Biet Hai, they struck at the enemy along the waterways from Saigon to the South China Sea and for a hundred miles up the Mekong River. No longer did the NLF move its supplies and troops freely by day or night without fear of being hit. With each successful operation, Boehm's Frogs and Ashcroft's "junkies" grew bolder and ventured deeper and deeper into the forest.

Ashcroft showed up with Boehm at the Majestic's open-air veranda to have dinner with me. Both wore faded dungarees, bush hats, and strapped-on .45 sidearms. Saigon was relatively safe for U.S. service members, so far, but it did no harm to be prepared. I carried a 9mm pistol tucked underneath my shirt.

Jerry Ashcroft and I shook hands. In his thirties, he stood square and stocky with what I soon discovered to be a perpetual grin on his face. As always, Boehm sounded like he was chewing on a mouthful of gravel. You never knew whether he was about to embrace you or kill you.

"You sonofabitch," he greeted with obvious pleasure as he wrung my hand in a grip like stone.

Amused, Ashcroft shook his head and quipped, "You should see how he behaves when he *doesn't* like you."

We sat down at a table to order with our backs to the front of the building and a view of the street in front. Another little precaution.

"Commander, thanks," Boehm said with gratitude. 'You saved my worthless ass again, sir. I was about to die at SERVRON 8 before I got orders that the CIA—*you*, commander—had requested me to train

Frogmen. I don't know how much longer I could have tolerated all that 'yessir, nosir, three bags full, sir' bullshit."

We ate and afterwards had drinks and smokes and talked about the war.

"What we're about to have here," Boehm said, "is a classic cluster fuck. It always happens when politicians start running wars. They have no fucking concept of what limited warfare means. Vietnam is becoming a war led by administrators and managers who shackle professional fighters with stupid and unworkable rules of engagement."

Boehm was a man hard to shackle.

When he relieved Navy Lieutenant Pete Willits, previous advisor to the LDNN, Willets met him carrying a briefcase containing automobile brochures and contracts. His nickname was Out to Lunch Willets.

"I work for Cars International on the side," he pitched with an oily used-car-salesman smile. "I can get you a good deal on any kind of car you can name. Buy it here, you beat the taxes, and it'll be waiting for you when you get home."

Boehm returned Willets's smile with a withering glare. "I'm not here to buy cars. I'm here to kick ass. Your ass will be the first one I kick if you try to sell me a car again."

Boehm's superior at Military Assistance Advisory Group (MAAG) was Navy Captain J. B. Drachnik, who plastered signs all over his Saigon office proclaiming PROGRESS IS OUR MOST IMPORTANT PRODUCT. Like General Electric or GMC. In Vietnam, administrators and managers took precedence over combat leaders.

"Had I uttered 'kill' or 'maim,'" Boehm remarked with disgust, "both of 'em would probably have filled their skivvies and fainted."

Willets had made little progress training LDNN while he had them. The Bos'n got one hell of a headache trying to *re-train* the forty-two Vietnamese assigned to him for "Frog work." Half the unit still couldn't swim well enough to begin basic underwater work. As for tactics, they couldn't have sneaked up on a sawmill going full blast. Boehm caught one Viet dragging a heavy box using detonating primo cord that might have detonated with a sharp blow. Another mistakenly pulled a grenade pin. The spoon pinged free.

"Incoming! Throw that sumbitch!"

That was one time when the Nguoi Nhai turned frog, hopping in all directions. Shrapnel caught a couple of them in the ass.

Boehm started with basics at the Nha Trang training base. Firing range. Demolitions. Physical conditioning. Swimming exercises. Small unit tactics. Leadership. Team building. He drove them relentlessly as he labored to turn them into SEaAirLand guerrillas.

"You will be ass-kicking, tiger-baiting, shark-riding, VC-throat-cutting, badass motherfucking killers. No more holding hands."

"Numbah One SEAL!" they responded with more enthusiasm than ability.

Jerry Ashcroft, whose junk force was already kicking VC ass at Cat Low in the Delta, stopped by to observe Boehm's training. He expected Boehm and his Nguoi Nhai would be moving in with him shortly.

"You were serious about making SEALs out of them, Boy-san," he said.

"As serious as a fart in church."

"You about ready to take them out and fight them?"

"There's about to be a new bad dog on the block."

Kicking ass was going to be *their* most important product.

"Welcome to Shit City," Ashcroft greeted him when Boehm transferred his Nguoi Nhai from Nha Trang to Task Force Base 33 at Cat Low. "With your SEAL types and my thieves and killers, we are going to control every river, creek, and mud hole in the Rung Sat."

The next day after having dinner with Boehm and Ashcroft in Saigon, I commandeered a Caribou and pilot to fly me to the TF-33 landing strip at Cat Low.

The base lay on a spit of land twelve miles from Vung Tau near the broad mouth of the yellow-brown Mekong. The compound was a typical fortress of the war—a triangle enclosed in concertina, razor wire, and fighting bunkers. One side of the triangle extended piers into the river to which were tethered the fleet of armed junks used to interdict VC shipping and movements. Swift Boats had not yet arrived. Vietnamese and their families lived in grass, mud, and tin hootches in the middle of the compound.

Boehm and Ashcroft had just gotten back in from a prisoner snatch mission upriver when I arrived. The target was a farmer's hootch near the junction of two canals. Recent intel said a cadre of VC officers would be meeting there. The Vietnamese CNO in Saigon provided them with a guide named Phan, a broad-faced, restless little man with serious eyes. He was from that region and knew the land and the location of the target.

"Keep an eye on him," Boehm advised Khe, his LDNN commander. Caution dictated you were always suspicious of strangers.

The mission had got under way with the captain of Ashcroft's lead boat throttling back and turning into a narrow canal that broke free of the river. A rising sliver of moonrise separated tree line from sky. Presently, the three blacked-out watercraft nosed into the dark bank and cut engines. For five minutes the raiders held still on a listening watch to pick up anything that might not be jungle or river sound.

"Khe, let's do it," Boehm whispered. His face was blackened and he wore jungle-filthy fatigues and boots from previous missions. He never washed them. He simply hung them out to dry, then re-wet them before each new mission so they smelled like the jungle.

Unloading eighteen heavily armed men over the sides of the junks in near-total darkness was a feat in itself. Ashcroft and a security detachment of Biet Hai remained with the boats as a rear guard. Other Biet Hai went along with the raiders to establish rally-point security along the way.

A well-used pathway ran alongside the canal. The trail ended at the farmer's hootch. The grass and palm frond hut remained in darkness and appeared unoccupied. Some geese in a pen nearby muttered sleepily. Boehm set up his men in jungle surrounding the target to watch and wait.

By midnight he was ready to give up on the intel he received, search the empty hut, and go home. Until suddenly a shadow materialized and glided across the front clearing to enter the little dwelling. Moments later, a candle flickered inside, its yellow glow edging a blanket covering the doorway.

Four more armed men arrived one at a time at quarter-hour intervals, like thieves and conspirators, and slipped inside the little building. Apparently, they felt so secure they didn't bother posting a guard.

Boehm passed Khe the signal. Khe set the plan into motion. He and two other Nguoi Nhai circled wide and dashed for the right side of the hootch, running low and quietly in their sneakers. Chanh and three others approached from the left. Boehm crept across the clearing straight toward the door with the assault party.

The VC proved more cagey than expected. One of them must have detected a stealthy footfall or the sigh of a fern as a body brushed against it. Dim candlelight flooded in an elongated rectangle across the clearing as someone pushed the blanket away from the doorway and stepped out cautiously with his AK unslung. One of the others inside rattled off an interrogatory phrase, to which the man at the door did not respond.

Instead, alerted by some movement, he pivoted in the direction of Khe's element, bringing his rifle up to bear. Candlelight silhouetted him.

Boehm sprang into a crouch, tipping the muzzle of his carbine upward. Before he could fire, a tracer from Khe's group streaked into the man. It took him low, above the groin, spinning him to the left in a complete circle. Another tracer caught him in the shoulder and spun him the opposite direction.

Boehm stitched him across the rib cage with a burst. Pink mist of pulverized bone, blood, and flesh clouded light pouring from the doorway. The guy vibrated on his feet, like a puppet manipulated by a puppeteer suffering a heart attack. He was dead by the time he hit the ground, but the body continued twitching.

A second man bolted from out of the hut, only to be felled by a hail of bullets. Boehm's Nguoi Nhai vaulted over his collapsed corpse and exploded into the hootch with a sound-and-light show. Vermillion tracers punched through the hut's grass walls and either arced across the black sky or spanged into the surrounding bamboo or banana trees where they smoldered in dry foliage.

Boehm glanced at the dead man in the doorway as he charged into the hootch.

Shooting ceased. The candle inside remained burning on a low table. One mortally-wounded VC writhed on the floor and screamed in agony. Another remained surprisingly unscathed. He groveled on his knees in front of his captors' guns. He looked about forty or so. Flickering candlelight tattooed fear across his features in large script.

A third VC sprawled dead across an ankle-high table from which teacups and self-rolled cigarette butts spilled onto the dirt floor. Blood oozed from the dead man's open mouth.

Boehm shouted, "Khe, give me a count."

"All count for, Boss-son. No one is hurt."

Boehm pointed at the prisoner. "Grab that cocksucker and let's get out of here."

Khe and Chanh bound the uninjured prisoner's hands behind his back with tape while Boehm searched the dead man and the wounded one, who was rapidly bleeding to death, and ransacked the hootch for documents and other intelligence. He shoved captured papers into his map case, then swept the scene with a final look.

"Di di mau!"

A spattering of rifle fire sounded from the direction of a nearby village. Apparently a VC reaction force shooting at shadows. Boehm dropped to one knee in the trees and snatched his radio mike. Khe knelt next to him, his eyes sweeping toward the sound of firing.

"Boss-san, what do with wounded VC?"

"Kill him if he can't keep up."

"Already do that, Boss-san."

Boehm nodded without comment and raised Ashcroft on the radio. "River Rat, this is Frogfoot . . . River Rat, we are hot. Leaving position and headed yours. Keep an eye peeled. ETA your position ten minutes."

They flew down the trail single file in the dark toward the boats. The surviving prisoner was tossed into one of the junks like a sack of rice. Raiders scrambled aboard not five minutes ahead of a swarm of pursuing pissed-off VC.

The three junks poured on the coal in leaving the canal to ride the middle of the Mekong out of effective small-arms range, bound for Cat Low. The men laughed and jabbered like a scene from a winning team's locker room.

"Those hoods of yours fight pretty good, like there's no tomorrow," Boehm complimented Ashcroft.

Ashcroft laughed. "There *would* have been no tomorrow if they were captured," he said.

Ashcroft, now back at TF-33, showed me what he meant by his remark. He asked some of his men to show me the tattoos on their chests: *Sat Cong*. The same slogan was now tattooed across the guide Phan's pecs. It was an effective way of ensuring loyalty. The VC automatically executed any man they captured bearing the tattoo.

Sat Cong. Kill communists.

CHAPTER THIRTY-FIVE

ON THE MORNING OF July 31, 1964, I was up early for a walk on China Beach, a luxury I indulged whenever I was in-country and had the opportunity. I wore khaki shorts, sneakers, and a green military pullover with the sleeves cut out. The red sun inched up from the depths of the South China Sea. Higher, the sky remained that dark blue-purple it was before the sun leached the night out of it. A cool breeze brought the sounds of gulls waking to squabble over scraps.

I kicked off my sneakers to wade in the gentle nibbling of surf at the sand. There were not actually *seven* seas. There was one vast ocean of interconnectivity. A man could sail around the world on many different azimuths without ever having to touch terra firma. The seas of the world helped keep people apart on their various land masses until the appearance of modern transportation and, at least to some extent, kept their constant petty bickering and wars separated.

Why *did* God have to put land so near the oceans?

I watched four Nasty boats rapidly materialize from out of the sunrise's red belly and barrel toward the finger piers below the black hulk of Monkey Mountain. I replaced my sneakers and long-legged it toward the pier to meet them and get in on the debriefing.

Operations had changed dramatically at China Beach after South Vietnam's president Diem and U.S. president Kennedy were assassinated eight months ago. Part of it came from the CIA's relinquishing operational control to the military, which led to the escalation of raids against North Vietnam by the new and faster Swift and Nasty boats I helped acquire and ship over. Crews were still made up of South Vietnamese naval personnel with a few West German and Norwegian mercenaries thrown in. No Americans *officially* accompanied the raids. Approval for all ops came directly from Admiral U.S. Grant Sharp Jr., CINCPAC in Honolulu, who received his orders directly from the White House.

For the past few months since Lyndon Johnson took over and ramped up activity in Vietnam, OP-34A, a military modification of CIA's previous OP-34, had clashed repeatedly with NVA naval forces based some 120 miles north of Da Nang at Quang Khe and on the two islands of Hon Me and Hon Ngu. The base at Quang Khe was a post for small boats smuggling high-priority arms and infiltrators across the DMZ, as well as for eighty-three-foot Chinese-built Swatow motor gunboats.

Attempts by OP-34 to sabotage Quang Khe and put the Swatows out of commission had failed. On a black night in early March, a Nasty boat inserted a Vietnamese swimmer team of dynamite saboteurs. In order to reach the target, the swimmers had to swim to a sandbar, creep across it, proceed up a river, dogleg left, swim in the dark to find the patrol boats, and attach limpet mines to their hulls. The mission failed; the team vanished.

Earlier in the week before I arrived, SOG slipped a covert long-term agent into North Vietnam. He got out a last message before NVA security swept him up.

In spite of failures by its predecessor, OP-34A experienced a number of successes. An NVA patrol boat had been seized, NVA storage facilities sabotaged and destroyed, a lighthouse shelled, a bridge knocked out—all of which caused a constant pain in Uncle Ho's ass.

The four Nasty boats now approached secure docking at China Beach where I waited for them, along with the command staff. They were dispatched early last night with saboteurs to plant explosives on the islands of Hon Me and Hon Ngu to destroy a gun emplacement and a communications station. Just as the armada's commander prepared to release his saboteurs, he received intel that the enemy had been alerted. Rather than risk losing dynamiters, he decided to hit the targets with machine guns and 57mm recoilless rifles.

A recoilless rifle fired a flat-trajectory shell with high muzzle velocity that might easily be mistaken on the receiving end as rounds fired from an offshore destroyer's five-inch guns. That and the fact that the U.S. destroyer *Maddox* happened at the time to be off the North Vietnamese coast in the Gulf of Tonkin on a secret electronics surveillance mission led me to believe it was on *that* night and with *that* mission that the Vietnam War actually began. It would be no stretch for the North Viets to believe the *Maddox* had fired on them with five-inch guns in support of the raid on the islands of Hon Me and Hon Ngu.

August was about to become the most critical month of President Lyndon Johnson's first year in office.

CHAPTER THIRTY-SIX

THE NORTH VIETNAMESE MAY have indeed taken U.S. destroyers in the Gulf of Tonkin as the source of fire they received against Hon Me and Hon Ngu. Two days after the raids, on the afternoon of August 2, Vietnam time, USS *Maddox* was approaching Hon Me Island inside the twelve-mile limit claimed by North Vietnam when she radioed being under attack.

John McCone telephoned me at home with the news. It was still dark outside; I had returned from China Beach less than twelve hours ago. Mary stirred in bed when the phone rang, then turned her back to me while I talked to the DCI. I hung up the phone and laid a hand on Mary's back.

"I have to go to work," I said.

She moved away from my hand and pretended to be asleep.

In the Gulf of Tonkin, three North Vietnamese P-4 torpedo boats had approached within five nautical miles of *Maddox* and released their torpedoes. *Maddox* evaded and returned fire with five-inch shells, scoring a direct hit on one of the P-4s.

Carrier USS *Ticonderoga* launched four F-8 Crusader jets that sank one of the two remaining boats and damaged the third as they retreated. *Maddox* suffered a single KPV heavy machine gun round through the destroyer's superstructure.

For the next week I watched history unfold either from Langley or Pentagon conference tanks while diplomats were hard at it on both sides of the ocean to either defend, justify, or neutralize actions undertaken by their respective nations.

In North Vietnam, General Phuong Tai accused *Maddox* of attacking peaceful fishing boats, thus compelling the honorable North Vietnam Navy to fight back. In Washington, President Johnson and SecDef Robert McNamara portrayed the engagement as an unprovoked attack in international waters.

There was a lot of scurrying about all day August 3 at the Pentagon, as well as at State and the White House. Every conference room was full. Coffee pots emptied as fast as they were filled. I must have guzzled five gallons myself.

That night off Vietnam, *Maddox* paired with another destroyer, the USS *Turner Joy*, to resume patrol off the North Vietnamese coast, beyond the international three-mile line but inside the twelve miles North Vietnam claimed. Three China Beach Nasties with 57mm recoilless rifles also raided two separate NVA coastal installations.

North Vietnam fired back on the Nasties and filled the Gulf of Tonkin with Swatow patrol boats.

Things were not going to be allowed to die down, not with these kinds of "mine is bigger than yours" posturing from both sides. I suspected President Johnson would push this to the limit. From what I heard, and what I saw, the president was itching for a fight.

Daniel Ellsberg, special assistant to SecDef McNamara, was on Pentagon duty the night of August 4, when he received an emergency incoming radio message from the Gulf of Tonkin. At 11:00 p.m., USS *Maddox* and USS *Turner Joy* were patrolling the Gulf as a two-destroyer task force under the command of Captain John J. Herrick when their radar and sonar indicated another attack by the North Vietnamese Navy.

Rough weather and heavy seas on top of a night turned black by low cloud cover added confusion to the situation. For four hours, firing repeatedly against what their captains described as torpedo attacks, the two U.S. destroyers maneuvered amid electronic and visual reports of enemy watercraft. No wreckage or bodies were ever recovered from the contact despite the Navy's claim of sinking two torpedo boats.

I accompanied John McCone to the Pentagon where SecDef McNamara, Secretary of State Dean Rusk, NSA's McGeorge Bundy, and a number of others were crowded into the communications center with Ellsberg. It was 6:00 p.m. Washington time. Tension seemed to cast off sparks as Captain Herrick's cables kept coming in at intervals. McNamara remained constantly on the horn relaying them to President Johnson at the White House. I could almost imagine LBJ grabbing the Soviet premier by his ears, as he famously did hound dog pups, and barking out something like, "You shithead, this is between me and that yellow sonofabitch in Hanoi—so stay out of it!"

Shortly before midnight local, the president interrupted national television to make his announcement.

"My fellow Americans: As president and commander-in-chief, it is my duty to the American people to report that renewed hostile actions against United States ships on the high seas in the Gulf of Tonkin have today required me to order the military forces of the United States to take action in reply. . . . That reply is being given as I speak to you tonight. Air action is now in execution against gunboats and certain supporting facilities in North Vietnam which have been used in these hostile operations. . .

"Finally, I have today met with the leaders of both parties of the Congress of the United States to pass a resolution making it clear that our Government is united in its determination to take all necessary measures in support of freedom and in defense of peace in Southeast Asia. . . ."

Congress passed the Gulf of Tonkin Resolution on August 7 by a unanimous vote in the House and only two nays in the Senate. The Resolution authorized the president to "take all necessary steps, including the use of armed force, to assist any member or protocol state of the Southeast Asia Collective Defense Treaty requesting assistance in defense of freedom."

It was the equivalent of a declaration of war and provided a legal basis for massive American investment. McCone's first reaction echoed mine: "Oh, shit! This thing has spun out of control."

CHAPTER THIRTY-SEVEN

I LOOKED AT DCI JOHN McCONE over our morning coffee together in his top floor office at Langley as the conversation shifted to Africa. My initial reaction was: *Sounds like a job for Humphrey Bogart and the African Queen.*

The communist bloc was at it again, poking and probing at the Third World, taking advantage of the escalation in Vietnam and our focus there to slip in something sneaky elsewhere to instigate insurrection. Sometimes I thought World War II had never ended, had in fact merely shifted into the shadows.

In 1963, a rebel army known as the Simba Rebellion had captured much of northern and eastern Congo, including Stanleyville, more than a thousand miles up the Congo River from the Atlantic seacoast, which they declared to be the capital of a new "Peoples' Republic of The Congo." When the central government in Leopoldville made moves in 1964 to drive out revolutionaries and reconsolidate the nation, Simbas rounded up hundreds of Belgians, Americans, and other Europeans, surrounded them with drums full of gasoline in the lobby of the Victoria Hotel, and threatened to burn them alive if government forces intervened. These hostages had now been held under threat for nearly four months.

"Bone," McCone asked, "can you take boats up the Congo to Stanleyville and get these folks out? We have to act fast. These Simbas are savages. They aren't bluffing."

Belgium had ruled the huge territory of the Congo for more than half a century before granting it independence in 1960. Violence erupted when the two provinces of Katanga and South Kasai seceded. UN secretary general Dag Hammarskjöld sent in UN peacekeeping forces.

Prime Minister Patrice Lumumba of the Central Congolese Government welcomed the UN at first but then turned against it when Hammarskjöld refused to aid him in driving out the secessionists and reuniting the Congo. He turned to the communist bloc instead. Russia, China, and Cuba poured in advisors and equipment.

"If we can take the Congo," China's premier commented, "we will have the whole of Africa."

Supported by the USSR, Lumumba and two thousand troops marched against South Kasai to get rid of Albert Kalonji, who had declared himself president. The ill-disciplined Congolese Army slaughtered more than 3,500 civilians. Thousands of others fled.

Although Lumumba succeeded in forcing Katanga and Kasai back into the fold, Congolese President Joseph Kasa-Vubu used the Kasai massacres as a pretext to get rid of Lumumba, who was becoming a powerful rival. Lumumba was arrested and subsequently executed, an action that provoked international outrage among communists and their sympathizers worldwide. Protestors attacked the Belgian embassy in Yugoslavia. Violent demonstrations erupted in London and New York.

A politician named Joseph Mobutu acquired sufficient power in the Congo to replace Kasa-Vubu with a college of commissioners; Moise Tshombe, who led the secessionist movement in Katanga, joined him to head an interim Congo administration while fresh elections were organized. Mobutu and Tshombe threw out the Soviets and returned to the UN for help.

Communists were not yet finished with African aspirations. Political instability they helped create coincided in 1963 with the widening escalation of the Cold War. In an orgy of savagery and bloodshed, the Maoist-inspired Simba Rebellion executed thousands of government officials, political leaders of opposition parties, provincial and local police, schoolteachers, and those they believed to have become "Westernized."

Simbas, meaning "lions" in Swahili, consisted mostly of an irregular militia of teenagers under the influence of a drug called khat. They were indoctrinated in witchcraft and juju and promised that bullets would turn to water if the Simbas first drank magic water and screamed a magic cry, *"Mai Mulele!"* America, they were told in a standard communist ploy, was the enemy.

Khrushchev sent in at least two hundred military advisors to train the Simbas. Castro dispatched one hundred Cubans under the command of an old nemesis of the United States, Che Guevara.

As far back as the Eisenhower administration, the United States feared a Soviet-aligned Congo could form the foundation for a major expansion of communism into Africa. DCI McCone pressed President Johnson to increase military aid to Mobutu and Tshombe.

"We give in to commies in Africa, we give in to others in Cuba and Vietnam—pretty soon we'll be giving in to them in Washington," he said.

Agents in the CIA's important outpost at Leopoldville stressed how the Congo "is experiencing a classic communist takeover" and might follow the same path as Cuba. However, President Johnson seemed too busy ramping up a war in Vietnam to pay much attention to Africa.

McCone's suggestion that I rescue the hostages at Stanleyville by running a fleet of boats hauling an armed force a thousand miles up the Congo River sounded unworkable to the point of delusion. After studying the situation, I concluded we had two other options to reach the Victoria Hotel in time to save the hostages—overland or by air.

Stanleyville was surrounded by a vast jungle with few roads. That left one practical option.

I reported my conclusion on Stanleyville to the DCI: "The hostages' lives depend on surprise and speed. The only way we can do it is by airborne troops. My SEALs can do it. Give us the chance. They're all airborne qualified—and they're the best in the world."

McCone nodded thoughtfully.

"I'll try it up the Congo River if that's the decision," I amended. "But the Simbas will slaughter those people in Stanleyville before we can get to them."

"There's one obstacle to the airborne option," the DCI pointed out. "The American military cannot be perceived as directly involved."

The Belgians operated under no such restrictions. McCone managed to squeeze C-130 airplanes out of President Johnson for use by the Belgians in a rescue attempt.

At 6:00 a.m. on November 24, 1964, Operation Dragon Rouge kicked off with 350 Belgian paratroopers commanded by Colonel Charles Laurent dropping onto Simi-Simi Airport on the western outskirts of the city, two miles from the Victoria Hotel. Simba rebels began massacring their captives. Panicked hostages broke out of the hotel and scattered with Simbas chasing after them, killing and mutilating in increasing fury as paras rushed down the main street toward the center of town. The Simbas slaughtered about two hundred foreigners before they dispersed, with rescuers chasing *them*. The death count may have been much higher but for the speed and surprise with which the paras arrived and executed the operation.

Over the next two days, Belgian soldiers, the Congolese National Army (ANC), and a contingent of mercenaries hired by ANC rescued more than 1,800 American and European hostages and 400 Congolese from Stanleyville and nearby Paulis.

At Langley, I watched with relief as events played out better than I expected.

"It's not over." DCI McCone said. "I have another assignment for you, Bone. You may have to go to the Congo after all."

CHAPTER THIRTY-EIGHT

I LOOKED OUT OVER THE African terrain from the cockpit of the C-130 Hercules as the pilots made final approach to the four-thousand-foot unsurfaced airstrip on the west shore of Lake Tanganyika near Albertville. I leaned forward in anticipation from my jump seat between the pilots. "Congo Joe" in the right seat turned his head and grinned at me.

"Welcome to the black heart of Africa," he said.

"*Heart of Darkness,*" I responded. The novella by Joseph Conrad: "*We penetrated deeper and deeper into the heart of darkness. . . . I should be loyal to the nightmare of choice.*" Africa as the "Dark Continent," a place of danger and nightmares, was the accepted popular perception of darkest Africa at the turn of the century when Conrad published his book. In many ways, the image lingered on.

Tanganyika was the longest and second-largest freshwater lake in the world, stretching 418 miles to separate the nations of Congo and Tanganyika. It was beautiful country with the narrow deep blue of the lake snugged into the remarkable emerald of forest. Albertville further down the lake presented a contrasting conglomerate of dusty mortar buildings and native thatched huts bisected by dusty roads.

The lake had 1,136 miles of shoreline and an average width of only thirty miles, and smugglers were able quickly to ferry across Soviet- and Chinese-supplied arms to be used in ground fighting by Simbas against the Congolese National Army and its Belgian and mercenary allies. The rebels' rout at Stanleyville had not stopped them.

Acting on Khrushchev's instructions, Castro sent in a small fleet of armed and armored high-performance boats under Defense Minister Che Guevara to dominate the lake and keep supply lines to the Simbas open. Lacking a naval capability to interdict smugglers, Congolese president Moise Tshombe appealed to President Johnson, who promised to send help.

DCI McCone passed the issue on to me. "You're our maritime expert. How do we handle it? How do we put a navy in there?"

I had helped design Swift Boats now being used on Vietnam's waterways. "We'll fly them in," I said.

Mickey Kappes in my Maritime Division was in many ways a look-alike for Lee Harvey Oswald, JFK's assassin, and a man who always seemed involved in some controversy or other, such as plots to knock off Fidel Castro. I sent him to Africa as a sort of advance party to pave the way and work with mercenaries to run down Che Guevara.

Out of sheer desperation when the Simba Rebellion first began, Tshombe and Mobutu in the Central Congolese Government had called up many former mercenaries to fight the revolutionaries. More than two hundred international hired fighters arrived in September 1964 to form a unit called 5 Commando led by "Mad Mike" Hoare to serve as the spearhead of the ANC. A more appalling horde could not have been assembled, gathered as they were from waterfront bars, jails, and back streets all over Europe. Thugs and brawlers, thieves, pickpockets, and muggers—just the sort to take on the killers and thugs of communism. They were widely feared all over the Congo for unsanctioned killings, torture of prisoners, looting, and mass rape in recaptured rebel areas.

"Suit your tactics to the enemy," was Hoare's philosophy on unconventional warfare. "Queensberry Rules when you are fighting gentlemen; no-holds-barred when you are up against savages. They do not think any more of you if you use kid gloves and soft talk. Less, as a matter of fact, as such are the traditional signs of weakness in Africa."

UW could be a dirty business.

From CIA's Miami Station, I collected sixteen Cuban exile boat-men. I brought in two SEALs from Vietnam with Swift experience, Lieutenants Phil Holtz and J. Hawes. They would be my officer staff. That made us a band of twenty, counting Kappes, who had already gone ahead, plus a half-dozen self-described "coon ass" workers from the Louisiana boat factory.

We had to disassemble the Swift Boats to transport them by air-planes. That meant splitting the hulls of the two 50-foot boats down the middle, snipping seven feet off the bows, cutting off the superstruc-ture, and removing the engines. My Swift Boat force along with work-ers from the factory, equipment, supplies, and logistics—everything needed to reassemble the boats—were loaded aboard two C-130s and four C-134 cargo planes and airlifted by way of Naples and Cairo to Lake Tanganyika.

Kappes was waiting at the airfield when I landed in the advance C-130. The other planes would be coming in at staggered intervals. After the heat and humidity of Vietnam, I was surprised to find, due to elevation, a temperate climate more like that of the Mediterranean than Equatorial Africa. Average temperatures ranged in the mid-sev-enties. No wonder European colonists settled in the area. This land could be a paradise with a proper government and the right approach to building a society.

The rest of the planes arrived the next afternoon and dumped fifty tons of boats in pieces by the side of the airstrip. Railcars on a nar-row-gauge rail spur delivered the boat parts to a makeshift "marina" on the lake. The Cajun workers, using Argon-gas welders, began putting Humpty together again. Lieutenant Hawes and some of the Cubans set up armed watches to either side of the marina. I stood by the water and looked out over the lake.

"Boss, we got company," Lieutenant Hawes yelled out suddenly from on top of a felled log.

A speck on the watery horizon approached fast. Lieutenant Holtz came up, pulling his ball cap low over his eyes. "Reception," he guessed. "Might be the bad guys."

It hadn't taken long for word of the new American presence to spread across the lake to communist operating bases in Tanganyika.

"We can give 'em a surprise reception of our own," Lieutenant Holtz suggested. He was in his early thirties, with a thick chest, muscled swimmer's arms, and a tanned face topped by a sun-bleached crew cut. He carried an M-60 machine gun over his shoulder. "I'll signal the Cubans to get ready."

I recognized the boat as a Soviet Komar.

"He's turning back," I said.

The enemy boat kicked up a wake in a kind of salute as it swerved past. It continued up-lake. I noticed a red flag popping at the bow.

"Commandante Tutu," Lieutenant Holt remarked drily, "has slapped us across the face with his gauntlet."

"Commandante Tutu" was Che Guevara's nom de guerre.

CHAPTER THIRTY-NINE

THE LOUISIANA CAJUNS REASSEMBLED the first Swift Boat within ten days; the second was ready for action two days later. After that, yearning for home, they airlifted out and returned to Louisiana, leaving only a small maintenance crew of three volunteers behind to help my Tanganyika force quell communist arms smuggling along nearly five hundred miles of lake. I found some irony in that my Cuban boatmen would be fighting Cubans on a continent halfway around the world from their homeland.

"*Por favor*, boss," enjoined Raphael Cruz, whom I appointed chief over the other boatmen fighters. He was older than the others, about forty, skinny with big sad eyes. "*Por favor*. Do not refer to Che's scum as *Cubans*. Che Guevara and Fidel Castro and all who are traitors with them are not Cubans. They are *communists*."

Communists were indeed a different breed of reptiles whose allegiances lay first of all with Khrushchev and the other comrades.

I divided my force into two elements and placed each of my SEAL lieutenants in charge of one. They took care of scheduling patrols and the day-to-day business of chow, rest periods, fuel, and the other necessities of maintaining our craft and keeping operations going. Whenever a Swift left our little makeshift marina, which consisted of a single short pier and a tin shed, it went armed to the gunnels with twin 50-caliber machine guns, a 50-caliber anti-aircraft gun, 3.5-inch rocket launchers, and small arms and grenades for the crew.

The two separate crews rotated on twenty-four-hour shifts. At least one Swift and crew prowled the lake constantly, hunting; the second remained in reserve/rest status as an immediate reaction force. I hired African women cooks from Albertville to supplement our daily C-rations and keep our Quonset hut–type barracks clean. One of the Cubans placed a hand-lettered sign above the barracks doors: CASA DULCE CASA. "Home Sweet Home." Below which Lieutenant Holtz attached another sign: HOME OF THE COMMIE KILLERS. THEIR DAYS END WHEN OURS BEGIN.

I felt in my element. I took patrol shifts same as the other men, running the lake, nosing up into streams, pulling night vigils at likely crossings to listen and look with night vision devices, searching for signs of activity. It was tedious and time-consuming.

Once or twice one of my boats spotted a fishing-type craft speeding across the upper end of the lake and darting into a channel too narrow and shallow for a Swift to enter. We questioned local fishermen through a Swahili interpreter and searched their boats; some of them were undoubtedly Simbas keeping a lookout on behalf of smugglers.

Soviet Komar gunboats kept a low profile, but sooner or later we were bound to run into them.

I kept in contact with the CIA station at Leopoldville through encrypted radios. Through it the American government supplied the Congolese Government with T-28 trainer-fighter planes, B-26 bombers, and C-130 cargo ships along with U.S. crews and support staff. Officially, none of the American planes and crews existed.

Our little airstrip near Albertville frequently bustled with planes skimming in and out to airlift ANC troops into hot spots to fight Simba rebels or run battlefield recons. I sometimes solicited T-28 pilots to run aerial recons. So far, nothing. The Komars were biding their time. For the moment I dominated Lake Tanganyika.

Nearby Albertville provided access to the lake and served as a staging base for offensives against Simba rebels to the north and west. Mad Mike Hoare's 5 Commando operated out of the town with the ANC.

Together, they began to squeeze Simba-controlled territory from all sides, forming a loose perimeter to push in on the Simbas with a variety of shallow and deep pincers. Mad Mike's fighters-for-hire became particularly adept at using the wilderness to outflank and reduce Simba positions. His cutthroats were brutal sonsofbitches, but they were fighting brutal sonsofbitches. I developed a great deal of respect for him and his soldiers-for-hire.

Hoare on a personal level turned out not to be quite the bloodthirsty psychopath I expected. He was a genial but flamboyant forty-six-year-old from Dublin with a ruddy Irish face, a bit of a burr in his voice, and a way of laughing at himself and the world. He played rugby, drank beer, lived for the fight, and took life as it came.

"What, you're a fighter pilot too, Hamilton?" he remarked during one of his visits. "I can pay you more than whoever's paying you now, what?"

"I suspect we may be getting paid by the same sources."

He let out one of his hearty laughs, not admitting it but not denying it either. "Chap, the nature of my sugar-tit nanny has been greatly exaggerated."

We walked down to the lake and stood on the pier. He pointed north up the lake.

"Hamilton, there is a creek that flows out of Uganda into the upper end of the lake. It's not on the maps, and the mouth of it is well-camouflaged. Some of the locals," he continued, "tell me there's a lot of activity upstream, may even be a Komar base up it. The Cuban named Kappes you sent in ahead says you're looking for Commandante Tutu? You might find him there."

CHAPTER FORTY

I CONCENTRATED PATROLS IN THE north end, where Uganda reached in and touched the lake. I requested one of the CIA trainer-fighter pilots fly over the area.

"There's a stream there all right," he reported. "Not much to it. It's overhung by woods. Looks to me like it may be too shallow for anything as big as a Komar."

Two nights later, Lieutenant Hawes's boat radar picked up a Soviet Komar screaming west across the lake toward the opposite shore. He maneuvered on it in moonlight, finally sighting it as it slowed to approach a blinking light signal coming from a narrow beach. Arms smugglers.

Hawes ordered his cox'n to pull throttle and wait. There was no way of knowing how many Simba warriors might be hiding in the woods. It was my night to sleep, but the radio watch at base awoke me. Hawes on his mike gave me the lowdown.

"Take the boat when it leaves," I advised. No way could he assault on land with only himself and four Cuban riflemen. "I'm scrambling the other Swift now, but we won't be there until midday. I'll see if I can get Hoare or the ANC to intercept the guns on land."

The Komar pulled out of its rendezvous, having apparently unloaded, and headed toward the concealed stream mouth. Hawes's Swift laid on full throttle and closed in. The Komar's machine gun went to work, blossoming red and yellow flames. Hawes's two 50-cals spat back. The speeding boats swerved and shifted and side-slipped to avoid targeting themselves, filling the night air with spray, the booming crackle of machine-gun fire, and dueling green or red tracers crisscrossing.

This first encounter between my people and theirs ended as suddenly as it began, with the Komar vanishing into the night-blind, forest-shrouded stream, leaving only the sound of its diminishing engines. Apparently, the creek was deeper than we thought.

"Pull out," I ordered.

The CIA chief at Leopoldville, whose station monitored all radio traffic, picked up an in-the-clear transmission between the Komar and another source identified as Che Guevara, a.k.a. Commandante Tutu. He sounded in a rage, vowing to kill every gringo on the lake and send him to hell in the belly of a crocodile.

"Boss, I will kill him myself, *verdad*?" pleaded Raphael Cruz, my appointed Cuban chief. "Che, he take to his prison my brother, my cousins, and he murder them with a bullet from his pistol. He kill for the pleasure of it. He laugh when he shoot them, and I am tell he piss in their dead faces."

I had heard such stories before of this sadist. If anyone deserved to die, it was Che Guevara. I clapped Raphael on the back.

"We will do what we can do," I promised.

"I will piss in his face," Cruz said.

It seemed Guevara might be directing his arms-smuggling racket from a hidden base somewhere upstream in the secret river. Since we couldn't approach him by water without being discovered and ambushed, I radioed Kappes, who showed up at our marina the next day with about thirty fighters from Hoare's 5 Commando. Those and my nineteen, including the lieutenants and me, added up to a good-sized, heavily armed platoon.

The Swifts dropped us off in the jungle at the mouth of the secret river where we cautiously made our way upstream. On the third day, while dodging crocodiles and snakes through a swamp, we came upon a crude camp of native-like huts concealed in the forest. The dwellings appeared hurriedly abandoned and professionally sanitized so that nothing remained behind to identify the previous occupants. Not a scrap of paper, a tin can, a bottle cap . . .

I ordered the camp torched. Flames popped and crackled and black smoke twisted into the sky as the column trudged back to the lake. Guevara had escaped again, but there was a new sheriff in town, and Che had to find a new base if he intended to stay.

* * *

Things settled down for about a week, until Leopoldville intercepted and cracked an encrypted transmission from Commandante Tutu. It seemed Guevara was planning a big powwow with Simba leaders near a village called Mpala on the Congo side of the lake.

I seeded out scouts and coast watchers to keep vigil and notify me of any movements. Intel from the station chief proved valid and timely. We had to move fast when one of my scouts spotted a Komar filtering in under darkness from a stream flowing out of Uganda.

As dawn approached, we located and trapped two Komars and an arms-supply trawler concealed back in a cove. I swung our Swifts wide to land troops down-lake while Mad Mike and his mercenaries slipped into the jungle to close in from the rear.

It was almost too easy. The Soviet Cubans and the raggedy-ass Simbas were either drugged up on khat or so overconfident they didn't hear us coming. They were laughing and hooting and chattering around a big kettle on a fire in the center of the little village when Lieutenants Hawes and Holtz planted M-79 incendiary rounds directly in the center, breaking up the party in dramatic fashion.

Caught in a crossfire between Mad Mike's fighters and my shooters, they didn't stand a chance. I saw two Soviet Cubans bite the dust, riddled with bullets but going down fighting with their boots on. One died immediately. The other screamed his guts out before somebody put him out of his misery.

Several Simbas took off into the jungle while a handful of Che's Cubans put up a fight from one of the grass huts. I emptied a clip into the hootch from my M-2 carbine, popped out the empty box, and slapped in another. When I looked up, I spotted a slight figure wearing camouflage fatigues and a black beret escaping out the back and racing for the trees. He carried a long package of some sort tucked underneath one arm.

"It's him. It's *him!*" Rafael Cruz shouted. "*Kill him!*"

He got off one shot from his M-14 rifle before Guevara vanished into the jungle. I gave chase with Rafael and Lieutenant Holtz spread out to my either side. We had the sonofabitch. He was fifty yards from the goal line and no chance of scoring a touchdown.

Or so I thought.

Ahead, two Cubans from a brush pile cracked down on us with rifles. Che had left a rear guard. Raphael yelped and went down, wounded. I hit the dirt and opened up with my carbine, throwing lead at muzzle flashes in the shadows.

"Cover me!" I yelled at Lieutenant Holtz.

He laid suppressive fire into the brush pile. I sprang to my feet and dragged Raphael back into the trees. He was conscious, but blood was spreading rapidly across his chest. He opened eyes filled with pain.

"Boss," he said, his voice cracking. "Kill him for me. . . . Kill him for my . . . brother and my cousins."

Suddenly, a Beechcraft appeared seemingly from nowhere, flying low and slow out of rifle range beyond where I was pinned down. It circled downwind, then returned almost immediately trailing a big hook attached to a long cable.

I couldn't believe it. Boehm and I and our men had experimented with skyhooks at Fort Bragg during the train-up for the commissioning of SEAL teams. They were developed by Army Special Forces for snatching spies and other operators into the air and out of danger. Guevara was one wily bastard with a contingency plan for any situation.

The big package he carried when he fled must contain his harness and grab bar for the hook.

The Cubans in the brush blocking the way realized they had accomplished their mission by delaying us long enough for Guevara to escape. They tossed out their weapons and surrendered. I saw the Beech gaining altitude as it fled. At the end of its cable clung Che Guevara, grabbed from the crocodile's jaws and whisked back into Uganda.

Right out of James Bond. You had to admire the little bastard's élan.

CHAPTER FORTY-ONE

C HE GUEVARA WAS HAULING ass out of Africa the last we heard of him. The Simbas proved to be a poor investment for Castro and the commies, so Khrushchev concentrated his support elsewhere. Communist presence in the Congo collapsed.

I went home.

While I was away, DCI John McCone resigned in a dispute with President Johnson over the Defense Department's takeover of CIA covert responsibilities in Vietnam. Kicking out the CIA left the agency in turmoil, confused by exactly what government expected of it not only in Vietnam but in other hot spots around the world. A man I trusted and valued for his cool common sense was replaced by Vice Admiral William Raborn, a squarely built man with thinning hair, gray sideburns, and a jaw, as wags asserted, that was as hard as his head. Why would LBJ appoint a man with absolutely no intelligence experience as DCI? Perhaps to reduce the CIA's influence in making national policy?

Vietnam was quickly ramping up into a *real* war. The U.S. ambassador to South Vietnam, General Maxwell Taylor, who opposed introducing combat troops, provided the president with disturbing assessments of conditions in the tiny besieged nation:

"We are faced here with a seriously deteriorating situation characterized by continued political turmoil, irresponsibility, and division

within the [South Vietnamese] armed forces, lethargy in the pacifi-
cation program, some anti-U.S. feeling which could grow, signs of
mounting terrorism by VC directed at U.S. personnel and deepen-
ing discouragement and loss of morale throughout South Vietnam.
Unless these conditions are somehow changed and trends reversed, we
are likely soon to face a number of unpleasant developments ranging
from anti-American demonstrations, further civil disorders, and even
political assassinations to the ultimate installation of a hostile government which will ask us to leave while it seeks accommodation with the
National Liberation Front and Hanoi."

Pitched battles occurred after August and the Gulf of Tonkin "sea
battle." On October 31, 1964, Viet Cong disguised as farmers floated
sampans past the U.S. airbase at Bien Hoa and let loose with mortars
that killed four Americans, destroyed five bombers, and damaged eight
more.

On Christmas Eve, a driver parked an explosive-crammed truck
by the Brink Hotel in Saigon, where a crowd of U.S. soldiers waited
for entertainer Bob Hope. The explosion ripped through the building,
killing two Americans and wounding more than seventy.

The event that prompted LBJ to take more extreme action occurred
on February 7, 1965, at Camp Holloway near the provincial capital of
Pleiku. About three hundred VC crept up while Americans of the 52nd
Combat Aviation Battalion were sleeping and turned the base into a
conflagration of exploding ammunition and burning aircraft, killing
seven Americans and wounding one hundred.

"They are killing our men while they sleep in the night," President
Johnson raged. "I can't ask our American soldiers to continue to fight
with one hand behind their back."

He activated Operation Flaming Dart in retaliation. American and
South Vietnamese pilots targeted NVA bases near Dong Hoi in North
Vietnam with forty-nine sorties; a second wave targeted VC logistics
and communications centers near the DMZ.

Soviet Union Foreign Minister Alexei Kosygin happened to be visiting Hanoi when the raids commenced. Khrushchev was furious and
promised to provide additional assistance to Ho Chi Minh.

A few days later, VC sappers blew up a hotel used as an enlisted men's barracks in the coastal city of Qui Nhom, killing twenty-three American soldiers.

Apoplectic, LBJ responded with Flaming Dart 2—155 sorties and air strikes against North Vietnam.

The USSR increased its aid to North Vietnam by supplying SAMs, jet fighter planes, technical support, and more "advisors." China said it was ready to send its personnel "to fight together with the Vietnamese people to annihilate the American aggressors."

Escalation of the war from a clandestine affair carried out in the dark seemed to be spiraling out of control. The 9th Marine Expeditionary Brigade began sending Marines. The first Marines ashore at Da Nang found the sleepy little place I remembered from my OP-34 days—bunkers left by the Japanese in 1945, blockhouses deserted by the French, a single unimproved three-thousand-yard runway. Their initial orders were to guard the base. They were not to "engage in day-to-day actions against the Viet Cong."

The airbase was soon to become one of the three busiest airports in the world. U.S. force levels increased from 23,000 to 185,000 within the year.

PFC Craig Roberts was among Marines in a follow-up landing on the beaches near Da Nang. Word on the USS *Pickaway*, a Navy World War II assault ship bobbing offshore, had it that VC were everywhere, that attacks could come from any quarter. The countryside belonged to the Viet Cong, Charlie, the gooks, VC—the enemy. For the first time, U.S. combat troops were going in with permission to shoot back if fired upon.

Christ, it was hot. The sun itself became a burden. Marines would get to know it like they would get to know the shit-smeared punji stakes, the Malaysian whips, the black-pajamaed Viet Cong who sniped at them during the night and turned farmer again with the rising sun, but they would never get used to it. It sucked the moisture through the pores in their skin until they felt like fish left on a gray and weathered pier.

"Ladies, get your fuckin' asses in gear," gunny sergeants shouted. "We goin' to war, Marines. Not to some old lady's tea party. You want to live, make damned sure you are locked and loaded when them boats hit the beach and the gates drop. Make damned sure."

Second Battalion, 9th Marines, went ashore in one of several World War II–style beach landings the 9th Marine Expeditionary Brigade had made since LBJ committed the first land troops to Vietnam. Marines heard the VC had fourteen combat units within fifty miles of Da Nang. Most of them would probably be waiting on China Beach when the Marines landed.

Growing up beneath the dark cloud of the Cold War, living under the threat of nuclear war and communist expansion, they were finally getting their chance to stop the commies by going to a foreign and exotic land and battling evil on its doorstep.

Roberts found himself on a landing boat asshole-to-belly button with the rest of his platoon, so packed in he was gasping for a breath of air. Long lines of gray flat-bowed boats kicked up a giant washing machine of froth and charged toward the beach, leaving wakes that spread out behind and made even the *Pickaway* bob like a fishing cork.

The only things missing were bugles.

"One hundred meters to sand!"

Still no fire from the beach. The gooks must be waiting for the landing gates to drop in the surf.

The gates dropped. Roberts glimpsed a sandy strip backed by palm trees. Almost like a postcard from Hawaii or Miami Beach—"Having a great time, wish you were here."

"Go, damn you, go! *Go, go, go, go, go . . . !*"

Caught up in the excitement, Marines charged toward dry sand, screaming and yelling rebel war cries. Ready for action. Expecting it. *Wanting* it.

They dove face first in the sand and executed combat rolls to keep the enemy from marking their positions. Weapons swiveled back and forth across the front of brown-and-white sand and rattling palm trees and shimmering heat devils, eyes darting and busy.

Where were the human hordes?

Roberts saw a kid. About eight years old with an eight-year-old's grin, yellow skin, no shirt, and a baggy pair of too-short black trousers.

His first gook. Holding out two bottles, the kid positioned himself directly in front of the weapons.

"Hey, Joe. . . You buy Co'Cola?"

All around, kids and toothless old women who grinned like kids. All up and down the beach—the enemy. Selling Cokes and beer and cigarettes.

Marines slowly clambered to their feet and looked stunned.

"Buy Co'Cola, Joe? Buy Co'Cola?"

* * *

I knew from the beginning that the escalation was wrong, that UW operations were the best method of countering insurgencies, that a war fought by conventional means seldom overcame guerrilla action. Unconventional warfare and terrorism were calculated to slowly bleed a conventional force of its will to continue. It had worked before in history—a numerically inferior force triumphing over a much stronger force, bleeding it dry by a series of small and repeated cuts. The French suffered from the strategy and withdrew from Vietnam in 1954.

I helped the new DCI present our assessment of Vietnam. The communist nations, we noted, would no doubt ally themselves with Ho Chi Minh, but we did not think they would do it actively as the Red Chinese had in Korea. Instead, they would contrive to win victory through supporting a continued guerrilla insurgency.

The U.S., we said, was "proceeding with far more courage than wisdom. . . . [The NVA and VC] appear confident that their course in South Vietnam promises ultimate and possible early success without important concessions on their part. They seem to believe that they can achieve a series of local military successes which sooner or later will bring victory through a combination of a deteriorating South Vietnam Army morale and effectiveness, a collapse of anti-communist government in Saigon, and exhaustion of the U.S. will to persist."

In the Cold War, Army and Navy special forces were designed to fight limited wars, clandestinely, in a way that averted the nuclear powers from squaring off against each other. Under CIA patrimony,

Army Special Forces established permanent headquarters in Nha Trang, from which they eventually established more than 250 CIDG (Civilian Irregular Defense Group) outposts throughout the country, each generally defended by a single A-team of a dozen SF soldiers and a few hundred local civilian irregulars. "Winning hearts and minds" by building schools, hospitals, government buildings, canals, and fish ponds, while defending against insurgents. Classic unconventional warfare.

SEALs also operated in classic UW but in a different capacity. In addition to training South Vietnamese in combat diving, river warfare, and counterinsurgency tactics, they made their bones and their reputation in sustained direct-action efforts along the seacoast and the Mekong River in the Rung Sat Special Zone. Harassment of the enemy, hit-and-run raids, recon patrols, intel collection, ambush and counter-ambush, interdiction of enemy troops and supplies coming from North Vietnam.

Far from using conventional warfare methods of firing artillery or dropping bombs from 30,000 feet, SEALs, who seldom numbered more than 120 in-country at any one time, experienced combat close and personal, killing at close range and responding without hesitation lest they be killed themselves. They made great headway with this style of warfare, bringing to Vietnam the most effective direct counterinsurgency of the war. Widely feared by the enemy, with their faces painted to blend into darkness and jungle, they became known as "the men with green faces."

Now, the "Invisible Front" war of Green Berets and SEALs began to fade into the background in the new U.S. policy toward full militarization. President Johnson placed the military in near total control of the CIA, Defense Intelligence Agency, the National Security Administration, and other intelligence organizations operating in Vietnam.

With LBJ's approval, the commander of all U.S. forces in South Vietnam, General Westmoreland, initiated a strategy of attrition by employing U.S. superiority in firepower, technology, and mobility. His methods, contrary to the shadow war that existed before, turned to a series of search and destroy operations in which large U.S. and

South Vietnamese units supported by air and artillery swept through an area to attempt to engage the commies in battle. In contrast, North Vietnam and the VC continued to rely on hit-and-run operations and ambushes, avoiding set-piece battle except at their own initiative. Classic guerrilla operations out of Mao and Clausewitz.

CHAPTER FORTY-TWO

ADMIRAL RABORN BARELY MADE it a year as DCI before he ducked out to be replaced by Richard M. Helms. I knew Dick from the Bay of Pigs and had run into him from time to time since. Former OSS during WWII, he had the appearance of a very successful business-man—tallish, handsome, with dark, slicked-down hair and a straight-forward look in his piercing eyes. We would get along.

"Bone," he said, "the Defense Department and the White House might think the CIA has been put back in its place. But they'll come running back on their knees."

Although CIA's role in Vietnam had been minimized, we weren't completely cast out. "Knuckle draggers" were still in demand to counter communist efforts at world domination. Communists never seemed to stop pushing and probing, instigating unrest and discon-tent and bringing death and destruction. I found it difficult to under-stand what deep pathologies must drive an ideology that led to famine, gulags, blind subjugation, and mass executions.

The DCI kept me busy. One month I might be slipping operatives into El Salvador, the next in India or the Philippines. Accompanied by a former EOD man, I slid overboard from a freighter in the Caribbean and SCUBA'd with my swim buddy toward the green outline of Nica-ragua. We towed a marker buoy full of nitro, dynamite, and plastic C-4 for use by insurgents combating the country's communist takeover.

In the Philippines I met with representatives of newly elected President Ferdinand Marcos to advise on maritime operations against Muslim fanatics influenced by communist insurrectionists.

Anti-Semitism ran high all over the Middle East as fanatics preached the destruction of the state of Israel and the rise of a new Ottoman Empire. Arab states led by Egypt attacked Israel across the Sinai Peninsula. The war lasted six days. Arab casualties were many times those of Israel—less than one thousand Israelis killed, compared to over twenty thousand for the Arabs.

Israel tripled its area of control, taking in the Sinai Peninsula, the Gaza Strip, Golan Heights, East Jerusalem, and the West Bank. Nearly a half million Palestinians and Syrians fled to become refugees across the Arab world. The Middle East was becoming a hellhole with repercussions that promised to continue for decades.

Not only in the Middle East but all around the world global chess pieces were lining up and taking sides. Events seemed to be unfolding as part of a grand picture, a scheme of things in which the world was slipping deeper into danger, in which both foreign and domestic affairs were interconnected and part of an enmeshed tapestry of violence and conflict.

The stench that began the Cold War lingered on in Frankfurt where the Auschwitz trials got under way to try mid- to lower-level Nazi officials who helped run the Auschwitz-Birkenau death and concentration camps.

China tested its first nuclear weapon. Put another nuke in the commie corner. Mao Tse-tung launched his "Great Leap Forward" to preserve "true communist ideology" to the tune of slaughtering millions of his own people.

America joined the chaos. In San Francisco, Anton LaVey formed the Church of Satan—to worship the Devil! Colleges held teach-ins and snake-dances against the Vietnam War. Race riots boiled up in the Watts neighborhood, resulting in thirty-four deaths during six days of looting and arson. Additional riots broke out all over the nation—Tampa, Detroit, Cincinnati, Buffalo, Durham. Hippies dropped out and dropped acid and smoked anything, including banana peels. Drugs, sex, and rock 'n roll.

Where the hell was this nation—this *planet*—bound?

My personal life was just as chaotic.

While I was running off to Cuba, Vietnam, Africa, Central America, or whatever other hot spot that required my attention, poor Mary, like wife Elinor before her, was stuck at home without attention. She should have known better than to marry me.

I came home from a job in Central America to discover she had packed up and left for parts unknown, the only clue to her whereabouts a note on the kitchen table saying simply that she had had enough and was leaving. No "kiss my ass," "sorry." Nothing. Just gone. Her lawyer served divorce papers.

Face it, Bone: my life didn't call for a wife. Like the ground pounders in the Army put it: "If Uncle Sam wanted you to have a wife, he would have issued you one."

I vowed not to make the same mistake again.

* * *

Mary's side of the bed hadn't even cooled off properly before I met my third wife-to-be. Her name was also Mary. I called her "Mary II," but not to her face. Call me a fool. But, hell, a man got lonely. This time the marriage lasted less than a month before, *whoops!* She was gone.

"You fucking dunderhead," Boehm said. "You do understand? You don't have to *marry* them."

The same evening that Mary II left I walked the late night streets of Washington, another anonymous tourist tossed among the monuments. I collapsed on the cold stone steps of the Jefferson Memorial and gazed at the Capitol Building at the other end of the Mall. I was so damned tired of fighting America's "shadow wars."

I got up presently and trudged home to an empty house.

The next week I found a new fixture added when I walked into the CIA rotunda and took the stairs to the SOD floor where my Maritime Office was located. A tall, willowy blonde on temporary assignment as an analyst. She introduced herself as Barbara.

I stared like the fool I knew myself to be when it came to pretty women.

CHAPTER FORTY-THREE

L AST TIME I SAW Che Guevara he was hanging from a Beechcraft James Bond–style in the middle of Africa. He dropped off the screen after that for more than two years. Rumors circulated Fidel executed him for political reasons. I didn't believe that. He and Castro were Siamese twins, asshole buddies since they met in Mexico. They overthrew Batista together in 1959, orchestrated the Bay of Pigs victory, worked together to bring Soviet nukes to Cuba. No, Commandante Tutu was alive, torturing and executing people somewhere.

In the file I kept on him was a copy of a letter Che sent to his parents: "My Marxism is firmly rooted and purified. I believe in armed struggle as the only solution for the peoples who are struggling for their freedom and I am acting in accordance with my beliefs. Many would call me an adventurer, and I am one; only of a different sort, one of those that risks his skin to demonstrate what he believes is true."

No matter that what he believed was a lie.

I wasn't all that surprised when the CIA station chief in La Paz informed DCI Dick Helms that Guevara might be fomenting Cuban-style insurgency in Bolivia. According to him, a man suspected of being Guevara entered Bolivia on December 2, 1965, using a forged passport bearing the name Ramon Beritz Fernandez. Soon after arrival, he disappeared into the countryside, where he assumed command of a small force of about fifty-five communists dedicated to overturning "capitalist exploitation" of Latin America by U.S. "imperialism."

In April 1967, the Bolivian Army's 8th Division captured a member of Ramon's band, a French communist writer named Régis Debray. He confirmed "Ramon's" true identity to be Che Guevara and provided the general area of his operations. His base camp lay somewhere south of Bolivia's Rio Grande River.

In early July, CIA's Ground Branch brought in veteran CIA operative Felix Rodriguez to recruit, train, and lead a team to track down and capture Guevara. Rodriguez was a twenty-six-year-old native-born Cuban who joined a group of exiles in 1960 for CIA-sponsored military training in Guatemala with Brigade 2506. I met him prior to the Bay of Pigs when UDT-21 inserted saboteurs into Cuba before the invasion; he was one of the infiltrators.

Rodriguez flew to Washington and went as directed to an Agency-rented apartment downtown. It was a bright, nicely-decorated place within easy walking distance of the memorials. I was one of the agents who briefed him. I had a score to settle with Guevara because of Africa, but the DCI denied my request to go along on the ops.

"The operation could take weeks, months," he said.

The basic plan called for Rodriguez and another exile to enter Bolivia under false documents posing as Cuban U.S. residents exploring business opportunities. In-country, they would train Bolivian soldiers in basic intelligence gathering and coordinate with government intelligence officers to help them react quickly to raw intelligence. At the same time, U.S. Army Special Forces Major "Pappy" Shelton of the 8th Group raised and trained a Bolivian Ranger battalion of six hundred soldiers. CIA officers from SOD oversaw the entire project—and the hunt was on.

In La Paz, "Jim" from the CIA spent long workdays analyzing intel reports and documents captured from guerrillas. He built a file for each member of Guevara's band, which included thirty Bolivians, seventeen Cubans, three Peruvians, one Argentine, and one East German.

The chase received its first major break on August 31 with the capture of a guerrilla named Jose Castillo "Paco" Chavez in a firefight on the banks of the Rio Grande River at Vado del Yeso. A second was also captured. "Ernesto" was hostile and arrogant, so someone shot him on the spot.

I telephoned authorities at Bolivia's Third Tactical Command and helped persuade them to turn the captive "Paco" over to Rodriguez for questioning. Felix interrogated him at Nuestra Senora de Malta Hospital, where he was recovering from wounds.

The poor, bedraggled prisoner sat in a chair surrounded by about a dozen soldiers pointing rifles when Felix arrived. He wore long, dirty hair, a droopy Fu Manchu mustache, and a wimpy little beard. He was thirty-three years old and looked frightened out of his wits.

"You're going to kill me," he kept saying.

"No, I'm not," Felix reassured him.

"I never wanted to be a guerrilla. I never wanted to fight. And now you're going to kill me."

Felix spent two weeks with Paco, gaining his confidence and debriefing him every day. Paco said he met three characters other than "Ramon" in the band who were important players in the guerrilla drama. One was the writer Debray, the other an Argentine named Ciro Roberto Bustos, and the third was Tania, Che's lover. She was an East German whose real name was Tamara Bider, later discovered to be a KGB agent assigned by Soviet Intelligence to keep watch on Guevara. These three served as messengers, carrying secret documents and money to the guerrillas from La Paz.

Paco recalled seeing Tania shot dead at Vado del Yeso the same day he was captured. He saw her fall into the river where her lifeless body wedged behind a rock by the weight of her backpack. Felix sent a group of Bolivia soldiers back to the scene of the firefight, where they found Tania's body, somewhat decomposed but still identifiable.

A diary recovered in the backpack of another shot-dead Cuban guerrilla lieutenant called "Braulion" gave some indication of what life was like in Ramon's band.

26 Feb. 67: We lost the first man at 3 p.m. It was our friend Serafin. He was passing close to the edge of the Rosita River and slipped in. He didn't know how to swim. Others tried to help him, but we were weak (from lack of food) and we could not help him.

2 March 67: We have no communications with the vanguard. I started having cramps in my legs and could not walk. Marcos could almost not walk too. The personnel was very, very weak. We were finally authorized to eat the reserve (food in our packs) because there's no hope of finding a farmer.

25 March 67: Ramon made a speech. He fired Marcos from his position and gave Miguel the position he had before.

12 April 67: We buried Rubio and we retreated a bit higher (into the countryside). We returned again to the base, where we stayed for two days, after which we returned again to Nancaguazu. There, we left the rear guard, while Ramon and the vanguard proceeded toward a little place called Ballipampa.

Going under the war name "Ramon," Che had escaped the firefight, although not in so dramatic a fashion as in Africa. Bolivian Rangers and U.S. Army Green Berets closed in on the guerrilla members and surrounded them in the wilds near the small mountain village of La Higuera. I kept careful monitor as the sequence of events sped up. I intended to be there at the end to see Che Guevara in bondage, a fitting end to a communist revolutionary dedicated to putting the world in chains and behind iron walls.

On September 26, a Bolivian combat patrol killed three guerrillas in the Vallegrande area near La Higuera. Felix Rodriguez urged Colonel Joaquin Zenteno Anaya, a Bolivian intelligence officer, to move the Ranger battalion into the area of operations. The Rangers began a series of search and destroy missions.

On October 7, one of the battalion companies received intelligence from a farmer who reported hearing voices at a place called Quebrada del Yuro; nobody was supposed to be there. Commander Gary Prado surrounded the area with less than two hundred men.

A firefight erupted the next morning, a Sunday, between the Ranger company and insurgents. One of the soldiers shot a revolutionary in his right leg, a flesh wound.

"Don't shoot! Don't shoot me!" he cried in Spanish. "I am Che. I am worth more to you alive than dead."

Shortly thereafter, Felix received the news by radio. *"Papa cassado."* *Papa* was code for a "top guerrilla commander." *Cassado* meant "captured" or "wounded."

Back at Langley, the DCI and I were at first skeptical that such a dedicated revolutionary and combat veteran could be taken captive so easily by green troops.

In Bolivia, Felix took off in a T-86 trainer plane for the scene. I made reservations to fly to Bolivia the next morning. On his flight to Villegrande, the nearest airport to La Higuera, Felix heard the words everyone had been waiting to hear: *"Papa—el estranjero."*

Che Guevara.

I waited up all night with DCI Helms to see what developed.

The next morning, early, Colonel Joaquin Zenteno Anaya and Felix caught a helicopter to La Higuera, a tiny place consisting of a few mud-brick houses and a single rutted street. Armed soldiers in combat fatigues waited in a fenced-off area between a thicket of trees and a small shack.

They escorted Felix and Anaya to an old schoolhouse, a one-story rectangular structure whose tile roof had long ago disintegrated from weather. Che was held inside with his arms tied behind his back and his feet bound. He looked like a filthy beggar in ragged clothing, not even a pair of boots, only pieces of leather tied to his feet. Nearby lay the corpses of two other guerrillas.

Colonel Anaya looked at his watch. "You have until two o'clock in the afternoon to interrogate him," he informed Felix. "I want your word of honor that at two o'clock in the afternoon you will bring me back the dead body of Che, and you can kill him any way that you want, because we know how much harm he has done to your country."

Felix held a last conversation with Che Guevara.

"You don't want to talk about Africa," Felix said, "but we were told by your own people you had ten thousand guerrillas and they were very poor soldiers."

"Well, if we had ten thousand guerrillas it would have been a big difference, but you're right. They were very poor soldiers."

Rodriguez asked him why he chose Bolivia for his guerrilla activities.

"One, it was far away from the United States," Che replied. "Second, it is a very poor country and I didn't feel the United States had that much interest. Most important, it has a boundary with five different countries, which we could use for our activities."

Asked if he wished any last words, Guevara said, "Well, if you can, tell Fidel he will soon see a triumphant revolution in America. . . . If you can, tell my wife to remarry and try to be happy."

Just before noon a soldier came to Felix with a phone call from Vallegrande. Felix picked up the receiver. A low voice on the other end said, "You are authorized by the Senior Command to conduct Operation Five Hundred and Six Hundred."

Rodriguez knew what that meant. He left the room. Minutes later, a soldier named Mario Teran walked into the room with an M-2 carbine and shot Guevara in the head.

A crowd of two thousand people waited in Vallegrande to view the notorious Cuban revolutionary when the chopper bearing his body landed and loaded it into an old gray ambulance. I arrived the next day to find his corpse covered with a sheet in a laundry room converted to a temporary morgue at the Nuestra Senora de Malta Hospital.

I pulled the sheet off his face. My Cuban killed in Africa, Raphael Cruz, would have liked to see it. Someone had placed on his head the trademark black beret he always wore. I looked at his emaciated, unshaved face for a long time. Alive, he was a vicious bastard with little regard for human life. Still, I had to hand him one thing: he was good at what he did, and at the end he hadn't begged for his life.

CHAPTER FORTY-FOUR

I WAS FORTY YEARS OLD, married and divorced three times, three kids on the other side of the continent. My track record did not include a finish line. And now here I had eyes for the new blonde analyst at Langley. At least her name wasn't Mary.

Close friendships rarely happened in the Agency. In fact, they were discouraged. Standard procedure in the operations sector required the use of pseudonyms. It was "Carl" or "Jim" or "Ron Smith." There were perhaps more "Smiths" and "Joneses" at Langley than there were "O'Haras" in Scotland. Plus, no one talked about his job. Everything was on a "need to know" basis.

Barbara wore no ring; neither did I, of course. Part of standard operating procedure, SOP, was to blend into the background while presenting as little as possible about private lives. Still, I made a point of stopping by her desk whenever I could.

"I've never seen you around before, Barbara. Where have you been?"

She laughed, delightfully and openly. "You mean, where have I been all your life?"

The girl had a sense of humor. That was good. She told me she had just returned from Paris.

"Paris? Why did you come back to headquarters?"

She laughed. "If I told you, I'd have to kill you."

I laughed with her at the old joke. Then she said, half-jokingly, but in a way that let me know she was single and never married and that she might be interested in me, "I was looking for a husband. I'm thirty-five years old and my age is creeping up on me and I couldn't find the marrying type in Europe."

I was nothing if not the marrying type. I fumbled for something to say. "Uh—"

"Yes?"

"Uh—gotta go. See you."

I was not going to fall into that old trap again. I didn't need any more pretty faces left in my wake. I tried to stay away from her desk, but I kept making excuses to detour into her piece of geography.

One of my men in Maritime was getting married on a Saturday afternoon. I telephoned Barbara at her desk and asked her to go to the wedding with me. I didn't know her home number; that sort of information was never given out freely at Langley. To my surprise, she said yes.

Call me a fish; I was hooked.

I remained secretive with her, out of long habit. She naturally knew I was in SOD, head of Maritime, but I told her nothing about my experiences in Vietnam, Cuba, Europe, or any of the other hellholes in the world. Perhaps it was because I didn't want to frighten her off. I had already lost three wives because of there always being "another side of the ocean," as the last Mary put it.

With me, Barbara was open and candid for someone who had worked inside the Agency since she got out of college. She was living at home with her folks in Pittsburgh, she told me, when she noticed an ad in the newspaper offering recruitment for people who would like to live and work overseas. Since Barbara always wanted to travel, she responded to the ad and soon discovered herself signed up in Washington, D.C., for an unspecified "government agency."

She had been all over the world since then working as an intelligence analyst for Agency offices in both primary and backwater U.S. embassies. Now she was back in the States on temporary assignment to the Directorate of Operations.

I didn't want another family. I fled for my life.

Barbara accepted a temporary assignment overseas. We didn't see each other for three months, which gave me plenty of time to think. This was an exciting, energetic, and accomplished lady. If there was ever going to be a right woman for me, this was she. I was known for taking chances. Why not one more time?

After she returned to Langley, we dated for about a year before driving to Rockville, Maryland, one Saturday afternoon, just the two of us, to get married at the Justice Building. I could almost hear Boehm growling in my ear, "You dunderhead, sir. You went and did it again."

CHAPTER FORTY-FIVE

For the past twenty years I had been involved in some form or another with the emerging development of unconventional warfare. My kids grew up and my wives left me while I went gallivanting around the globe making the world "safe for democracy" and all that. I couldn't stand the thought of my marriage with Barbara ending like the others.

I retained my reserve commission in the U.S. Navy with the rank of full commander, but decided to resign from the CIA and take a more conventional job. Barbara remained with the Agency in long-term station at Langley while I took several GS-rated civilian government positions. Although these jobs required some travel, we still lived, more or less, a "normal" lifestyle. Little house in the suburbs, two-car garage, postage-stamp lawn.

I served stints with the Merchant Marine & Fisheries and the National Transportation Safety Board before being offered a post with the National Oceanic and Atmospheric Administration as its worldwide activities manager for "Manned Undersea Science and Technology." I was considered one of the nation's foremost experts on unconventional warfare when it came to the world's bodies of water.

One CIA-DOD research project had to be the epitome of clandestine warfare—the utilization of animals as warrior surrogates. The concept of training dolphins to assist in war had been on man's mind for a thousand years. In water pens bigger than Olympic pools at Naval Station Key West, a top secret experiment tested the concept of training bottlenose dolphins for combat tasks.

Dolphins are extremely intelligent mammals. I often donned SCUBA to roughhouse with them in the pool. They were affectionate, intelligent animals who wanted to play endlessly.

During one test, I pretended to be drowning by relaxing my arms and floating slowly to the bottom of the pool. A female named Gloria dove to the rescue. She nosed and pushed my 225 pounds to the surface and held me above water until I indicated I was breathing again. A marvelous demonstration. I grabbed her and hugged her as we tumbled playfully across the pool.

She "kissed" me on the face.

"Sorry, ol' gal, I'm already married."

It was good to be working in the water again. Back during my early days with UDT-21, I volunteered for a water project at the Naval Air Development Center in Johnsville, Pennsylvania, for the National Aeronautical and Space Administration. Guinea-pig Frogs submerged ourselves in a swimming pool one degree below body temperature for eighteen hours to simulate extended weightlessness in space. At the bottom of the pool, we performed various tasks such as eating liquid food out of plastic bags, playing chess and checkers, writing notes with grease pencils on whiteboards, using underwater sign language, and even watching TV in a waterproof case. All this subsequently became part of the normal training routine for astronauts preparing for their duties in space.

That wasn't nearly as exhilarating as this was now with dolphins. The graceful creatures had a natural sonar ability to detect intruders from the sea. We trained them to press a buzzer to sound an alarm to a sentry on shore, then intercept. Divers failed every time to get through. A three-hundred-pound dolphin made a formidable defensive tackle.

Dolphins could also tow or push through the water packages of explosives that weighed up to one hundred pounds and magnetically attach them to a target.

The project remained top secret for another half-dozen years before a disgruntled civilian scientist leaked it to the news media. It was immoral and a waste of taxpayer money, he testified before the Senate Intelligence Committee, to train dolphins to detect and attack enemy Frogmen and place electronic monitoring devices or explosives on enemy ships.

Actually, the sleek animals were first-rate night fighters.

We deployed our dolphins to Vietnam to patrol Cam Ranh Bay; one dolphin attempted to recover a nuclear weapon lost near Puerto Rico. Another entered Havana Harbor and attached an electronic device to a Soviet nuclear-powered ship to measure the ship's efficiency. Still others tracked Soviet submarines and stole mines from Chinese waters.

My sweet Gloria attacked a Soviet Komar boat off Cuba that was chasing fleeing refugees trying to reach Florida. The explosive she carried blew off the gunboat's stern. The refugees got away. Gloria died. I put up a marker for her on the beach at Key West.

Dolphins were another victory in the battle against the dark forces of communism. Gloria and all our other aquatic freedom fighters should have been awarded medals.

* * *

The science and art of unconventional warfare followed me like shadows, even though I had left the UW business.

Camcraft, Inc., of Marrero, Louisiana, a company that participated in the development of the Swift Boat, contracted with Washington to build a river patrol boat for use by our "Brown Water Navy" in Vietnam. Riverine Forces and SEALs along the Mekong required souped-up, heavy-duty boats for their continuing quarrel with communist guerrillas. Since I had worked on the Swift Boat, I represented the government in discussions over how these new boats, called PBRs (Patrol Boat-River), should be constructed.

I recommended my old friend and "First SEAL" Roy Boehm for the task of training Riverine Forces in use of the PBR. Boehm, now in his late forties, was about to be medically discharged from the Navy because of a knee injury acerbated by a terrorist bombing in Saigon. He was in the hospital when he received orders to report to the Naval Amphibious School at Coronado as senior instructor for a new curriculum in counterinsurgency training on inland waterways. Commander Jerry Ashcroft from Junk Force Base TF-33 in Cat Low, and Boehm's former combat partner, commanded the new program. I flew out to greet Boehm's arrival since the PBR was partly my creation—and since Ashcroft confided in me how Roy's morale needed a kick in the butt.

The walls at the Special Operations Center were closing in on the craggy-faced old bos'n. He stood at the office window watching a class of Basic UDTR trainees jog past on the beach in their helmets and wet fatigues chanting a Jody call. UDT had not yet merged with SEALs, but there was talk of it happening soon.

I recognized the longing on Roy's face. How he missed the excitement, the adrenaline flow, even the frustrations of being one of these special men. Sometimes I experienced the same yearnings.

"Instead," Roy lamented, "I'm a *teacher*."

He turned slowly away from the window to face Ashcroft and me. "Let me off the hook?" he pleaded. "I don't belong here."

Ashcroft straddled a chair backwards. "Boy-san, haven't you always said someone needed to educate troops before we sent them off to become cannon fodder? You said they needed to know *why* they were going, *where* they were going, *who* they were fighting, *what* to expect when they got there, and *how* to fight."

"They need a *teacher* to teach them, not me."

"What the hell do you think you were doing when you were a bos'n mate on a five-inch gun in the South Pacific? How about all the years you were diving, experimenting with it, and passing that knowledge on? How about when you trained UDT Frogs? How about the SEALs? The SEALs were *your* creation as much as any other man's. You *trained* them. You *taught* them. How about the Nguoi Nhai in Vietnam? Who *taught* them? You did. You're a *teacher*, Boy-san. One of the best. Teaching is more than being able to spell 'unconventional warfare.' Hell, you don't need to spell it. You *lived* it. Boy-san, there ain't gonna be no walking out on this."

I nodded agreement. "Roy, teach these guys. Teach them how to stay *alive*. Now get the hell out there and do your job."

The first PBRs were of armored fiberglass, thirty-one feet in length, nine and a half feet across the beam, heavily armed with twin 50-caliber machine guns and M-60 machine guns, and an assortment of small arms. Operation Game Warden in Vietnam operated on brown waters in boats I helped design, with crews Roy Boehm trained. PBR warriors became both feared and famous as the process of war further tempered naval special warfare.

CHAPTER FORTY-SIX

T HE VIETNAM WAR ENDED in 1975 with the last U.S. personnel in humiliating flight by helicopter from the roof of the American embassy to offshore ships. Ho Chi Minh's troops enveloped Saigon and immediately began imprisoning and executing hundreds of thousands of South Vietnamese. Score a victory for international communism and a defeat for the Free World.

The American public was sick of war, wanting only to withdraw from the world and pursue life in peace isolated between the nation's two oceans. Unfortunately, a restless and resentful world was not going to let that happen. General anxiety as residue from previous wars, from communism's worldwide aims, and from the rise of Middle East terrorism spread gospels of terror and violence around the world: Islam against Israel and the "Great Satan"; Muslims bitter and resentful over the dissolution of the Ottoman Empire after World War I; ultra-left wings fomenting revolution; populist uprisings against imperialism and colonization; fanatics of the political left and right seeking "social justice" and willing to kill for it; communists like the late Che Guevara spreading out into Third World countries to overthrow governments. Throwing tantrums to get their way. Bombing civilians, hijacking aircraft, kidnapping people for ransom or concessions, taking hostages, committing assassinations.

Insightful military officers realized that the United States must respond in the only way terrorism and violence understood—by force.

In late 1977 on a remote twenty-seven-acre site in North Carolina near Fort Bragg, the U.S. Army conducted a "coming out" exercise for a group of "special soldiers." The mission/demonstration exercise that midnight for Delta Force under the command of Colonel Charles Alvin Beckwith was to rescue hostages simultaneously from a hangar and a commercial aircraft seized by "terrorists."

While government and military dignitaries watched, Delta soldiers blew hinges off doors, cleared rooms, took down the aircraft, "killed" or captured terrorists and rescued hostages—all within thirty seconds.

The nation's first specifically tasked counterterrorism unit was up and operational.

Delta Force owed its origins to the jungles of Vietnam in 1965. Colonel Bill McKean, CO of 5th Special Forces Group, assigned Captain Charles Alvin Beckwith to form a special unit within the group called Project DELTA, or Detachment B-52. Its mission was to conduct long-range reconnaissance, venture out ahead of divisions or brigades to look the country over and test the water. It was also tasked with bomb damage assessments, hunter-killer missions, and special-purpose raids. The job was so hairy that Beckwith's Detachment B-52 initially ended up with only seven volunteers.

Beckwith distributed flyers to other SF teams in-country:

Wanted: Volunteers for Project DELTA. Will guarantee you a medal, a body bag, or both.

Colonel McKean scoffed. "You won't get a swinging dick."

He underestimated the nature of men who gravitate toward special forces. Beckwith was inundated with replies within a week of stuffing flyers into mail sacks going out to the ninety or so Green Beret A-team detachments in-country.

Three years previously, beginning in 1962, Beckwith pulled a year's duty with Britain's 22nd Special Air Service Regiment in an exchange program between SAS and the Green Berets. The SAS was organized in World War II to operate deep behind enemy lines—to disrupt, collect intel, sabotage, assassinate, and work with indigenous peoples. It required skills not expected of ordinary soldiers.

After the war the SAS penetrated deeply into the Malaysian jungle to hunt down and defeat a large, well-armed communist guerrilla force known as MRLA, Malayan Races Liberation Army. Having been unable to gain power by political means, the MRLA turned to terrorism in accordance with Chinese general Sun-Tzu's prescription to "kill one, frighten a thousand."

The guerrillas were trying to make a comeback in 1962 when Beckwith linked up with the SAS. Operating in Malayan jungles with the Brits, he contracted such a severe case of leptospirosis that he was not expected to survive—but eventually recuperated.

Three years later, Project DELTA in Vietnam was a result of some of the skills he learned from SAS about counterterrorism and operating within the enemy's own yard. A 50-cal slug from a North Vietnamese machine gun put him out of action before he had a chance to try out all his ideas in the field. Again he was not expected to survive—and again he beat the odds and recovered.

He refused to give up what he learned from the SAS unit that had trained and dedicated itself primarily to combating terrorism. He even proposed a name for his unit—1st Special Forces Operational Detachment-DELTA (SFOD-DELTA).

He envisioned highly adaptable and completely autonomous teams possessed of a broad array of special skills for direct action and counterterrorist missions, in some ways like the Jedburghs and OSS of World War II that went out into enemy land in small patrols to blow up bridges and dams and railroad lines, collect intel for air strikes or for attacks by conventional forces. They would be hand-picked volunteers thoroughly trained to battle terrorists on their own grounds and terms. Men who could break into buildings or planes besieged by terrorists, who were snipers and experts in weaponry and explosives, locksmiths, medics, electricians, men who hot-wired a Chevy or a Mercedes, soldiers with skills to climb mountains and buildings, fly airplanes, speak other languages, men with guts and purpose to operate decisively in absence of orders.

Beckwith kept submitting his ideas for years after he healed from his gunshot wounds. But Vietnam was over, the American people were weary of fighting, and it seemed no one wanted to listen. His was a lone voice crying in the wilderness about the threat of terrorism.

In 1977, radicalized Muslims hijacked a commercial airliner and flew it to Mogadishu in Somalia. The West German counterterrorism unit called GSG-9 (Grenzschutzgruppe 9) stormed the plane, overwhelmed the terrorists, and released all the passengers safely. The incident exposed weaknesses in the U.S.'s own response plans for similar incidents.

"Is the United States prepared to carry out a mission like this?" Beckwith wanted to know.

The Pentagon went frantic trying to find an answer to the question. People running back and forth. Meetings and conferences in the JCS "think tank," buzz sessions in the White House ready room, debates in Congress, hand-wringing at Langley, and a national counterterrorism forum at the Fort Benning Infantry Conference, during which Beckwith's proposals were dusted off and discussed.

Delta drew its first official breath on November 21, 1977 by order of Headquarters, Department of Army. "Chargin' Charlie" Beckwith was given command of it.

Beckwith sent out feelers for volunteers in much the same "medal or body bag" manner he did with Project DELTA in Vietnam. Requirements were so stiff that he retained only seven out of the first thirty who took part in the selection. The second selection was even worse, with only five out of sixty retained. Eventually, however, Delta drew in a thousand soldiers, of whom about three hundred trained to conduct direct operations against terrorists. The rest were highly specialized support elements.

Delta set up its headquarters at Fort Bragg in an old stockade centered on about nine acres of fenced-in real estate. A long corridor bisected the concrete fortress-like building. Off the corridor extended a half-dozen major cell blocks, each converted to the unit's needs in maintaining weapons, explosives, supplies, specialized equipment, and training. Instead of girlie pinups, walls displayed photos and clippings of recent terrorist activities.

The shooting house—also called "Haunted House" and "House of Horrors"—allowed firing of live ammo in various scenarios against mannequin terrorists and hostages. Each room presented a different situation for operators to overcome—an aircraft passenger area, a private residence, offices, warehouses. . . . All were designed to provide Deltas practice and training in different kinds of gear while confronted with various restrictions of vision and movements.

Operators were not only allowed but encouraged to appear other than as soldiers in order to blend into any environment. The headquarters stockade soon became known as "The Ranch" due to the propensity of some to wear cowboy boots and chew tobacco.

Delta Force did not have too long to wait for its first mission.

CHAPTER FORTY-SEVEN

Historical events occur in a cause-and-effect sequence, one leading inexorably into the next. History has a way of taking events and applying to them unexpected consequences.

As America continued to try to pull back into its shell, it elected in 1976 President Jimmy Carter, a pacifist president who exemplified America's longing for isolationism and its eagerness to avoid confrontation by compromise.

On his second day in office, Carter unconditionally pardoned all Vietnam War draft dodgers. He returned the Panama Canal Zone to Panama, and concluded Strategic Arms Limitation Talks (SALT II) with the USSR by making concessions. Perceived U.S. weaknesses under President Carter emboldened terrorists and lent impetus to communist aspirations of expansion.

In February 1979, the hard-line Iranian Islamic Revolution overthrew the Shah of Iran, Mohammad Reza Pahlavi. Pahlavi fled to France while Ayatollah Ruhollah Khomeini returned *from* France, where he had been exiled for the past fifteen years, to assume power in Iran. The Shah had been allied with the U.S. for decades. President Carter further angered anti-Shah Iranians with a televised toast to the Shah and a declaration of how beloved he was by his people.

Days after the coup, on February 14, in an incident known as the "Valentine's Day Open House," Fedayeen militants stormed the U.S.

Embassy in Teheran and took U.S. Marine Kenneth Kraus hostage. Rocks and bullets shattered most of the embassy's front windows. Upon Carter's advice, Ambassador William Sullivan surrendered the embassy to the militants in order to save lives.

Kraus, who had been injured during his kidnapping, was tortured, tried in a kangaroo Sharia court, convicted of murder, and ordered put to death. Only the intervention of Iranian foreign minister Ebrahim Yazdi saved the Marine's life and returned him and the embassy to American control by the end of the week.

For the next eight months the embassy remained on alert and under a state of near constant siege. On October 22, 1979, Carter permitted the Shah to come to New York to be treated for cancer. This intensified anti-American sentiment in Iran and spawned rumors of a U.S.-backed coup and reinstallation of the Shah. Khomeini heightened rhetoric against the "Great Satan" and spread talk that he possessed "evidence of American plotting." He called for street demonstrations.

Beginning at 6:30 a.m. on November 4, Fedayeen ringleaders herded approximately five hundred Muslim students to the American embassy. A female student with metal cutters concealed beneath her chador snipped the chain locking the gate. Embassy guards brandished firearms, but it quickly became apparent they were ordered not to shoot.

Occupiers ended up with fifty-two hostages, whom they bound, blindfolded, and paraded in front of photographers. Large, angry crowds congregated to jeer the Americans and cheer the occupiers. Ayatollah Khomeini issued a statement on Iran radio supporting the seizure and calling it "the second revolution." The American embassy, he charged, had been an "American spy den in Teheran."

President Carter called the hostages "victims of terrorism and anarchy." He vowed the United States "will not yield to blackmail." However, the only direct action he took was to appeal to the ayatollah for the release of hostages on humanitarian grounds.

Days dragged by with nothing done. *CBS Evening News* anchor Walter Cronkite began ending each of his newscasts by noting the number of days the hostages remained in captivity.

* * *

Things were happening in the world. I simply could not stay out of the fray.

"I'm not cut out for the civilian world," I complained to Barbara.

"Bill, you ninny. I knew that when I married you."

"But . . . but, Barb, I've lost three wives because of it. I couldn't stand to lose you too."

"You're not going to lose me, Bill. That I promise."

Barbara was a confident, independent, self-sufficient woman. We made a good team.

The next day I walked into BUPERS (Bureau of Naval Personnel) at the Pentagon and filled out paperwork to return to active duty in the U.S. Navy. In short order, I was assigned to the CNO's office in the Pentagon as a Special Warfare Officer in the Special Operations Division, refining proposed protocols for unconventional warfare.

I was back in the game.

CHAPTER FORTY-EIGHT

NEWS ANCHOR WALTER CRONKITE closed his broadcast of April 24, 1980 with, "American citizens at our embassy in Teheran have today been held hostage for 171 days." At this point he didn't know about Operation Eagle Claw, which the president and National Command Authorities had ordered activated to rescue the hostages.

That night passed long and tense for those of us at the Pentagon listening with mounting apprehension and anger to frantic satellite radio passages coming out of Iran in the early hours of April 25.

About forty of us stuffed ourselves into a SCIF—Special Classified Intelligence Facility—across the corridor from the Big JCS situation "tank" with its wall-sized screens and state-of-the-art communications where the upper echelon of Washington politics and military gathered. The SCIF was a sixteen-by-thirty-foot room suspended within a larger room in order to preclude penetration by eavesdropping devices. Armed guards at three SOD—Special Operations Division—checkpoints cleared each person before he was allowed to proceed. The room's low ceilings and fluorescent lights cast everything in a greenish light.

Junior action officers, planners, spooks, and SpecOps warriors in the SCIF sat on molded plastic chairs around two long meeting tables in the center and worked ourselves into tension headaches compounded by caffeine overload. Moldy coffee cups, crumb-laden paper plates, and butt-filled ashtrays littered the tables. A half-dozen small, square loudspeakers attached to cables running across the floor to wall jacks carried intercepts from NSA, Wadi Kena, Masirah, Desert One, and from Teheran where an American agent on the ground had his own PRC-101 radio transmitter tied into the satellite network.

The entire Eagle Claw mission operated on the same frequency, which allowed us to hear Delta's transmissions, the aircraft pilots' chatter, and the various commanders' comments and orders all in real time as it happened. I would rather have been there with them, but by now I was at a point in my career when I had to be content with relegation to the planning stages.

Under cover of darkness, eight RH-53D helicopters lifted off the carrier USS *Nimitz* on station in the Arabian Sea for the six-hundred-mile flight inland, while six C-130 tankers and troop planes departed Masirah Island at Oman. The plan was for them to assemble at a secured prearranged site in the wastelands of Iran, code-named Desert One. From there, Chargin' Charlie Beckwith, on-ground commander, and 120 Delta Force operators would proceed in refueled helicopters to a hide site near Teheran where in-country operatives would then transport them surreptitiously to the American embassy in vehicles.

Once the hostages were extracted, everything went into reverse: trucks to helicopters, helicopters to waiting C-130s, and then everybody the hell out of Dodge. It was a good plan and should have worked. Except for Murphy's Law, which states that anything that could go wrong, *would.*

Inside the Pentagon's SCIF we heard the first chopper report "feet dry" as it crossed the Iranian coastline just west of Chah Babar on its way to the Desert One rendezvous. The rest of the eight made landfall shortly thereafter. That was when things started to fall apart.

Two of the choppers had to abort and return to *Nimitz* because of mechanical failures. A third suffered a hydraulic leak. It auto-rotated down into the desert, where another RH-53D dropped in and picked up the stranded crew. The remaining choppers arrived late at Desert

One due to a desert storm known as a *haboob*. That left five choppers, when Beckwith and other planners deemed a minimum of six were needed to complete the mission.

About this time an Iranian bus appeared on its scheduled route. Guards detained the driver and about forty-five passengers.

Shortly thereafter, a gasoline tanker truck drove up from the opposite direction. Seeing the bus and airplanes, the driver pounded pedal to the metal. A rocket from a LAW (Light Antitank Weapons System) stopped the truck. The driver leaped out as it burst into flames and fled down the road until another car picked him up, screeched into a U-turn, and headed back toward Teheran. Flames from the abandoned tanker truck leaped more than one hundred feet into the desert sky.

In Washington, one of the spooks in the SCIF expressed the group's common distress: "This is gonna be a goatfuck."

Our chins dropped onto our chests, and the room fell totally silent when Colonel Beckwith came up on the air to announce that he was calling the mission off.

But Murphy and his law weren't finished yet. A helicopter repositioning itself to refuel from a C-130 for the long flight back to *Nimitz* collided with the plane. Both aircraft exploded and became engulfed in flames. Sounds of explosions, screams, and total confusion erupted from SCIF speakers.

"Oh, my God!" someone exhaled from the stricken room.

Fires from the burning aircraft and the tanker truck could be seen for miles. Iranian air defenses were expected to arrive within a very short time. Beckwith loaded his team on the C-130s and fled Iran, evacuating five injured Americans and leaving eight dead behind. Operation Eagle Claw had turned into Operation Goat Fuck.

Doom hovered like a dark cloud over official Washington, D.C. Failure in the attempted rescue proved a major embarrassment for the military and for Delta Force's first major mission. Iranian TV showed the burned bodies of dead U.S. servicemen left behind. Footage of it rebroadcast on U.S. networks.

"And tonight," said Walter Cronkite, "our hostages remain in captivity for 172 days."

* * *

Following the disaster, panels and committees throughout government rushed into session to determine what went wrong at Desert One and how problems with the nation's special operations forces might be remedied. The Holloway Commission, the DOD (Department of Defense), the Joint Chiefs of Staff, the Special Operations Rescue Group, and the Rescue Mission Report all came up with the same criticism—the lack of a central overall control. They also presented a common recommendation that a Joint Special Operations Command be created at Fort Bragg to place all special ops forces—SEALs, Green Berets, Delta, Marine Recon, Rangers—under their central commanding authority, which would coordinate and oversee, plan, train for, and conduct counterterrorism activities.

I was appointed a member of the Special Operations Advisory Panel and of the Counterterrorism Joint Task Force charged to come up with specific recommendations. One of the most important of these was that SpecOps be provided dedicated aircraft rather than drawing whatever might be available from conventional assets. The suggestion was immediately implemented in the formation of the 160th Special Operations Air Regiment—160th SOAR.

"All we need now," I confided in Chief of Naval Operations Admiral Thomas B. Hayward, "is a president with balls instead of marbles."

CHAPTER FORTY-NINE

I RAN'S KIDNAPPING OF OUR embassy personnel and holding them month after month made America more aware of the rise of international terrorism. Growing turmoil around the globe, especially in the Middle East, made the planet a much more dangerous place. War and general bedlam formed a kind of backdrop for terrorism's upward trend.

Part of my duties as a member of the Counterterrorism Joint Task Force was to gather data on terrorism, its nature, and genesis and to predict its evolution and offer solutions. I wasn't surprised that terrorism and global unrest fed upon each other and upon the blood of victims. Terrorism did not occur in a vacuum; it increased according to the general condition of the world.

During the period our countrymen were held hostage in Iran, Soviets sent troops into Afghanistan to support a pro-Soviet coup, and Iraq invaded Iran. Both wars continued throughout the months of the Iran Hostage Crisis and bore every indication of continuing for years longer. I was certain in my own mind that they in turn would metastasize into even more conflicts and wars.

"We in government," I commented to CNO Admiral Hayward, "have a tendency to look at acts of terror as unrelated incidents. We can, in fact, make predictions upon trends."

"And your predictions, Commander Hamilton?"

"You're not going to like this."

I showed him a chart I made of terrorist acts within the last two decades or so and how they fed upon the instability of the world and themselves created new instability. Since 1962, I pointed out, there had been fifty-seven airliner hijackings or attempted hijackings, fifteen of which originated in the United States. There were also hundreds of other terrorist incidents directed against the United States, Israel, or the West, among then 8,200 bombings and bomb threats inside the United States between January 1969 and April 1970 attributed to campus disturbances and student unrest.

Incident	Location	Date and details
"Sunday bomber"	New York City	1960. Series of detonations in New York subways and ferries resulting in one dead and 51 injured.
American Airliner hijacking	Marathon, Florida	May 1, 1962. Hijacked to Cuba.
Political assassination	Los Angeles	1968. Presidential candidate Robert Kennedy shot and killed by Palestinian-Jordanian-Muslim.
Massacre	Munich, W. Germany	August–September 1972. Black September Palestinian terrorists at Olympic Village. Eleven Israelis and one German police officer killed. Five terrorists died.

Incident	Location	Date and details
Bombings	New York City	1973. Puerto Rican terrorists FALN. 40 bombings.
Assassination	Chevy Chase, Maryland	1973. Israeli Air Force attaché shot outside home.
Airport bombing	LaGuardia Airport	1976. 11 killed, 75 injured.
Car bombing	Washington D.C.	1976. Former member of Chilean government and assistant killed.
Kidnapping	Kabul, Afghanistan	1976. Kidnapped U.S. ambassador killed during gunfight.

My chart went on for page after page. The CNO threw up his hands. "Jesus Christ!" he exclaimed.

"Yeah," I said. "Look at history and we see how they grow out of events. Radical Islam will be our next terrorist challenge."

The United States' first official war after the Revolutionary War was because of terrorism.

During and after the seventeenth century, Barbary pirates operating primarily in the Mediterranean from ports in the North Africa Ottoman provinces of Tripoli, Tunis, and Algiers seized ships for ransom and made raids along the seacoast as far north as the British Isles, the Netherlands, and even Ireland. Other than for loot and ransoms, the pirates' main purpose was to capture Christians for the Ottoman slave trade and the Arabian market. An estimated one million Europeans were taken for slavery from the sixteenth to the nineteenth centuries. England and Spain lost thousands of ships. Out of fear, civilians in Spain and Italy abandoned long stretches of their coast.

Pirates seized the first American merchant ship in 1784, then two more the next year. They had their own ambassador in Tripoli, who represented them before the North African Ottoman states of Tripoli, Algiers, and Tunis. These rulers offered the pirates safe haven and encouraged them to enslave, kidnap, and pillage on the high seas, for which the princes received a cut of the spoils.

Diplomats John Adams, Benjamin Franklin, and Thomas Jefferson went to London to negotiate with Tripoli. They demanded an explanation from Tripoli's envoy, Ambassador Sidi Haji Abdrahaman, who explained that the piracy was "founded on the laws of Prophet Mohammed. It is written in the Koran that all nations who should not have acknowledged our authority are sinners. It is our right and our duty to make war upon them wherever they can be found and to make slaves of all that can be taken as prisoner. Every Musselman who should be slain in such endeavors is sure to go to Paradise."

The United States at the time did not have a navy. President George Washington had no choice but to pay hundreds of thousands of dollars in "tribute" and for "protection." In effect, for ransom.

One of President John Adams's first undertakings after succeeding Washington to the presidency was to build a navy. Thanks to him, the U.S. had its Navy when Thomas Jefferson followed Adams to the presidency in 1801. "I was very unwilling that we should acquiesce in the humiliation of paying a tribute to those lawless pirates," Jefferson said. "I very early thought it would be best to effect a peace through the medium of war."

Jefferson dispatched the Navy and Marines overseas. General William Eaton led a successful military campaign against Tripoli, freeing captured seamen and crushing the terrorist force. After four years of fighting, Tripoli signed a peace treaty on America's terms.

"Point being," I stated to the CNO, "that the only way to deal with terrorism is by the sword."

Modern Islamic terrorist tactics could be traced through Adolf Hitler and World War II. At the start of the twentieth century, over one million Jews were living peacefully alongside Arabs in Palestine. As Hitler began his rise, vast numbers of Jews fled Europe for the Middle East, creating anti-Jewish unrest. The Grand Mufti of Jerusalem, a title granted by the British protectorate of Israel to Amin al-Husseini, was virulently anti-Jew. His idolization of Hitler led to the Islamic-Nazi pact. Throughout the war years, al-Husseini instigated violence and terrorist actions against Jews in Palestine. He also supported the Nazi war effort by raising an SS division of twenty-six thousand Muslims in Hungary.

During the last days of the war, Hitler looked to his favorite commando, Otto Skorzeny, to raise a band of soldiers trained to cause chaos and terror and spread fear in the enemy's rear—a mobile army of Nazi terrorists called Werewolves.

It was Skorzeny who pioneered the theory of guerrilla cells operating independently behind enemy lines with no centralized command, blending in with the people so they wouldn't be noticed. He wrote what was in effect the first terrorist handbook, a manual on techniques for "dirty fighting" that included everything from how to apply psychological pressure and blow up a fuel dump to planting booby traps and decapitating motorcycle couriers by stretching piano wire across roads.

After Germany lost the war, Skorzeny and a network of former SS officers escaped through "rat lines" to Egypt where they trained Muslim werewolves to operate against Israel and the West. Yasser Arafat, who rose to become head of the Palestine Liberation Organization (PLO), was among those whom Skorzeny trained. Arafat and Skorzeny spread the disease of Nazi terror throughout the Middle East.

Former Nazis obtained such a foothold in Egypt under Gamal Nasser that Nasser appointed Skorzeny to be his military advisor. Under Nasser, Egypt melded fully into a Nazi-like state. He banned political opposition, assassinated opponents or sent them to prison, and expelled or killed 75,000 Jews.

Skorzeny relocated to Spain in the early 1960s, where he organized the "Paladin Group" that offered his own brand of consultation to put down any opposition to his client regimes and organizations and advise them on consolidating their power. Among his clients were Muammar Gadhafi, Saddam Hussein, and various terrorists from the PLO, Hamas, and Hezbollah.

"Terrorist groups in the Middle East," I said, while the CNO nodded his head in understanding, "still pattern their tactics after Skorzeny and his Nazi Werewolves. Terrorism from Islam will soon threaten the future of Western civilization—unless we stop them."

"How do we stop them?" Admiral Hayward asked.

I shook my head and grinned. "With brains and balls," I said.

CHAPTER FIFTY

NAVY COMMANDER DICK MARCINKO was sometimes known as "Dynamite Dick of the Delta," for his daring SEAL team operations behind enemy lines in the Mekong Delta. During one six-month period, his team performed an incredible 107 combat patrols that resulted in more than 150 confirmed enemy KIA and 84 captured. His two tours in Vietnam won him the Silver Star for Valor, four Bronze Stars with Combat "V," two Navy Commendation Medals, and the Vietnam Cross of Gallantry.

I ran into Marcinko in one of the seventeen miles of corridors at the Puzzle Palace, while the Pentagon was in a frantic scramble to offset and respond to the humiliating blow of Desert One. He told me he was assigned to the Special Operations Division in the CNO's office. I was assigned to a CNO SpecOps Advisory Panel while he was detailed to a TAT—Terrorist Action Team. Both of us were among those planning a second hostage-rescue operation against Iran.

Rather, we were the hands behind the scenes. Action officers for each branch of the armed services worked for their respective chiefs of staff. If the JCS had a question, they dropped it down the line, where we hustled to do research and draft an answer. Superiors then either "chopped" our work or approved it to pass on up the chain.

Over cups of coffee with Marcinko in the cafeteria, talk turned to counterterrorism and the changes in naval special warfare each of us hoped to see in response to Iran and the growing terrorist threat. Marcinko leaned across the table toward me with an intensity some men found unsettling. He was a big man of about forty with a dark olive complexion and eyes nearly as dark as his hair. "Rough at the edges" expressed itself in a vocabulary liberally sprinkled with "fucks" and "assholes." He reminded me of Roy Boehm. Both were the kind you wanted with you in a barroom brawl.

"Delta Force screwed the pooch on Eagle Claw," he said, "but that wasn't Chargin' Charlie's fault, although the pencil dicks will have to find someone to blame it on. Bone, listen. We need to be preaching for the Navy to form a real counterterrorist team of our own. Let the pussy Army have Delta; they can play in the dirt. We'll target maritime objectives—tankers, cruise ships, military assets like navy yards, aircraft carriers, nuclear submarines."

"I've been preaching it since before Vietnam," I replied.

Marcinko growled in his throat. "The goat fuck at Desert One is the catalyst to get her done."

He was right.

In fact, SEAL Team One on the West Coast and SEAL Team Two in the east had already established some counterterrorism training. At Little Creek, Team Two dedicated two of its ten platoons specifically to CT activities and gave it the name MOB-6, or Mobility-6. MOB-6 conducted joint training exercises with Britain's SAS and its Special Boat Section, with West Germany's GSG-9, and with CT units from France and Italy in boarding ships and oil rigs to rescue hostages and take out bad guys.

Marcinko had written a memo outlining his ideas, a copy of which I had in my possession. The original went to CNO Hayward.

"Commander Hamilton, you're our UW authority," CNO James Hayward said. "What do you think?"

He was a tall, gaunt naval pilot who projected formality and always looked as though he should be wearing oversized aviator-frame sunglasses.

"I'm considering Marcinko to command a new CT unit," the CNO went on before I had a chance to respond.

I nodded noncommittally. "He's abrasive, sir, he's an asshole. Hide him when the women and kids are around, but otherwise he's definitely the best man for the job."

"Done. He builds and trains the unit. You oversee it and make sure he does it right."

Marcinko promised the Joint Chiefs and CNO that he could have the unit operational within six months. We called it SEAL Team Six to confuse Soviet intelligence as to the number of actual teams. He started with seventy-five shooters and fifteen officers, most of whom were handpicked original members from UDT/SEALs. MOB-6 disbanded, and many of its members transferred to him.

SEAL Team Six came on line officially in October 1980 and set up shop at Little Creek in two "chicken coops" located fifteen yards behind SEAL Team Two's headquarters. Both buildings were World War II wooden structures forty feet wide and eighty feet long, built on concrete slabs. They had been previously used as a Navy Wives Club meeting house and a Cub Scout den.

There was nothing at all military looking about the members of Six, nothing to identify them on-base or off. Marcinko wanted lean and mean. He got that and more. They were scruffy looking and wore civilian clothing with no base stickers on their vehicles. But what they did have was the best equipment available: high-tech Gore-Tex parkas and boots, parachutes, climbing gear, helmets and goggles, backpacks and ballistic nylon soft luggage, skis, SCUBA, camouflage for every environment . . . S&W .357 revolvers in stainless steel, Beretta 9mm autos, H&K submachine guns with and without silencers, stainless steel Ruger Mini-14s, silenced .22 caliber automatics, sniper rifles, stun grenades, C-4 explosives, claymore mines, radio-controlled remote detonators, and an annual ammunition training allowance larger than that of the entire U.S. Marines.

CNO Hayward's orders to Marcinko had been curt: "Dick, you will not fail."

SEAL Team Six's training program emphasized realism in various scenarios: ship boarding, oil-rig takedowns, plane hijacking recoveries, air ops, structural entry. . . . Naturally, training entailed a great deal of combat shooting and specialized techniques. Shooting had to be both accurate and instinctive. Shooters must be able to bring down their targets with one or two shots under any conditions. Six Team operators each shot a minimum of 2,500 rounds every week, more than most SEALs shot in a year.

In the Kill House, they practiced entering and clearing rooms and determining friend from foe on pop-up man silhouettes. Entries began with a single man coming through a doorway. Then in pairs, groups of four, finally in sixes, weaving a lethal, complicated choreography until every man mastered the art of dancing through a doorway and entering a room without getting killed or killing the man in front. After a while, maneuvers were all conducted with live fire.

Marcinko then added a twist. He attached a three-by-five index card somewhere on each silhouette target—head, torso, shoulder, groin. . . A shooter had to hit the card in order to score. Miss it and he started all over.

The scenario came with certain hazards. Concrete walls and floors created ricochets which occasionally dinged a guy. It was a dangerous game, but a necessary one in order to have men face the worst monsters terrorism produced. Better that men be injured or even die in training than that more of them be killed because they were not ready for the major leagues.

"We will not fail" became Marcinko's mantra.

Having conducted initial training at Little Creek, SEAL Six moved to Eglin Air Force Base in Florida to continue even more demanding CT training in a secluded corner of the base. Marcinko stood before them.

"Gentlemen, this will be a no-shitter," he began. "You know what we are here to do—counterterrorism. And what does counterterrorism mean? It means that we will fucking do it to them before they fucking do it to us. First, you do not have to like everything you do. Fact is, I don't give a shit whether you like everything you do or not. All you have to do is do it.

"Second, you are the system, gentlemen. The buck stops with each one of you. You assholes have the very best toys money can buy. If your equipment fails, it's because *you* fucking failed—not it. So I will not accept any goddamn excuses—'the gear didn't work, sir' or 'I got the wrong lung, sir,' or 'I didn't bring the right weapon, sir.'

"*You* are the fucking system. Failure is on your shoulders. I will accept no excuses. None. CNO Hayward sent me down here. You know what he fucking said, gentlemen? He said, 'Dick, *you will not fail.*'

"So, I *will not* fucking fail, gentlemen. Nor will *you* fucking fail."

He walked to a covered easel and threw back the black drape, revealing a map of Iran. "We have been assigned a mission. We aren't even a unit yet, but we have a mission. You see the map. You know where that is. You know who's still being held there. We are on call. Our number has been posted.

"It comes down to this: I'm giving you the tools. I'm giving you the opportunity. I'm giving you the support. If there is shit, I will take it for you. If there is flak, I'll absorb it for you. All you have to worry about is getting so fucking good at your jobs that you can fucking do anything."

I nodded with approval. Marcinko was an abrasive sonofabitch, but he knew how to motivate men. SEAL Team Six was up and running.

"Dick, you've got the best unit in the world," I complimented him. "Don't abuse it."

CHAPTER FIFTY-ONE

RESCUE OF THE AMERICAN embassy hostages would not, as it turned out, be SEAL Team Six's first CT mission. Ronald Reagan ousted Jimmy Carter for the presidency in the 1980 elections. The evening before Reagan's inauguration, Walter Cronkite reported, "Americans in Teheran have been in captivity 443 days." The next morning, January 20, 1981, the newly sworn-in fortieth president of the United States announced that Iran had freed the fifty-two hostages and that the plane carrying them had crossed the border and was no longer in Iranian airspace.

Apparently, the new president knew how to deal with terrorists. During his presidential campaign he referred to the Iranians as barbarians and implied that the sun wouldn't set once he became president before Americans with big guns were in Teheran looking for the ayatollah. As he stated later, his was a very simple philosophy regarding what the nation should do whenever an American was held captive abroad: go in and get him, "wherever it took us, anywhere in the world the person was."

I stood up in front of the TV set with Barbara and cheered. Ronald Reagan would have made a hell of a SEAL.

Commander Richard Marcinko settled for a lesser mission as the team's first—recovery of a stolen nuclear device from a clandestine terrorist training camp on Vieques Island in the Caribbean, seven miles due east of Puerto Rico. Alerted by JSOC, the Joint Special Operations Command at Fort Bragg, Marcinko had his team ready to go within hours. Each man carried a beeper. When it went off, he had four hours to show up at a prearranged location with all his equipment.

A terrorist group known as *Macheteros*—"machete wielders"—had broken into a National Guard airfield outside San Juan, where they took a hostage along with a pallet load of equipment that included a nuclear weapon. They evaded police dragnets, roadblocks, and SWATs and disappeared. U.S. intel assets tracked them to Vieques.

Macheteros were a small, well-financed, tightly organized guerrilla force of ultranationalists who vowed to wage war against "U.S. colonialist imperialism." Active since 1978, they received training courtesy of the Soviet KGB and had staged a number of lethal attacks resulting in the shooting of half a dozen Puerto Rican policemen, the murder of two U.S. sailors, and the wounding of three other American military personnel in separate ambushes.

The attack on the National Guard armory made front-page news—minus reference to the nuclear device—as Marcinko and a team of fifty-six operators arrived by HH-53 helicopters at Eglin Air Force Base in Florida. Never had Marcinko coordinated so many elements at once—a clandestine insertion via a massed night HAHO (high-altitude, high-opening) parachute jump into hostile territory, a target takedown, snatching the hostage and the nuke, and a synchronized extraction by choppers from a hot landing zone. Executing the plan successfully called for intricate timing.

The C-130 with Team Six detachments aboard went wheels-up from Eglin at 2:00 p.m. for the six-hour flight to the island. Marcinko was a detail man when it came to planning and executing a plan. On the flight he checked preloaded magazines for the team's Beretta and H&K submachine guns. To his astonishment he noticed that the weight of the rounds seemed considerably lighter than the custom loads he helped design.

He removed one of the cartridges and noticed it was a compound bullet. A *training* round. This was just another fake JSOC exercise, a full-mission training profile based on a real incident to make team members think they were playing for keeps. Although Macheteros, as reported in news accounts, *really had* attacked the National Guard armory, the rest of the scenario was pure bullshit.

Marcinko's first reaction was to go ape over the charade. Why hadn't he been informed it was a war game? But, then, on second thought, he understood. What better way to test an outfit than to let it think it was actually going into combat? He kept his mouth shut and went along with it.

Out over the Caribbean, 8:00 p.m., ten miles off the coast of the island and over ten thousand feet above it, Marcinko and his fifty-six SEAL CTs jumped out both doors of the C-130 into the black wind. Remarkable how quickly jumpers can exit an aircraft. They "flew" their square chutes over the Caribbean for ten miles and landed almost silently in the clearing a SR-71 Blackbird flying at twenty-eight thousand feet overhead had picked out for them.

OPFOR (opposing forces) at the terrorist site were Americans also equipped with blank ammunition. Everything went down smoothly. SEAL Team Six flew three thousand miles, put out four SEAL platoons in a high altitude–high opening night jump, parasailed ten miles to the objective, landed in a single cluster on a DZ no bigger than a couple of football fields, assembled, took down the bad guys, rescued a hostage, and snatched back a nuke without the loss of a single SEAL.

The scenario was so realistic, with everyone playing his part, that the SEALs' only surprise came when Marcinko informed them that the mission had been a training exercise, the team's certification exam. This was the first time the CTs had practiced all the risky skills of their profession in a real-time, full-tilt war game. So they had busted their asses for a *game*?

"The more you sweat in training, the less you bleed in combat," goes an old military axiom.

Marcinko received a message from JSOC. "You did wonderfully— better than we expected. The Joint Chiefs are impressed."

SEAL Team Six's next mission—*all* missions after that—would be for *real*. The nation's newest counterterrorist unit, brother to Delta Force, was certified and ready for action.

CHAPTER FIFTY-TWO

C OMMANDER DICK MARCINKO DESIGNED and trained the best group of warriors in the nation's history. Still, I wasn't shocked when he was relieved of command and chopped over to the operational control of the CNO at the Pentagon in July 1983 with a fourth-floor office down the corridor from mine. Marcinko admitted himself that he was an obnoxious sonofabitch who rubbed just about everyone he came in contact with the wrong way. He had pissed off, threatened, alienated, provoked, offended, and screwed with SpecWar commanders on both coasts. Now he was paying the price for it by sitting on his ass behind a desk.

He and I were both confined to offices in a crowded corner of the Navy Command Center, a bustling series of rooms where lower ranking officers—lower than admiral, that is—kept track of naval movements and crisis incidents worldwide. One day in September 1983, Marcinko and I entered a SCIF to find a group of intel types gathered around a nautical chart on the wall. Marcinko bulled his way into the center of it and in his smirking boom of a voice inquired, "Hey, guys. What country are we losing today?"

"Grenada," someone said.

It seemed people moved in and out of the Pentagon more often than deck swabbies changed their skivvies. Admiral Hayward retired and Admiral James D. Watkins replaced him as CNO. Through him,

CAPTAIN WILLIAM H. HAMILTON JR., USN

I already knew the United States was about four days away from over-running the island nation of Grenada with the most massive invasion force since the Inchon landing more than thirty years ago.

I accepted that with my age and rank I had to be content with studying, evaluating, and preparing actions to be carried out by younger SpecWar fighters. Marcinko, on the other hand, seemed desperate. He had spent much of his life preparing to lead a unit like SEAL Team Six into combat. He cultivated the team, built it—and now he was side-lined. He appealed to his old friend and sea daddy, Vice Admiral James A. "Ace" Lyons Jr., now deputy chief of naval operations.

"I'm fucked!" he groaned. "Anything is better than sitting in a win-dowless room and listening to reports coming in over the radio. Sir, I know damned well I'm better'n anybody else you can get at leading men into a fight."

Lyons assigned him to the secretary of Navy as his briefer.

"Cocksuckers," Dick bellyached to me. "You and me, Bone, we started all this shit with SEALs and Team Six and CT. So what do they do? They bend us over and fuck us. So here we sit it out like a couple of old whores."

Grenada was the southernmost island of the Grenadine chain, only ninety miles north of South America. Great Britain managed the island until 1974, when its citizens won independence within the British Commonwealth. The first prime minister, Eric Gairy, proved corrupt and heavy-handed, whereupon he was overthrown by the Marxist New Jewel Movement led by Maurice Bishop.

Bishop proved worse than Gairy. As new prime minister, he imposed an oppressive communist dictatorship enforced by a People's Revolutionary Army (PRA). Soviet Premier Khrushchev recognized the advantages of Grenada's strategic location within the American sphere. Although only 130 square miles in size, it was ideally positioned as an aircraft fueling base and as a supply depot and training center for guerrillas and terrorist groups throughout the Caribbean and southward. Castro, who supplied the Soviet premier with much of the Marxist muscle in Africa and Latin America, moved Cuban forces onto the island.

In 1983, Prime Minister Bishop fell out of favor with his colleagues. Deputy Prime Minister Bernard Coard, also a communist, ousted Bishop from office on October 14, 1983, with the aid of other so-called politburo members.

Six days later, a mob in the capital, St. George's, tried to forcibly free Bishop and other members of his former government. At Coard's orders, the PRA opened fire and killed more than fifty people, wounding many more. Coard ordered the PRA to take Bishop and four of his ministers and three of his supporters to nearby Fort Rupert and shoot them. Afterwards, he imposed a shoot-on-sight curfew on the entire island.

An estimated one thousand Americans, of whom six hundred were students at St. George's University Medical School, found themselves trapped on the island. President Reagan had previously proclaimed that no American would be abandoned to a foreign power. The United States was also concerned in this Cold War era about the construction of a nine-thousand-foot runway on the island capable of accommodating strategic bombers from the Soviet Union.

In Washington, the National Security Council ordered the Joint Chiefs of Staff to prepare a military plan to rescue U.S. citizens in Grenada. President Reagan expanded the mission. It would now take over the island and rescue former governor general Sir Paul Scoon, who was being held under house arrest. Scoon seemed receptive to denouncing communism and installing a democratic government.

"Well," President Reagan rationalized, "if we've got to go there, we might as well do all that needs to be done."

Joint Task Force 120, code-named Operation Urgent Fury, assembled under the overall command of Vice Admiral Joseph Metcalf. It was a curious juxtaposition of conventional forces and special warfare units from the Army, Navy, and Air Force. It would be carried out in complete secrecy.

CHAPTER FIFTY-THREE

THE GRENADA LANDING FORCE consisted of thirteen ships, hundreds of fixed-wing aircraft and helicopters, and more than seven thousand men. All four services operated together for the first time since the Vietnam War. Special Operations forces—Navy SEALs, Army's Delta Force, and two Ranger Battalions—would bear the brunt of the fighting.

The general plan called for Marines to make an amphibious landing to seize the northern half of the island while Rangers and elements of the 82nd Airborne secured the southern half by parachuting or air-landing onto the airfield at Point Salinas. SEALs and Delta Force were assigned four crucial missions, beginning on the night of October 23.

A pair of MC-130 Combat Talon deep-penetration transports flew south separately in radio silence for almost seven hours. Aboard were sixteen SEALs from Teams Four and Six, eight on each aircraft. As evening approached, the Talons linked up and descended to a radar-evading six hundred feet above the Caribbean Sea. SEALs prepared to parachute-drop a pair of blunt-nosed Fiberglass Boston Whaler assault boats with 175hp outboard engines.

Plans called for the SEALs to use the boats to pick up a four-man Air Force Combat Control Team from the destroyer USS *Clifton Sprague*, then transport the zoomies ashore to emplace radio beacons at the Port Salinas airfield to guide in C-130s at dawn to airdrop Rangers.

Darkness had fallen by the time the SEAL planes arrived at their destination. Winds gusted at twenty-five knots and the seas were six to eight feet, conditions that ordinarily precluded parachute ops. C-130 tailgates opened. Men kicked out the boats and followed them into the blackness, jumping with static lines at this low altitude, each jumper laden with nearly one hundred pounds of weapons, ammunition, and other gear.

Chief Engineman Johnny Walker hit the water so hard it ripped off much of his equipment. Wind re-inflated his parachute and dragged him skipping across the waves, nearly drowning him before he managed to cut free. He found himself separated in the darkness from the boats and his teammates.

Other SEALs were not that fortunate. Four of the sixteen— Machinist Mate Kenneth Butcher, Quartermaster Kevin Lundberg, Hull Tech Stephen Leroy Morris, Engineman Robert Schamberger— vanished in the pitch-black night to become the operation's first casualties. One of the boats was lost.

Survivors found each other and the remaining Whaler and regrouped on the destroyer with the Air Force team and set out to complete the mission. Bad luck continued to follow them. They spotted a Grenadian patrol boat approaching on their way to the island and cut power. Seawater swamped the overloaded little Whaler. The motor refused to start again and the boat drifted out to sea on a strong outbound tide. Its occupants were rescued several hours later. Rangers would have to make their combat jump on the airfield unassisted by radio beacons.

* * *

In the meantime that same Monday night, the 22nd Marine Amphibious Unit dispatched a SEAL element led by Lieutenant Michael Walsh to scout beaches for the Marines' landing on the island's northern end. SEALs conducted a World War II UDT-type hydrographic survey and discovered that reefs offshore made the landing unapproachable except by very shallow-draft boats. Undetected, they beached their rubber boats in a driving rainstorm and found themselves within listening distance of a Grenadian work party digging defensive emplacements.

They slipped back to sea and reported their findings. Navy Task Force Commander Admiral Joseph Metcalf changed plans. Instead of making the amphib assault, Marines would be helicoptered to land at Pearls Airport and nearby Grenville.

Marines began choppering ashore at 5:20 a.m., Tuesday, October 24, in coordination with Rangers paradropping onto Point Salinas in the south. Cuban troops guarding the airport opened fire on the Rangers, who responded and dropped two dozen Cubans dead, then rounded up and took 661 prisoners. Eight Rangers died in the brief battle. By 11:00 a.m. the Salinas airport was secured. C-130s and helicopters began landing gun jeeps and 82nd Airborne troopers.

* * *

Gunfire at Point Salinas still sputtered when an eight-man SEAL detachment from Team Four landed in a rubber boat around the coast and north of the airport. Its mission was to capture the Beausejour radio station and keep it off the air until U.S. forces took over.

Radio Free Grenada was a 75,000-watt transmitter capable of blanketing a large area of the Caribbean. Built from Soviet-supplied equipment, it sat on a hill overlooking St. George's less than a mile east of the sea. About a hundred yards southeast of the station, a north-south highway bridged a river, beyond which lay a settlement suburb of St. George's.

Only a handful of PRA soldiers guarded the transmitter. They surrendered to the SEALs. Lieutenant Donald K. Erskine prepared his swimmers to hold the radio against counterattack and sent a two man security team to the road north of the station. It used an M-60 machine gun and a light antitank weapon (LAW) to ambush a truck filled with militiamen, killing five, wounding several others, and scattering the remainder.

Shortly thereafter, an enemy reaction force of infantry led by a Soviet BTR-60 armored personnel carrier roared up from nearby Fort Frederick to exchange fire with the defenders at the radio station. A SEAL slapped a rocket into the BTR's turret, disabling its guns. Other militia with automatic weapons continued to advance in overwhelming numbers. Four SEALs, including Lieutenant Erskine, suffered non-life-threatening wounds.

Realizing that defending the station was hopeless, Erskine destroyed the transmitter and he and his men made a dash for the sea. They hid out until dark, then swam out toward the invasion fleet until helicopters spotted their strobe lights and hoisted them to safety.

* * *

SEAL Team Six, under Commander Robert Gormly, who had replaced Marcinko, drew the mission to rescue Governor General Sir Paul Scoon and his staff from house arrest at Government House on the outskirts of St. George's.

Shortly after dawn following the Ranger paradrop at Point Salinas, two Black Hawk helicopters piloted by Night Stalkers, as members of the 160th SOAR were called, lifted off with Commander Gormly and his twenty-three-man force and streaked for Government House. They intended to insert SEALs in two elements inside high walls that enclosed the residence: one element in the front yard, the other in the backyard.

As the choppers circled, trying to locate the house in dense tropical forest, they began receiving withering machine-gun fire. The chopper at the rear of the house took the hardest hit. The thirteen SEALs aboard it managed to fast-rope to the lawn. Commander Gormly, who had the team radio, was unable to get out of the Black Hawk. That meant the detachment on the ground had no commo with the tactical operations center.

Intense fire drove the second helicopter and its SEALs back to the fleet.

That left the rescue mission up to thirteen SEALs and Lieutenant John Koenig in the backyard. They fought their way across the lawn and into the mansion, where they found Scoon, his wife, and nine staff members hiding in the basement. Unable to fly the freed hostages to safety as planned, Koenig set up defensive perimeters inside the house and on the grounds outside and prepared to hold out until relief arrived. The loss of the radio put them out of touch with the rest of the invasion force.

Fortunately, the residence was located on a hilltop, which provided SEALs excellent fields of fire across the lawn. The siege raged throughout the day with intermittent attacks by Grenadian forces. A SEAL sniper picked off a number of attackers while moving from window to window upstairs.

The PRA commander called up three armored personnel carriers (APCs). Inside the mansion, to team member Lieutenant Bill Davis's surprise, he discovered the little nation's landline telephone system still worked. He dialed Rangers at the Salinas airfield and asked for gunship protection.

Anti-aircraft emplacements from Cuban military headquarters at Fort Frederick shot down two of the Sea Cobras that responded to Davis's request. Shortly thereafter, an AC-130 Spectre gunship from the Air Force's Eighth Special Operations Squadron arrived over target. It possessed more firepower than a tank—a battery of 20mm Vulcan and 40mm Bofors cannon, even a 105mm howitzer capable of firing as many as eight forty-pound explosive shells per minute.

Its massive firepower destroyed an APC and laid down a curtain of fire against attackers. A laconic radio transmission from the C-130 reported the number of enemy dead and wounded: "I see twenty flappers and kickers and seven runners."

The Spectre circled for the rest of the day and throughout the night, out of range of ground fire and prepared to stop further movements against the trapped SEALs. Lieutenant Bobby McNabb inside the mansion reported one incident that occurred during the night.

"We called in a strike on an APC on my side of the house. He was trying to hit the plane. You could hear the plane, kind of see it outlined up there. The plane shot the 20mm at him. Every time one of those rounds hit, they kind of gave off a spark. The Spectre hit the APC so many times it had a hellish glow over the top of it. You could see the bodies getting blown about. Oh, man, it was brutal."

* * *

In the meantime, the war continued elsewhere, with A-7 fighter bombers from the carrier USS *Independence* knocking out anti-aircraft defenses around St. George's. Two companies of Marines from the 22nd MAU (Marine Amphibious Unit) landed under cover of darkness at St. George's and at Grand Mal Bay. Reinforced with five M60A1 Abrams tanks, they moved toward Government House and the encircled SEALs.

* * *

Delta Force entered the fray, its objective Richmond Hill Prison to release political prisoners. The only intel Delta commanders had about the prison was its general layout. No one realized the prison perched on a ridge overlooking a deep canyon and that the twenty-foot-high walls projected from an extremely steep incline overgrown with jungle—or that PRA headquarters lay only three hundred yards away at Fort Frederick.

Two Black Hawks loaded with sixty Delta commandos closed in on the prison prepared to land one on each side and discharge the commandos as a blocking and security force while four other choppers raced in to evacuate prisoners.

Alarms sounded inside the prison as the choppers approached. A company of riflemen armed with AR-47s and a pair of ZPU-4 anti-aircraft machine guns firing six hundred rounds per minute ran toward the prison from Fort Frederick and drove the air assault back. Pilot Keith Lucas was killed, his copilot's head grazed. The smoking Black Hawk made it to a nearby hill crest before it skidded into a clearing.

One Huey managed to slide in underneath the fire to fast-rope nine Deltas into the prison yard while a UH-60 Black Hawk provided cover with its guns. The rest of the air fleet headed out to sea with several wounded. The nine commandos inside the prison held out for three more hours until they were rescued.

* * *

Over at Government House, besieged SEALs were relieved by Marines at 7:12 a.m. and Scoon and his staff evacuated. Miraculously, the SEALs suffered no casualties during their day and night in battle.

* * *

At Point Salinas on the southern tip of the island, giant C-141 Star-lighters airlifted in additional elements from the Army's 82nd Airborne Division. Thus relieved, Rangers headed out on their own in a forced march to rescue American students at St. George's University Medical School. The school was in Ranger hands by 7:30 a.m. However, they were astonished to learn about a second medical school campus at Grand Anse on the west coast of the island, where 223 Americans were trapped.

Having heard they were to be rescued, students and staff at Grand Anse marked their dormitory roofs with white sheets and covered windows with mattresses to protect against flying glass. All wore white armbands to identify themselves and flattened out on the floors as Rangers arrived to take charge that afternoon. There were no American casualties.

* * *

The Rangers had one final objective—Camp Calivigny, the main training base atop a seacoast promontory five miles east of Salinas, where as many as six hundred Cubans and thirty Soviet advisors were believed to be holed up.

Destroyers blasting with their five-inch guns, 82nd Airborne howitzers thundering death from the airfield, and Navy A-7s and Air Force Spectres on strike missions leveled the camp. Black Hawks carrying Rangers rushed in to mop up. Three choppers either crashed or were shot down during landings. Three Rangers died and four were injured before what was left of the camp's defenders either fled or surrendered.

That ended most of the island's resistance. Mopping up continued for several more days. By mid-December, U.S. combat forces went home and a pro-American government took power in Grenada. Nineteen Americans died and 123 were wounded in the action.

As with the after-action report from Desert One in Iran, pencil necks like me in the Pentagon rushed in to investigate the Urgent Fury operation. What went wrong and what went right? Every movement came under intense scrutiny.

Almost unanimously, we concluded that the operation was a debacle, a cluster fuck of screw-ups from start to finish. We tabulated the failures: poorly coordinated communications; leaks of pending action to local communist officials; and lack of intelligence about the island, its terrain, and its defenses. On top of all that, a series of mechanical and electronic malfunctions, miscalculations, and SNAFUs added to the turmoil.

Still, for the United States to mount and execute such a complex operation with only four days' advance notice was a triumph in itself. Governor General Scoon, his staff, and a number of political prisoners were liberated, and 662 American students rescued without a single death or serious injury among them. An unquestionably brutal communist regime was eliminated and another Soviet-Cuban adventure nipped in the bud. This was the first time since before World War II that an avowed communist government was replaced by a pro-Western one.

Perhaps the main lesson to come out of all this was a better understanding of the nature of special warfare. SpecOps by its very definition was delicate and highly complex, requiring time to plan, time to rehearse, time to reconsider and re-plan and rehearse again. Above all, success at low cost depended on detailed, up-to-the-minute intelligence. Only the foolhardy exposed relatively few men, no matter how well trained or dedicated they were, to an intensely hostile environment without precise information about the enemy.

The lesson had been a costly one for special operations forces.

"We have to get better," I said.

CHAPTER FIFTY-FOUR

GENERAL IBRAHIM TANNOUS, LEBANON's Armed Forces chief of staff, and Brigadier General Carl Stiner, commander of the U.S. Joint Special Operations Task Force (JSOTF), sat over early-morning coffee in Tannous's Beirut office when a tremendous blast rocked the building. The two men, Stiner lean and fit, Tannous rather chunky, rushed to the window to see a full black column of smoke tipped by a white spinning smoke ring—like an atomic explosion—rising from an area approximately two miles away, from the direction of the airport.

"I hope it's not the Marines!" Tannous exclaimed.

U.S. Marines at the airport had been under constant threat ever since they arrived in Lebanon to help restore sanity to the savage civil war raging between Israelis, Syria, and elements of the terrorist Palestine Liberation Organization (PLO). Defense Secretary Caspar Weinberger insisted the U.S. must take the lead in the United Nations to bring peace.

A new form of warfare emerged in the 1970s, or perhaps it was a new way of practicing a very old form of warfare—state-supported terrorism. Nations not militarily powerful learned to use terrorist tactics to achieve objectives and concessions they might never win through diplomatic or military means.

Turmoil in Lebanon traced back to the breakup of the Ottoman Empire after World War I. France, as the dominant power of which

Lebanon was a protectorate, granted the nation independence and pulled out its troops in 1946, leaving a complex ethnic mess more or less evenly distributed between Muslims and Christians, with Muslims divided into two sometimes-opposing groups, Sunni and Shiite. A third sect called Druze combined Christian and Muslim teachings. Add a fourth group to the mixture in the 1970s, the Palestinians, who had been driven out of Israel and Jordan, and the pot became even more chaotic.

Yasser Arafat's PLO migrated to West Beirut in 1975 to establish a main base of operations in its continuing feud with Israel. This did not set well with many Lebanese, especially with the Christian militia, the Phalange. Full-scale war broke out between the PLO and the Christian militia, resulting in the deaths of forty thousand Lebanese and Palestinians. The Lebanese Army fell apart and became incapable of enforcing the peace as the various factions turned against each other. Most of Lebanon became a battleground, with surrounding nations choosing sides to support.

Syria first sided with the Palestinian Fedayeen, then switched allegiance to the Christian militias. The USSR supported the Druze and its People's Socialist Party, or PSP. Israel occupied a security zone in the south where Christians, Palestinians, and Shiite Muslims lived together but hated each other. Iran became the most dangerous of the sponsors when it sided with the Shiite Muslims to spread Islamic revolution through subversion and terrorism. Iran's sponsorship introduced new forms of terrorist warfare that included suicide bombings and hostage-taking.

U.S.-educated Hosein Sheikholislam, a disciple of Ayatollah Khomeini, formed Hezbollah, or "Party of God," as the militant arm for fanatical fundamentalist Shiites drawn from all around the world. Trained by Iran's Revolutionary Guard, they were the most fearsome of all terrorists, willing to martyr themselves in the name of Allah. They saw Westerners, and particularly Americans, as the "Great Satan" and therefore primary targets.

Hezbollah located its main Lebanese base and terror training facility at Baalbeck in Syrian-controlled territory in the Bekaa Valley, only an hour's driving time from Beirut.

In June 1982, Israel finally got fed up with PLO terrorism and launched a full-scale invasion of Lebanon to clean out the Palestinian terrorists once and for all. In two weeks it drove the Palestinian army from strongholds near Israel's northern border, destroyed a major part of Syria's forces occupying the Bekaa Valley, and pushed all the way to Beirut, where it linked with the Christian Phalange militia and surrounded Muslim West Beirut, the center of militant Muslim activity in the capital.

Lebanese president-elect Bashir Gemayel, whose daughter had been killed earlier in an ambush meant for him, was bomb-assassinated on September 14, 1982, by a Syrian agent. The Phalange then massacred more than seven hundred unarmed Palestinians in West Beirut refugee camps, from September 16 to 18. In April 1983, a suicide bomber rammed his vehicle into the U.S. embassy in Beirut, killing sixty-three people in the explosion, among them seventeen Americans, including the CIA station chief and all but two of his officers.

In spite of his reservations, President Reagan sent 1,500 Marines to Lebanon in July 1983 to protect West Beirut. They settled in at an airport barracks, one of the strongest buildings in the city.

General Stiner arrived in Beirut at about the same time with orders from General Jack Vessey, JCS Chairman: "The Lebanese Army is the only effective institution of government to which we can tie our assistance program. I want you to work closely with General Tannous in coordinating the timing of Israel's withdrawal with the development of Tannous's forces, so the Lebanese will be able to effectively relieve the Israel forces. We want to eliminate the possibility of a void that will encourage renewed fighting by the factions."

Renewed fighting. It had never stopped. Beirut remained an armed camp where fighting might break out at any time. Lebanon began a more rapid and uncontrolled descent into a deeper hell as Israel began withdrawing on September 3, 1983. At midnight, a heavy Druze artillery and rocket barrage killed two Marines at the airport.

Marine Detachment Commander Colonel Tim Geraghty dispatched a sitrep (situation report) through his chain of command: "The stakes are becoming very high. Our contribution to peace in Lebanon since 22 July stands at four killed and 28 wounded."

"We're nothing but sitting ducks for all sides," a Marine complained.

At approximately 6:30 a.m. on October 23, a yellow nineteen-ton Mercedes-Benz stake-bed truck drove onto the Beirut International Airport. The driver of the hijacked truck circled the parking lot before accelerating through a barrier of concertina wire. It sped past two sentry posts, over an open vehicle gate in the perimeter chain-link fence, crashed through a guard shack and into the lobby of the barracks building where U.S. Marines were billeted and headquartered.

The force of the explosion, equivalent to approximately twenty-one thousand pounds of TNT, collapsed the four-story barracks, sheared the bases of steel-reinforced concrete support columns, dug an eight-foot crater through a seven-inch floor of reinforced concrete, and reduced one of the strongest buildings in Beirut to a pile of pancaked rubble. Generals Stiner and Tannous felt the massive shock wave from two miles away and watched the ball of flaming gas scald the morning sky. Twenty-four Marines died in the bombing.

Ten minutes later, a similar attack against a French military barracks six kilometers away in the Ramlet al Baida area brought down a nine-story building and killed fifty-four French paratroopers.

U.S. intelligence intercepted a cryptic message minutes after the bombing: "We were able to perform the spectacular act, making the ground shake underneath the feet of the infidels."

That same afternoon, a previously unknown group calling itself Islamic Jihad telephoned a Beirut newspaper. "We are soldiers of God and we crave death," the terrorist spokesman gloated. "Violence will remain our only path if the foreigners do not leave our country. We are ready to turn Lebanon into another Vietnam. We are not Iranians or Syrians or Palestinians. We are Lebanese Muslims who follow the dicta of the Koran."

Terrorists further celebrated their "victory" by spreading picture-posters of both "martyred" truck drivers throughout the Shiite suburbs of Beirut. Sheikh Fadlallah, Hezbollah's spiritual leader, had blessed the drivers before they set out on their missions, apparently promising them an easy life in Paradise surrounded by their seventy-two virgins.

CIA-intercepted messages between Iran's Foreign Ministry in Teheran and the Iranian ambassador in Damascus exposed Iran's complicity. One of these messages, dated a few days before the bombings, urged a major attack against all Americans.

Suspiciously, Iran's chief terrorist, Hosein Sheikholislam, checked out of the Sheraton Hotel in Damascus on October 22, the day before the attack on U.S. Marines. Also, the Iranian embassy in Damascus inexplicably evacuated just hours before the bombing occurred.

Two weeks later, a young woman astride an explosives-laden mule rode up to an Israeli outpost on the edge of the southern buffer zone. The mule blew up, killing its rider and fifteen Israelis. The woman's picture-poster went up in Beirut, Damascus, and Teheran alongside those of the two suicide truck bombers.

The U.S. embassy, the U.S. Marines, the French barracks, the mule—clear evidence that we in the United States were faced with a virulent pattern of state-sponsored terrorism.

"Islamic jihad?" CNO James Watkins mused. "Is this something new, Commander Hamilton? What's your assessment?"

CHAPTER FIFTY-FIVE

Islamic jihad, while not exactly a new term, was one not so familiar with many of us in the U.S. military. I was both intrigued and horrified at the fanaticism demonstrated in someone strapping dynamite to himself and committing suicide in order to kill not only a military enemy but also innocent civilians who might not share his particular philosophical or religious convictions. My God, how did you stop a people who "crave death"? Who were not only willing but even seemingly *eager* to blast themselves into the afterlife in Allah's name?

What is the Muslim religion? I asked. What is jihad? Charged with providing the CNO an assessment, I pored over an English translation of the Quran, striving to decipher the motivations behind the violence and fanaticism rising throughout the Middle East and understand what it portended for the United States and the world.

Barbara looked quizzical when she found me in my recliner puzzling over a hand-marked and dog-earned copy of the Quran.

"What are you doing, Bill? Converting?"

"Barb, what's the Agency doing about Islamic jihad?"

She knew the term. She still worked as an analyst for the CIA. "Ronald Reagan is convinced that the heart of all evil resides in the Soviet Union."

"You find the Russkies nipples-deep in insurrection no matter where it occurs. They agitate in Beirut, in Iran, creating unrest and revolution among Muslims. What's that old phrase? Something about the Devil and his playmates?"

"Bill, you need to talk to Bill Casey."

I had met Casey after the Iranian hostage crisis when President Reagan appointed him new director of Central Intelligence. He was a balding older man with a ring of white hair above his ears and wire-framed glasses perched on his nose.

"You're a smart girl, Barbara. That's why I married you."

We had set a record. We had been married to each other more years than I had been married to my previous three wives together.

"Get back to your studies, you big lout." She smiled and kissed me. What a woman!

Jihad? Defined as "struggle in the way of Allah." Both a personal spiritual struggle as well as a military struggle. Innocuous enough in the first instance. Not so much so in the second.

The long struggle between Christianity and Islam that began with the Crusades had succeeded in containing Islam and eventually dissolving the last caliphate, the Ottoman Empire, after World War I. However, Muslims still yearned for a "new caliphate." In Islamic theology, there is a strong conviction that the world is disintegrating and Allah will usher in a new era in which Muslims rule the globe. Shiites especially believe that only catastrophic violence against infidels will bring Allah to earth, and that in the meantime jihad continues until the populations of every nation convert.

DCI Bill Casey and I understood that only a small fraction of Muslims were terrorists. However, for would-be terrorists seeking to achieve world domination, passages in the Quran and in Muhammad's recorded sayings in the Hadith supplied sufficient ammunition for them to justify their actions:

It is the duty of those who have accepted Allah's word and manage to strive unceasingly to convert or at least to subjugate those who have not. This obligation is without limit or time or space. It must continue until the whole world has either accepted the Islamic faith or submitted to the power of the Islamic state. . . .

Killing unbelievers is a small matter to us. . . .

Allah deserves killing them to manifest the religion. . . .
Fight everyone in the way of Allah and kill those who disbelieve
Allah. . . .
I will cast terror into the hearts of those who disbelieve. There-
fore strike off their heads. . . .
And the stone behind which a Jew will be hiding will say, "Oh,
Muslim. There is a Jew hiding behind me, so kill him."
I have been made victorious with terror. . . .
I have been commanded to fight against people till they testify
that there is no god but Allah. . . .

The second genocide of the twentieth century occurred beginning in 1915 when Muslim Turks rounded up and slaughtered more than a million and a half Armenian Christians. (The first occurred when a mercenary army raised by German settlers in what is now Namibia attempted to exterminate the Herero people.) The *New York Times* quoted Doctor M. Simbad Gabriel on the genocide in its September 25, 1915, issue:

The doctor said that greed, religion, and politics all combined to induce
the Turks to massacre the Armenians. The government was always
behind every massacre, and the people were acting under orders.
When the bugle blows in the morning, Turks rush fiercely to the
work of killing the Christians and plundering them of their wealth.
When it stops in the evening, or in two or three days, the shooting
and stabbing stop just as suddenly then as it began.

Hitler may have been as much inspired in his "final solution" by the example of the Armenian massacre as Islamic terrorists were by the Grand Mufti of Jerusalem and by former SS officer Otto Skorzeny with his Werewolf campaign after World War II.

Modern international terrorism sprang out of the rise of Marxist nationalist and revolutionary movements with their view, especially in the Islamic world, that terrorism was effective in reaching goals. Radical Palestinians unable to confront Israel militarily led to plane hijackings, kidnappings, bombings, and shootings. By the 1980s the

Palestinian network supported by various state sponsors such as the Soviet Union and Iran had created an extensive transnational network that became the major channel for terrorist techniques worldwide.

Hezbollah, Hamas, Muslim Brotherhood, Egyptian and Palestinian Islamic Jihad, PLO, Al Fatah, Amal . . . none of these groups expected to destroy the West in a single blow or in a series of blows, not unless one of them first obtained nukes. What they did was exploit weaknesses—economic, political, psychological, physical—to create tension and erode the will of their enemies to continue the struggle. It was a process that could take a very long time. Years, even decades of patience. But, after all, radical Islam had been on this path to conquer the world for Muhammed and Allah since 1632.

Training camps for jihadists to learn their bloody work sprang from fertile soil in the hidden valleys of Lebanon, the deserts of Libya and Iran, the desolate mountain passes of Afghanistan. . . . After releasing the American Embassy hostages, Ayatollah Khomeini established an international training camp in Manzareih in Iran. His faculty included translators, commandos from North Korea, security experts from Syria, Soviet KGB officers, Palestinian veterans, advisors from Libya, and radical experts from terrorist movements all over the world. The first class of 150 graduated in July 1981.

A year later, 240 terrorist organizations from eighty different countries met in Tripoli for the International Conference of the World Center for Resistance to Imperialism, Zionism, Racism, and Fascism. Organized by the Soviet Union, Iran, and Muammar Gadhafi of Libya, the conference formed a committee consisting of representatives from Libya, Cuba, Iran, Syria, and North Korea with the goal of forming an international terrorist training program to prepare revolutionaries to battle the "oppressors," primarily the United States.

It was difficult to believe the preparations these nations and movements were taking for war against the West. As many as eighteen functioning training facilities staffed by experts in modern combat and sabotage—in effect Nazi Werewolves—were turning out thousands of terrorists. The largest of these camps, Sikilabad, boasted a Western-style airport mockup complete with modern equipment and supplies. Students became trained in sabotage, aircraft boarding, hostage taking, political kidnapping, and control of airport facilities. Special camps trained women and suicide fighters.

Insanity on a global scale. During the 1970s, the total number of confirmed domestic and international terrorist incidents numbered 8,114, with 4,978 people killed and 6,902 injured. These statistics were already more than tripling into the 1980s with nearly thirty thousand incidents worldwide. Over sixty thousand people had been killed and forty thousand injured in aircraft hijackings, kidnappings, suicide bombings, and random other acts of mayhem—and the decade was not yet over.

DCI William Casey and CNO James Watkins weren't going to like my assessment: Eventual war on a scale that eclipsed all wars combined since the beginning of the nineteenth century. And, sooner or later, Islam jihadists would obtain nuclear weapons and would have no qualms about using them.

CHAPTER FIFTY-SIX

THE DEPUTY CHIEF OF naval operations for plans and operations, Admiral James "Ace" Lyons, summoned Dick Marcinko and me to his office one morning in early 1985.

"All right, you two. You've been bitching about this long enough. Sit down."

I glanced at Marcinko. He shrugged. I pulled up a chair. Marcinko stood; he always said it was better to take an ass-reaming standing up than sitting down. Maybe Ace would kick us back out into the fleet if we screwed up badly enough. I was up for promotion to captain. A captain should have a command.

"As an institution," the admiral began, "the Navy is so focused on the Soviet threat that we don't take the time or energy to deal with other equally dangerous potential adversaries."

I looked at Dick. He shrugged again.

"We're a peacetime Navy, and we think like a peacetime Navy," the admiral continued. "That makes for liabilities when it comes to dealing with terrorism. The Germans, the Italians, the French, the Brits—they all deal with terrorism on a daily basis while we just go blithely along. Then all of a sudden the shit hits the fan. Some asshole blows up our embassy in Beirut or we get intel the Iranians are going to target the Sixth Fleet with remote-controlled boats and we go ape-shit because we're not prepared."

I was beginning to understand. Dick and I had been trying to convince the chain of command that defensive counterterrorism measures were something the Navy needed. Most fleet commanding officers were more concerned about wives' clubs than they were of being blown up by a terrorist operative.

The Joint Special Operations Task Force commanded by Brigadier General Carl Stiner had developed force packages for virtually any anticipated crisis situation. Databases covered every known terrorist organization on the planet. My beef with JSOTF was that it was largely reactive, not proactive. We thought about offense *after* we were attacked, not defense before it happened.

"The bottom line is that the Navy is not prepared," Lyons continued. "The Navy doesn't have a damned manual about what to do if we're faced with the possibility of a suicide bomber or a remote-controlled speedboat filled with Semtex. We stamp millions of papers *Top Secret*, but our most sensitive installations are open to attack twenty-four hours a day. You can't lead people to change their thinking about terrorism. You have to push them.

"That's why I'm going to turn you two loose to shake up the whole system. Rattle the Navy's cage like it's never been rattled before. I want our base commanders to see how vulnerable they really are. I want to stick it to them—and have them learn from the experience, learn something they won't put in a file drawer and forget. I want an end to all the complacency. The jihad threat is real. I know it. You know it. And it's about time they knew it too."

Despite his impish smile and merry fifty-seven-year-old cheeks that made him look like a cherub, Lyons was viewed around the Pentagon as a hard-line rabble rouser with an intractable stubbornness that other four-stars found difficult to tolerate in the D.C. political climate. His was a warrior's mentality, audacious and unconventional. Through him, Dick and I had finally caught someone's attention.

He appointed me immediately to a new special staff section charged with testing the security of key naval installations against sneak terrorist attacks.

"Bone, you're appointed titular head of this with Marcinko as your deputy because Marcinko hasn't the finesse to do anything but piss off everybody he comes in contact with. Keep Marcinko out of sight when there's brass around, but otherwise give him the rein to build this thing. The two of you have been carping about this for years, and now we've got authorization from the CNO to do something about it."

Admiral Lyons dispatched a memo to CNO Watkins outlining our concept: "I have established the Red Terrorist Cell under the Code of OP-06D. This cell will plan terrorist attacks against U.S. naval ships and installations worldwide. They will identify the vulnerabilities of the targets and plan the attacks within the known capabilities, ethnic characteristics of the terrorist factions, and the political objectives of the sovereign states involved. In conjunction with the attack scenario, this group will also recommend actions which can be taken which will either inhibit or so complicate any planned terrorist action that they will not occur."

The new outfit would be formally known as Naval Security Coordination Team, but informally it became Red Cell. During war games, commies were the Red Team. Good guys were the Blue Team. Red Cell would play the part of commies and jihadists in exposing installation weaknesses to encourage commanders to beef up security against *real* terrorists.

"Stray from what we've agreed on, and you and your boys will be history," Admiral Lyons warned. "The idea is not that you assholes shoot and loot like a bunch of crazies. The idea is that we teach the Navy how to make life difficult for terrorists. Now go out there and build me a Red Cell."

Red Cell originally consisted of fourteen men. All but one were former members of SEAL Team Six; the whole team wanted in on the action when it heard Marcinko was involved. Steve Hartman was the one non-SEAL exception. He was a former Force Recon Marine who won two Silver Stars on secret missions into Laos and North Vietnam. His talents included lock-picking, motorcycle racing, parachuting, and saloon brawling. He possessed black belts in three different forms of karate.

Red Cell soon looked like a band of pirates and terrorists. Dick was good at that kind of transformation. A thick book of guidelines made sure we played fair and didn't go too far. A Navy lawyer traveled with the unit to enforce rules. Each scenario we developed had to be approved by the CNO and the commander of our targeted victim. Umpires were used, as in any war game. We videotaped each exercise for later study.

The world was our playground. We operated like real terrorists. Traveling incognito, scoping out targets, improvising demolitions by buying what we needed at hardware stores or stealing from military bases.

The waves we stirred up became a tsunami that put the entire Navy on edge.

CHAPTER FIFTY-SEVEN

Red Cell conducted its live dress rehearsal at the Norfolk Naval Base, Virginia. The SEAL Marcinko called Minkster phoned the base commander and in his best Arab accent threatened, "This is the Movement for the Free Ejaculation of Palestine. Free all our prisoners, or you Zionist infidels will suffer."

We successfully infiltrated the installation and placed mock explosives on the roof of the command center where more than a dozen admirals worked. Within the next few days we wreaked havoc on Second Fleet and Atlantic Fleet Headquarters with bombs, booby traps, and smoke grenades. Adding insult to injury, we returned a few weeks later and captured the base commander's home and took his family hostage while others of us carried out a mock attack on planes and docked ships.

I laughed with Barbara when I told her what we had done.

"You're like a bunch of rowdy boys on Halloween turning over the preacher's outhouse," she said.

It was, for a fact, great fun, but with a serious purpose. I couldn't always tag along, but I took every opportunity to join Dick and the Cells and get away from the Pentagon and its stuffy atmosphere. Admiral Lyons seemed to enjoy poking the brass as much as Dick and I did.

After Norfolk, we went for the Navy's nuclear submarine base at New London, Connecticut. Three years earlier, dope-smoking hippie

activists armed with hammers attacked a Trident ballistic missile submarine in the vicinity—base security was that weak.

We set up shop among civilians down the road and began to probe.
Marcinko rented a small plane. Our unit pilot, Horseface, flew him
under the I-95 bridge and buzzed the submarine pens. No one waved
the plane off.

On another day we rented a fishing boat and, flying the Soviet flag
on its stern, chugged past the base and openly shot film of submarines
in dry dock. We could have rammed or booby-trapped the subs had
we been so inclined.

Terrorists love to scout bars and clubs near military posts where
servicemen hang out. It was easy while lounging around drinking beer
and smoking cigarettes to pick sailors' pockets for wallets containing IDs and everything else from the combination to safes containing classified documents to details of the next fleet movements. Add
a good-looking babe from the local population, throw in a few beers,
and we could have almost owned our own submarine.

Hell, it was embarrassing to me how easy it was to breach security.
Marine guards manned a side gate where a single road led to
the submarine base hospital. Avoiding the road, Red Cell operators
came in from even further to the rear, rappelled down cliffs and crept
through a wide-open "back door" while everyone watched the front
door. Marcinko and his rowdies burrowed underneath a chain-link
fence, sneaked around the dark side of an ordnance facility, and "shot"
a security guard with a silenced pistol. That left the place wide open.

Our intruders picked the lock on a side door and entered. Inside,
working quickly, they attached a timer-detonated charge next to a
nuclear weapons prep area and hid IEDs (improvised explosive devices)
among an arsenal of torpedoes. They slipped back out again and disappeared, leaving an insulting sign inside on an office door: KA-BOOM!
LOVE AND KISSES FROM THE MOVEMENT FOR THE FREE EJACULATION
OF PALESTINE.

The base commander, a captain, was not happy when he saw the
film evidence of our night's work. He came complaining to Dick and
me. "You didn't play fair. You didn't play by the rules."

"What rules?"

"Well, you climbed down the cliff to raid my ordnance facilities. You never told me you'd do that—you only said you'd attack it. You swam downriver and came up under the docks when you attacked the submarines. If we knew you'd come from that direction, we'd have been waiting. We can't have people watching everywhere."

"I'm sure the *real* People's Front for The Liberation of Ejaculstan will take your views into account if they decide to stage an actual hit on your base, sir."

He kept pissing and moaning. "Your so-called terrorists phoned up and said they were going to hit the PX. We were ready, but they didn't."

"We attacked the commo center instead. This may surprise you, sir, but terrorists don't operate by rules. You have a nice, neat base here. I'm sure you run it very efficiently. But as far as security is concerned, you're very vulnerable. The tapes we took show how we blew up two of your nuclear submarines and could have blown 'em all up. All the bad guys have to do is bend a shaft or screw up a diving plane and your fleet of multimillion-dollar nuke subs is bottled up."

Each month we terrorized another installation. Our "attacks" proved acutely embarrassing, especially since, according to the rules, we gave advance warnings. They were frighteningly realistic, and that led to a number of bitter complaints. Rumors always floated out ahead of our pending operations.

No one could ever accuse Marcinko of having tact or sensitivity. During a pre-attack briefing, Dick would come out with something like, "We won't break any skin. We won't draw blood. No broken teeth. Everything else is mine."

To a woman, he might say, "We're not going to pull your skirt over your head and tie your hands behind your back."

"Dick, you could be a bit more subtle," I scolded him.

"Huh? You mean that wasn't subtle enough?"

In Naples, Italy, the team kidnapped an admiral and his wife by forcing their car off the road following a speech he delivered at a Navy club. Marcinko released him—and kidnapped him again the following morning.

At Subic Bay in the Philippines, Red Cell stole a native's boat and rammed it into the carrier *Kitty Hawk* as it steamed into harbor.

Our pirates captured a local ice cream store in Japan and used its employees and customers as hostages to test a base hospital's mass casualty capabilities.

Marcinko and I and the Minkster penetrated the Charleston, South Carolina, naval base using IDs we stole from a couple of civilian base workers at a bar downtown. Dressed in scroungy clothing, unshaven, we drove unchecked through the front gate and spent the next several days sabotaging a nuclear storage area and sneaking aboard nuclear-powered submarines. No one ever challenged us; I don't think they even saw us.

Even the president of the United States, Ronald Reagan, proved susceptible to our tender ministrations. Whenever he vacationed at his California ranch 125 miles south of Point Magu, Air Force One remained tethered at the Point Magu Naval Base.

The base was like a sleepy little southern California town in the hours before Labor Day weekend when its commander received *the call*: "This is the Movement for the Free Ejaculation of Palestine. If the Israelis do not free 173 of our political prisoners within two hours, your facilities will be bathed in American blood. The mother of all wars will begin on your accursed Zionist-loving territory."

For the next three days Red Cell brought down chaos and anarchy.

It began when Lieutenant "Trailer Court" used a stolen ID and wore a purloined commander's uniform to check in to the base at 7:00 p.m. Friday, saying he was reporting in for duty early to avoid paying for a motel room. After obtaining quarters at the BOQ, he and other Red Cell operatives, who had infiltrated by various other means, stole a weapons carrier, drove it to an ordnance warehouse, broke in and loaded the carrier with bright blue dummy 500-pound bombs. They rigged the bombs with remote-controlled detonators and parked the vehicle and its load covered in a tarp in the BOQ parking lot.

In the meantime, Red Cell SEALs infiltrated the base from off the Pacific Coast Highway and through a wildlife refuge that ran north of the base. As the weekend progressed, they videotaped themselves planting "explosives" in the air intakes of F-18 Hornet jets, "destroy-ing" the main Point Magu communications antennas, setting off smoke grenades in the headquarters building, "kidnapping" dependent women at the Magu cafeteria, and racing a car up and down the aircraft flight line pursued by jeeploads of security personnel.

By Monday, local cops and firefighters were bouncing off the walls, doctors were ready to stage a sit-down strike, and the FBI packed up its goodies and went home because no one was playing fair. There remained one target that Marcinko could not resist. Air Force One was scheduled to depart for Washington at midday.

Dressed in mechanics' overalls, two men climbed into the weapons carrier left parked over the weekend at the BOQ and drove it to the far corner of the field where Air Force One was being fueled and serviced. They climbed out of the vehicle, activated "explosives" rigged to the pallet load of 500-pound bombs, set the timer, and walked off. The carrier "exploded" minutes later.

From what I heard, President Reagan was quite jocular about the entire episode. "I'm just happy real terrorists are not as smart as these guys," he said.

Embarrassed naval officials moved quickly to correct security deficiencies uncovered by Red Cell. My reports backed up by video-tape led to U.S. senators Pete Wilson and John Glenn goading the National Security and International Affairs Division into a complete review of the Navy's internal controls for protecting assets and facil-ities. Secretary of the Navy John F. Lehman Jr. ordered an extensive reorganization of naval security. Marcinko, Red Cell, and I had cer-tainly made our bones.

Admiral Lyons recommended my promotion to captain. My fit-ness report for the period read, "His aggressive leadership was instru-mental in developing the navy's 'proactive' antiterrorist stance, and he has helped shape our antiterrorist program for years to come."

Promoted himself, Lyons shipped out for Honolulu as commander-in-chief Pacific fleet (CINCPAC), safely removed from the political mainstream in Washington and the Pentagon. Admiral Donald Jones, Lyons's successor, was a balding, bureaucratic "team player." He offered a handshake that felt like a dead fish.

I knew we were in trouble when, in a cold voice, he greeted Marcinko with, "I'm surprised you're not in jail yet."

Marcinko had twisted too many tails and, because of our successes in Red Cell, accumulated a deluge of complaints describing him as a maverick unfit for command. Partly because of that, partly because of actual irregularities in the books of SEAL Team Six when he commanded it, the Naval Investigative Service (NIS) opened a probe.

On April 6, 1986, he was dismissed from Red Cell and later court-martialed for conspiracy, bribery, conflict of interest, and making false claims against the government, all of which were connected with his extralegal methods of obtaining equipment and materiel for the creation of SEAL Team Six.

I used what influence I had in attempting to intervene on his behalf with the CNO and Department of Navy. I argued that, well, maybe he had gone too far in carrying out his obligation to build the best CT team in the world, but, damn it, didn't results show that it took men like him and like former Bos'n Mate Roy Boehm to build tough and effective CT units? We *needed* two-fisted brawlers in the trenches, not broad-beamed bean counters behind desks.

"Be careful," CNO Watkins cautioned me. "You'll step on your own dick."

Eventually, this man Marcinko, who with his crass manners and rogue attitude I considered most instrumental in creating both SEAL Team Six and Red Cell, was convicted and went to jail.

CHAPTER FIFTY-EIGHT

WORKING AS SHE DID for the CIA, my wife understood completely when I called her at the Agency. "Honey, I'll be late."

"How late?"

"A day or two. Maybe longer."

"Make sure you eat. See you when you get home."

We seldom spoke about the details of our work. There was never any, "Well, honey, how was your day? Do anything interesting today?"

* * *

Most of the 750 tourists aboard the 23,000-ton Italian luxury cruise liner *Achille Lauro* went ashore for pyramid-watching in Alexandria, Egypt, that Sunday morning, October 7, 1985. The ship sailed on toward Port Said with the remaining ninety-five passengers aboard, the majority of whom were elderly.

Somewhere along the route, the ship's radio operator transmitted a frantic SOS picked up by a ham operator in Sweden. The hurried message disclosed only that "terrorists" had hijacked the liner in the Mediterranean off the coast of Egypt. The ship then lapsed into radio silence and seemed to vanish.

As soon as the news reached Washington, President Ronald Reagan convened the Terrorist Incident Working Group and put JSOTF on alert, along with units of Army Delta Force and SEAL Team Six. The incident occurred at sea; SEALs would take the lead if American interests were determined to be involved.

The Terrorist Incident Working Group was one of a hodge-podge of organizations that cropped up in the U.S. government in response to the rising tide of terrorism in the Middle East. I had pushed for a unified approach against terrorism since I arrived at the Pentagon five years ago. Seemed things were finally going my direction.

Aircraft carrier USS *Saratoga* was on maneuvers in the Mediterranean. President Reagan ordered its jet fighter assets along with U.S. Air Force electronic intelligence aircraft to join in the search for the missing cruise ship.

As soon as Brigadier General Carl Stiner, commander of Joint Special Operations Task Force at Fort Bragg, learned of the hijacked ship, he and his staff began planning to take the ship down. He ordered his deputy commander and his ops officer to ready CT units for deployment and arrange transport with Military Airlift Command. The Task Force Command Group consisted of operations and intelligence staff officers along with communications and medical personnel; SEALs with their assault, sniper, and special boat teams; Air Force Special Tactics operators for airfield control and para-rescue; Delta Force operatives; and an Army special helicopter package of ten Black Hawks, six Little Bird gunships and four Little Bird lift ships. It was a major test for JSOTF just to move such a massive force halfway around the world, never mind conducting the operation when it arrived.

U.S. counterterrorists had never taken down a ship in real life. We had only trained for it, such as when Marcinko and I were building SEAL Team Six and persuaded a Norwegian "love boat" to go along with a mock terrorist scenario in Miami. What we learned was that a cruise ship was the toughest of targets. It required a large boarding party to subdue terrorists before they harmed their hostages while searching rooms, nooks, and crannies for hidden terrorists and possible explosives, controlling passengers and crew, securing everyone aboard, and taking care of any wounded or injured.

A lot of people at the Pentagon and White House were understandably anxious. I smoked a pack of cigarettes and drank a pot of coffee of my own while we denizens of the Pentagon waited either in SCIF rooms, the second floor "tank," or in various offices for an announcement that the *Achille Lauro* was located.

A week earlier, on October 1, the Israeli Air Force had bombed the Tunisian headquarters of the Palestinian Liberation Organization, Yasser Arafat's bunch, in response to a terrorist attack the PLO conducted against a civilian Israeli yacht. The strike destroyed PLO headquarters and killed sixty terrorists. Washington assumed the *Achille Lauro* hijacking to be in retaliation for the bombing. Terrorists weren't that particular who they attacked, as long as the targets were from the despised West.

On Monday, October 8, the liner reappeared four hundred miles away, bound for the Syrian port of Tartus. Syria was a haven for terrorists. President Hafez Assad exercised considerable leverage and influence over several regional terrorist groups, among them the PLO.

Pressured by the U.S.—more accurately, *threatened*—Assad refused to allow the *Achille Lauro* to dock. That left the ship alone and isolated on the sea. Hijackers were seen from the air singling out passengers and placing them in plain view on deck surrounded by a wall of fuel drums. For the first time the hijackers broke radio silence to negotiate.

"If we are attacked," they vowed, "we will set afire these infidels and burn them till they no longer are alive."

They demanded the release of fifty Palestinian terrorists captured by Israel. If Israel did not release them by 3:00 p.m., all passengers aboard the ship would be executed.

After the fact, we learned who the hijackers were and what occurred during and leading up to the hijacking. It was masterminded by the Palestinian Liberation Front (PLF), an affiliate of Yasser Arafat's PLO. Pretending to be tourists, Majed Molqi and three henchmen boarded the cruise ship in Egypt with a plan to accompany it to the Israeli harbor at Ashod, its next port-of-call after Egypt. There they would commandeer the vessel, hold the passengers hostage, and negotiate for the release of the Palestinian terrorists.

Things didn't work out that way.

At lunchtime while the ship was under way, the steward had thought it a good time to check out staterooms while everyone was eating. He entered Molqi's cabin and surprised four men cleaning automatic weapons. His unexpected appearance forced the men to make their move prematurely.

Most of the ninety-five passengers and ship's crew remaining aboard the liner, including twelve Americans, were in the dining room when Molqi and his terrorists slunk out of Cabin 82 armed with Soviet AK-47 rifles, pistols, and hand grenades. They burst into the dining room shouting and wildly discharging firearms into the overhead. Two people were slightly wounded. Terrified, the others were quickly subdued and sequestered in the dining room.

Two of the terrorists immediately stormed the bridge and took control. Molqi ordered the ship's captain, Gerardo de Rosa, to put the ship into radio silence and head for the Syrian port of Tartus.

Now, isolated on the sea off Tartus, the terrorists threatened to murder everyone aboard unless their demands were met.

To show he meant business as his deadline of 3:00 p.m. arrived, Molqi singled out sixty-nine-year-old Leon Klinghoffer, a retired Jewish-American from New York. Klinghoffer was partially paralyzed from two recent strokes and confined to a wheelchair. He and his wife Marilyn were on the cruise to celebrate their thirty-sixth wedding anniversary.

"The terrorists ordered me to leave him," Marilyn later related. "I begged them to let me stay with him. They responded by putting a machine gun to my head and ordered me up the stairs. That was the last time I saw my husband."

Molqi shot Klinghoffer with a pistol once in the chest and once in the head, then forced the ship's barber and a waiter to throw the body and wheelchair overboard. His body washed ashore on the Syrian coast a week later.

Molqi then selected a second victim, another American named Mildred Hodes, and issued a threat over the radio that he would kill her unless Syria allowed the ship refuge in Tartus. Before he carried out his threat, however, the PLF and PLO leaderships appeared to be rethinking the situation. Abu Abbas, PLF leader and mastermind behind the hijacking to begin with, one of Yasser Arafat's chief lieutenants, broadcast a message over an Arab-speaking radio station directing the hijackers to return to Egypt without harming the hostages. Kling-hoffer's murder had not yet been revealed to the world.

Achille Lauro set sail at 4:30 p.m. to take advantage of the coming darkness. U.S. E2-C Hawkeye electronics surveillance airplanes and warships from U.S. European Command shadowed the liner until it anchored at Port Said that night.

Back in the United States, General Stiner received President Reagan's go-ahead to launch his Task Force. Elements began arriving at Cyprus and Sigonella the same night the cruise ship anchored at Port Said. Italian military leaders and General Stiner's Americans hammered out a takedown plan in which SEALs from Team Six approached the *Achille Lauro* after dark Wednesday night in small boats with silenced engines, climbed aboard, found the terrorists, and eliminated them.

International politics tossed a monkey wrench into the plan before it went into production. Politics in the Cold War could be deceitful and treacherous.

Yasser Arafat dispatched two emissaries to Egypt to negotiate a peaceful settlement, one of them being Abu Abbas. They, along with ambassadors from Italy and West Germany, went aboard the *Achille Lauro* bearing a guarantee from Egypt that the hijackers would receive safe passage to their country of choice if they released the hostages without harming them. Up to this point, no one off the ship knew of Klinghoffer's fate. Earlier, Molqi had forced Captain de Rosa to make a statement as the liner neared Egypt.

"I am the captain," he radioed. "I am speaking from my office; and everybody is in good health."

Intelligence the CIA picked up indicated Arafat had "under the table" agreements with Egypt and Italy that he would not attempt to bring down their governments if they allowed the PLO to operate freely within their countries. These two countries, therefore, were willing to negotiate with terrorists.

To Israel and the United States, however, a terrorist attack was the same as a military attack—not to be met with appeasement but with military force. SEAL Team Six continued to refine its plans for a Wednesday night assault on the ship.

Wednesday afternoon, the Egyptian government announced, "At four twenty p.m. the hijackers, whose number is four, agreed to surrender without preconditions. They surrendered at five p.m."

Another announcement followed shortly thereafter, "The four hijackers have left the ship and are heading out of Egypt."

That was a lie. While the hijackers had indeed left the ship, they had not departed the country. As soon as he was freed, a distraught Captain de Rosa exposed the truth about Klinghoffer.

I had never seen CNO Watkins so furious. "Those bastards! Egypt knew the terrorists killed that old man and they still promised to let them go."

Nicolas Veliotes, U.S. ambassador to Egypt, contacted Egyptian foreign minister Abdel Meguid. "I want those sons of bitches prosecuted," he demanded.

Meguid dodged, insisting the terrorists were already out of the country. President Hosni Mubarak told Veliotes the same thing the next morning. "The terrorists have already left Egypt. I don't know where they went, but they possibly went to Tunis."

Another lie. The hijackers were still sitting in an EgyptAir 737 at Al Mazi Air Base near Cairo while Egypt attempted to find a country that would take them. U.S. Marine Lieutenant Colonel Oliver North, President Reagan's National Security Council representative for counterterrorism, suggested that it was not too late to take possible action. Since the EgyptAir flight had not taken off yet, why not use planes from the USS *Saratoga* to force it down at a friendly airport? He proposed the NATO base at Sigonella in Sicily where SEAL Team Six was staged.

President Reagan agreed.

CIA sources reported the terrorists intended to fly to Tunisia. The Egyptian Boeing 737 left Cairo on Thursday carrying Arafat's PLO negotiators and security officers from an Egyptian counterterrorism unit in addition to the four terrorists. Aerial tankers, an E-2C Hawkeye radar plane, and a C-141 with SEALs aboard took off from Sicily to intercept while six U.S. Navy F-14 Tomcats zipped into the sky from the USS *Saratoga*.

Four of the jets pulled into escort formation around the 737. U.S. electronic countermeasures jammed the airliner's transmissions so it could not contact Egypt. Tunisia succumbed to pressure from the U.S. and now refused to allow the Egyptian plane to land. F-14 Tomcats directed the airliner to put down at the NATO air base in Sicily, under orders of U.S. Secretary of Defense Caspar Weinberger.

Italy at first refused the plane permission to land, apparently out of fear of offending Arafat and the PLO. But the chairman of JCS, Admiral William J. Crowe, directed it to land whether the Italians liked it or not. A U.S. Navy lieutenant in the Sigonella tower pushed the Italian controller out of the way, took the mike, and ordered the airliner to obey or be shot down. As the plane went wheels down on the runway and rolled out onto the apron, Commander Robert Gormly and a contingent of his SEAL Team Six met it in pickup trucks and surrounded it, prepared to assault the aircraft and take its passengers into custody.

Fifteen minutes later, with the plane surrounded by eighty or ninety SEALs and Delta operators, squads of Italian troops and carabinieri showed up from everywhere. In pickup trucks and cars, on motorbikes, running on foot, even piled onto three-wheeled construction carts with five or six men in the dump buckets. Like an old Laurel and Hardy movie from the 1920s.

The outer ring of Americans, outnumbered three to one, faced the Italians. Two heavily armed allied forces squared off against each other with guns pointed, an impasse so tense those of us in SCIFs or in the Tank at the Pentagon felt it vibrating the air. I overheard radio transmissions of a SEAL officer, whose voice I failed to recognize, discussing with Commander Gormly whether he should order his men to open fire on the Italians.

"The 737 isn't going anywhere," Gormly vowed to another American over his radio.

We at the Pentagon heard veteran SEAL Bobby Lewis, who had the front of the plane blocked with a truck, radio Gormly as a furious Italian officer declared he and his men were boarding whether the Americans liked it or not.

"Boss, you'd better get over here. The Italians are about to assault my position."

"Damn! *DAMN!*" was all Admiral Watkins seemed able to manage as American and Italian diplomats and military officials on the ground in Sigonella frantically negotiated over who took custody of the hijackers.

General Stiner called Vice Admiral Arthur Moreau, Admiral Crowe's assistant at the Joint Chiefs of Staff. He laid out the situation in his typically calm and controlled manner while some of us crowded around Moreau in the Tank to listen.

"I want to bring you up to speed and to re-verify my mission," Stiner said. "Here is the situation: we have the plane. I have verified that the four terrorists are on board, along with eight to ten armed guards from the 77 Force, which I do not consider a threat. Also, there are two other men, one a tough-looking Arab in his mid-forties, who has to be important, and a younger redheaded, freckled-face guy sitting at a table with him. We have not been able to identify these two. I have already taken the pilot off the plane, along with another individual who claims to be an ambassador. He is now calling back to Egypt and we are monitoring his phone conversations. Mostly, he is requesting guidance to deal with the terrible situation they have ended up in.

"The Italian base commander here at Sigonella felt that he had to react. I think more to save face than anything else. In my estimation, they have positioned about three hundred or so troops in a perimeter around us. We are eyeball to eyeball. I have an Italian three-star with me. He has called all the way back to his Ministry of Defense and can find no one with any knowledge of an agreement to turn over the terrorists to us. I have also talked to Ambassador Rabb, and he has no knowledge of such an agreement.

"I am worried about our situation. We have the firepower to prevail. But I am concerned about the immaturity of the Italian troops, some of whom are green conscripts, as well as the absence of anybody with the ability to control them in this tense situation. A backfire from a motorbike or construction cart could precipitate a shooting incident that could lead to a lot of Italian casualties. And I don't believe that our beef is with our ally, the Italians, but rather with the terrorists.

"I just want to re-verify that my mission is to take the terrorists off the plane and bring them back to the U.S."

The Joint Chiefs went into a huddle. Five minutes later, Admiral Crowe responded to Stiner: "You are the ranking American on the scene. You do what you think is right."

Sounded to me like he was passing the buck in case everything went to shit.

Diplomats finally resolved the five-hour impasse as dawn broke over the NATO airfield. Secretary of State George Shultz received assurances from the Italians that the terrorists would be retained and tried for murder in Italy. Molqi and his band surrendered to SEAL Team Six. General Stiner turned them over to the Italians.

Not trusting the Italians to keep their word, Commander Gormly and a contingent of SEALs in a U.S. C-141 Starlighter shadowed the Egyptian airliner when it flew the prisoners to Rome. Claiming engine trouble, The C-141 even landed directly behind the hijackers and their carabinieri guards.

Italian authorities had balls the size of BBs. The freckle-face traveling with Klingenhoffer's killers was a political officer of the Cairo PLO, a man named Hassan. The tough-looking character was Abu Abbas, wanted by the United States for terrorism. After the plane landed at Rome, Italian authorities refused to turn him over to us. They seemed to want nothing more than to appease the PLO. Hassan and Abbas were tucked safely into passenger seats when the EgyptAir 737 returned to Cairo.

If it were up to me, I think I would have shot the bastards out of the sky and claimed temporary insanity. What a bunch of chicken shits we had for allies.

I yawned. It was over. I went home emotionally and physically drained. Barbara was waiting for me.

"What's for dinner?" I asked.

CHAPTER FIFTY-NINE

OST OF MY LIFE up to this point had been filled with various tyrants and killers. Terrorists in Lebanon, Cold War insurgents in Vietnam and Africa, communist guerrillas in Cuba and Nicaragua. . . . It was a never-ending cycle requiring we either continue to fight or succumb. There seemed to be no middle ground.

I was at home one evening in my favorite reading chair when Barbara sat on its arm and leaned over wearing that amazing smile of hers. "What are you reading, Bill?"

She reached to see the front cover. Sir Robert Thompson on insurgency.

"Sounds thrilling," she teased.

"We have counterinsurgency down," I said. "It worked for us in Vietnam, but we lost the war to politicians at home. We're infants, though, when it comes to building insurgencies to fight against the communists. Things are about to fall down around our ears in Nicaragua."

Shortly before I left the CIA to return to the Navy in 1979, the Frente Sandinista de Liberacion Nacional (FSLN) led by Daniel Ortega ousted Nicaragua's current dictator, Anastasa Somoza, and set about fundamentally transforming the little nation, Cuban style.

"You are either with the Soviets or you are against them," declared Humberto Ortega, Daniel's brother and the new regime's minister of defense. "We are with the Soviets. . . . Sandinism without Marxist-Leninism cannot be revolutionary. Because of this they are indivisibly united and, therefore . . . our political force is Sandinism and our doctrine is Marxist-Leninism."

Daniel Ortega aligned himself with Castro, Moscow, and the Eastern Bloc and began exporting revolution to El Salvador and other Central American countries. In Nicaragua, he simply replaced the Somoza dictatorship with his own and crushed any signs of democratic sentiment more ruthlessly than Somoza ever had. He seized television and radio stations, censored newspapers, and set about on the path of Stalin to nationalizing means of production, seizing and redistributing wealth, and initiating what passed for land reform in communist nations. That meant stripping farmers of private ownership and casting them onto collective farms patterned after the *kolkhozes* of the Stalinist era that led to famine and the starvation deaths of some ten million peasants.

Sandinista tanks and troops attacked Miskito Indian farmers who resisted relocation, burning their houses and leaving bodies where they fell.

Supermarket shelves where food was once abundant went bare. Poultry, beef, pork, fish, and staples like rice and beans were rationed and often unobtainable. Homemakers stood in lines all day for a roll of toilet paper or a can of cooking oil. Ragged, half-naked children prowled the streets and fought over scraps of food.

A military draft made it illegal for a teenager to leave the country for any reason other than advanced military training in Cuba or some other Soviet Bloc nation. Mail was censored, telephone calls monitored, and "block captains" reported directly to the Sandinista Defense Committee in a system of "people control" modeled after Cuba's. Thousands vanished into Managua's infamous El Chipote prison.

At least 400,000 people out of a 1979 population of 2,800,000 fled Nicaragua. Most of them were poor. Laborers, campesinos, factory workers, white-collar day workers, the so-called proletariat that Marxists always claimed to champion and protect.

Liberation theology was the going philosophy throughout Latin America. Left-wing priests, Jesuits, and nuns claimed Jesus advocated the violent overthrow of ruthless capitalist systems and replacing them by compassionate communism.

The official head of the Human Rights Office in Nicaragua was an American nun who assumed the moniker Sister Mary Hartman. She assured nosy reporters that no political prisoners were being held by the Ortegas. Not a single one.

"Your problem is that you don't understand the poor," she scolded. "I think the U.S. is evil. I am afraid to go back home very often because of fear of an outbreak of fascism in the streets."

I always found such people incomprehensible in their thinking. It wasn't like they got drunk at a Managua cantina one night, picked up a lovely senorita, then awoke the next morning to find themselves in bed with a slut. They should have known she was a communist slut when they entered the bar.

President Jimmy Carter seemed to have been among the most eager to jump into the bed. During Danny Ortega's first eighteen months as new dictator and avowed communist, the Carter administration provided him with 100,000 tons of food, $142.6 million in economic aid, and helped the Sandinistas obtain $1.6 billion from international lending institutions and Western governments.

Even while the Carter administration helped the new collectivist state get on its feet, the CIA discovered a combat brigade of Soviet troops setting up in Cuba. I remembered all too well the Cuban Missile Crisis. At first, Carter took a Kennedy stance and called the presence of Russian troops on our doorstep "unacceptable." Nonetheless, he capitulated almost immediately and abandoned his stand.

In a major address to the nation, he said he was "satisfied by assurances . . . from the highest level of the Soviet government that the Soviet personnel in Cuba are not and will not be a threat to the United States or any other nation."

The Soviet brigade remained on the island.

During his 1980 campaign for the presidency, Ronald Reagan had vowed to stop the spread of communism throughout Latin America and the world and to take on international terrorism. Iran released our American hostages as soon as he moved into the White House in 1981, and Jimmy Carter received that year's Nobel Peace Prize. Nobel chairman Gunnar Berge took a swipe at the new president's stance against communism.

The award to Carter, he said, "should be interpreted as a criticism of the [anti-communist] line the current administration has taken. It's a kick in the leg to all that follow the same line as the United States."

The Reagan Doctrine piqued the ire of opponents by advocating military support for movements opposing Soviet-sponsored communist governments around the world. An increasingly liberal Congress, intent on "détente" with the Soviet Union, fought to block President Reagan's efforts to provide assistance to anticommunist Nicaraguan guerrillas known as Contras, who were training and organizing in Honduras to fight Ortega's Sandinistas.

Prior to an important Congressional vote on aid to the Contras, the communist Nicaraguan minister of interior, Tomas Borge, employed the law firm of Reichler & Applebaum in D.C. to research "human rights abuses by Contras." By no coincidence, that attorney, Reed Brody, released the report just prior to the vote. During his "research" in Nicaragua, he was housed and given office space by the Sandinistas. Naturally, his report reflected unfavorably on the Contras.

Even while Nicaraguan campesinos were being slaughtered and dissenters by the thousands imprisoned, Democratic Senator Tom Harkin of Iowa and Massachusetts Senator John Kerry met with Ortega and proclaimed him "a misunderstood democrat rather than a Marxist autocrat."

The Democratic leadership in the House of Representatives dispatched a "Dear Commandante" letter to Ortega, commending his efforts to install "democracy" in his country. The letter expressed regret over the declining relationship between Nicaragua and the U.S. and pledged the congressmen's support for the Sandinistas. The letter was signed by House Majority Leader Jim Wright and nine other congressmen.

Congressman Newt Gingrich, Georgia Republican, called the letter "a remarkable statement to a foreign dictator. It shows sympathy and support for his actions against the U.S. government."

Sometimes I felt like batting my head against the wall in frustration. What was the matter with all these people? Didn't they know the history of how communism always arrived in a country by force and ended up murdering and enslaving millions? The Iron Curtain was not intended to keep people *out*; it was built to keep people *in*.

American "progressives" swarmed Managua to witness and celebrate the rise of another socialist utopia. Celebrities and politicians donated blood for communists injured by campesinos who fought back. They returned to the United States singing joyous hallelujahs to Marxism. We called them "Sandalistas." They arrived on their buses, chanting, "We are Sandinistas too!"

"People are afraid," said a former Sandinista now in exile. "Sandinistas hold the power because they hold the guns. They are killing those who oppose them."

American UW and counterterrorism efforts suffered serious setbacks at a time when worldwide Islamic terrorism was exploding, literally, and when Islamists and communists seemed to be cooperating with each other. It seemed all the Sandinistas had to do in order to survive and spread communism throughout the southern American hemisphere was to outlast the Reagan administration.

The third Boland Amendment passed by the U.S. Congress cut off all funds to the Contras in 1985. It prohibited the CIA, the Defense Department, in fact all U.S. government agencies from aiding the anti-communist Contras in any way. American resistance to communism and terrorism was rapidly being torn to shambles in Washington, D.C.

Perhaps I was tired after all these years as a Cold War warrior, a night fighter against evil. There seemed to be fewer and fewer of us willing to keep up the good fight. Optimism about my country and future seemed to be draining from my pores.

"Barb," I said, "I am afraid that the generations that follow us will soon give up and live in tyranny."

CHAPTER SIXTY

Efforts to keep the Contra insurgency alive were about to collapse around the ears of the president of the United States and generate a political scandal exceeded only by that of Watergate and the impeachment of President Richard Nixon.

At 9:50 a.m. on October 5, 1986, a World War II era C-123 transport aircraft filled with automatic M-16 rifles, ammunition, and rocket-propelled grenade launchers lumbered off Llopango Air Base in San Salvador on its way to a supply drop for the FDN (Nicaraguan Democratic Front, the Contras) inside Nicaragua. The three-man crew—pilot Bill Cooper, copilot Buzz Sawyer, and dropmaster Eugene Hasenfus—were veterans of CIA air ops in Vietnam and Southeast Asia.

Later that morning, a Sandinista Soviet-made SAM-7 ground-to-air missile brought the plane down. Cooper, Sawyer, and a Contra security officer died in the fiery crash. Hasenfus, a lanky, red-haired Midwesterner, parachuted from the stricken plane and was captured by Nicaraguan authorities.

I knew the shit was about to hit the propeller when the Lebanese magazine *Ash-Shiraa* published a piece on Hasenfus's capture that exposed a secret U.S. arrangement with Iran to trade weapons for hostages.

After Congress blocked all aid to the Contras, the Reagan administration had arranged funding and military supplies for the FDN through third countries and private sources. It raised some $36 million between 1984 and 1986. Marine Lieutenant Colonel Oliver North, deputy director for military affairs at the National Security Council, ran the secret assistance. A highly decorated platoon commander in Vietnam, North created "The Enterprise," which served as the secret arm of the NSC. It had its own transport airplanes, pilots, access to the airfield in El Salvador, a ship, clandestine operatives, and a secret Swiss bank account. In effect, the NSA was what the CIA used to be.

At the Pentagon, we turned a blind eye to what was going on and kept our mouths shut. After all, most of us agreed with President Reagan that *something* had to be done to stop the commies from taking over the hemisphere. What we did not know until afterwards, although there were rumors, was that President Reagan may have gone a step too far in his efforts to aid the Contras.

The president had been recovering from colon cancer at Bethesda Naval Hospital in 1985 when NSA Security Advisor Robert McFarlane told him that representatives from Israel had contacted the NSA with confidential information that a "moderate" Iranian faction opposing Ayatollah Khomeini's hard-line anti-American stance wanted to establish a quiet relationship with the United States. To demonstrate their seriousness, the "moderates" offered to persuade Hezbollah militants to release U.S. hostages seized in Lebanon.

In return, the U.S. must provide weapons to the politically influential factions in their struggle to depose Khomeini. These weapons would be used to run out terrorists that had prompted the U.S. to declare Iran a state sponsor of terrorism and establish a secular democratic government in Iran. The scheme was for Israel to ship weapons to the Iranian moderates, whereupon the U.S. would resupply Israel and receive payment from Iran through Israel. Secretary of State George Shultz and Secretary of Defense Caspar Weinberger opposed the deal, since U.S. law prohibited negotiating with terrorists.

"Look, we all agree we can't pay ransom to Hezbollah to get the hostages," Reagan argued. "But we are not dealing with Hezbollah, we are not doing a thing for them. We are trying to help some people who are looking forward to becoming the next government of Iran, and they are getting the weapons in return for saying that they are going to try to use their influence to free our hostages."

Oliver North offered an adjustment to the plan. Instead of selling arms through Israel, why not sell direct and use a portion of the proceeds to aid the Contra freedom fighters? Although U.S. law also prohibited sales of weapons to Iran, which presumably included any of its factions, arms sales began on August 30, 1985, with one hundred American-made TOW antitank missiles, followed by 408 more the following month. Other arms shipments continued over the next several months.

Hezbollah released David Jacobsen and Father Lawrence Jenco, former head of Catholic Relief Services in Lebanon, and promised to release the remaining two hostages. They never did. In fact, a different terrorist group in Lebanon abducted three more Americans in September/October 1986—Frank Reed, Joseph Cicippio, and Edward Tracy.

The scandal broke on November 24, 1986, when Attorney General Ed Meese and White House Chief of Staff Don Regan discovered a memo indicating that Ollie North was working with an Iranian faction to arrange release of American hostages through weapons sales and that part of the money from the sales went to the Contras.

Investigations followed through the Reagan-appointed Tower Commission. Felix Rodriguez, who had run weapons to the FDN out of El Salvador, testified before congressional investigators in a highly charged confrontation with Senator John Kerry. I sat in on the hearing and felt like standing up and cheering for Felix.

"Mr. Rodriguez, you have to understand that there are many allegations about the Contras that we have to probe," Kerry began.

"Senator, *you* should know that there is a disinformation apparatus within the Soviet and Cuban intelligence services. It is in the best interests of the Soviets and the Cubans that the Nicaraguan Freedom Fighters do not prevail."

It quickly became apparent that Kerry was simply speaking to hear himself talk, to make a record for his own benefit and pave the way for higher political aspirations. At one point, he even asked Felix why he did not try harder to save Che Guevara's life in Bolivia.

The verbal sparring continued until Felix lost his temper. "Senator, this has been the hardest testimony I ever gave in my life."

Kerry looked up, glasses perched on his nose. "Why?"

"Because, sir, it is extremely difficult to have to answer a question from someone you do not respect."

I almost *did* jump up to cheer.

Secretary of State Caspar Weinberger and thirteen other administration officials were indicted, eleven of whom were convicted. Most of the convictions were vacated on appeal. President Reagan was absolved of direct knowledge of North's Contra-Iran weapons arrangement, but the Tower Commission criticized him for not properly supervising subordinates in his administration.

Lieutenant Colonel Oliver North took the biggest fall and kept his mouth shut. He was convicted on three felony counts. He received a three-year suspended prison term, two years' probation, a fine, and community service. His convictions were later vacated.

I shook his hand the next time I saw him at the Pentagon. "Fighting terrorism and communism is getting harder and more dangerous ever year," I commented.

"We can't ever give up, Bone. It's all over if we do."

Chapter Sixty-One

I WAS CURLED UP IN my easy chair, wearing glasses, reading a paperback novel.

"It's the end of the world. I've never had to imagine anything like that before."

John Osborne laughed. "It's not the end of the world at all," he said. "It's only the end of us. The world will go on just the same, only we shan't be in it. I dare say it will get along all right without us."

Dwight Towers shook his head. "I suppose that's right. . . ." He paused, thinking of the flowering trees that he had seen on shore through the periscope, cascaras and flame trees, the palms standing in the sunlight. "Maybe we've been too silly to deserve a world like this."

Barbara entered the room, wearing her nightgown. "Honey, it's late. This isn't like you."

I showed her the garish cover. *On the Beach* by Nevil Shute. I summarized the plot for her. "There's been this nuclear war, and the whole world is gone. Radiation has killed everybody. Now some people are setting out in a submarine to see if they can find other people alive."

"I know, honey. I've read it."

Of course she had. Barbara was no stereotypical blonde.

"Heavy stuff," she acknowledged.

"Doll, it *could* happen. You know that, right?"

The window next to me was dark, as though nothing existed beyond it. After a long moment, I added, "In fact, it may be happening now."

Seldom has a time existed in my life that I hadn't thought of that day at Annapolis when our instructor entered the classroom to announce that the United States had dropped an atomic bomb on Japan. It marked the beginning of my interest in unconventional warfare as an alternative to the world's destroying itself. That was nearly forty years ago, and the drama of nuclear terrorism had not yet reached Act III.

After President Reagan assumed the White House in 1981, I was appointed to various panels and advisory and consulting groups to discuss the U.S. official position on nuclear war. Conferences, meetings, discussions, summits . . . seemed to consume politics. All we did seemed to be to *discuss*—while we dug ourselves deeper and deeper into the insane philosophy of Mutual Assured Destruction. Reagan referred to MAD as a "suicide pact" strategy.

I learned of "Star Wars" in a conversation with Secretary of State George Shultz. According to him, shortly after Reagan became governor of California, he attended a lecture by physicist Edward Teller held at the Lawrence Livermore National Laboratory. Teller had worked at Los Alamos in developing both the atomic bomb and the hydrogen bomb. His lecture was on the feasibility of defending against nuclear missiles *with* nuclear missiles.

Nothing came of Teller's ideas for more than a decade afterwards. But the concept apparently continued to ferment in Reagan's mind. In 1979 as he prepared for his second run at the presidency, he visited the NORAD command base at the Cheyenne Mountain Complex where he was shown extensive U.S. missile tracking and detection systems that extended throughout the world and into space. What struck him most was a comment that while the system could track incoming missiles and thereby warn individual targets, *nothing* could be done to intercept and stop them.

Reagan requested Lieutenant General Daniel O. Graham, a campaign advisor, to come up with a strategic defense concept using ground- and space-based weapons now theoretically possible because of emerging technologies. Reagan and Graham referred to it as "High Frontier."

Shortly after Reagan won the election and moved to Washington, he called a meeting of the Joint Chiefs of Staff. I attended as an advisor to the CNO, Admiral James Watkins. It was my first meeting with Ronald Reagan, who reminded me of an elderly uncle until you saw the shrewd intellect behind the septuagenarian appearance. He exuded confidence and purpose. The United States, I thought, might be in good hands.

The president stood at the head of the long polished table. He said, "Every offensive weapon ever invented by man has resulted in the creation of a defense against it. Isn't it possible in the age of technology that we could invent a defensive weapon that could intercept nuclear weapons and destroy them as they emerged from their silos?"

After Reagan finished explaining his "High Frontier" concept, the Chiefs of Staff looked at each other, then asked if they could consider among themselves for a few moments. Reagan nodded and walked out of the room. So did us advisors.

Shortly, the JCS came out of its huddle. "Let's do it," said the JCS Chairman, General John Vessey, a rail-thin army officer with a hawkish face.

The Strategic Defense Initiative (SDI) was born.

CHAPTER SIXTY-TWO

"**N**UCLEAR FREEZE" WAS THE current buzzword among peaceniks in the United States, who saw as the path to peace the U.S. and USSR "freezing" their production of nuclear weapons at the current level. As much as I would have liked to bury the genie, I had to agree with the president. The Soviets were way ahead in numbers of nuclear weapons; Reagan, thought to support a freeze, would leave the Russians in a position of nuclear superiority and amount to a unilateral disarmament by the United States.

On March 8, 1983, Reagan delivered what soon came to be known as the Evil Empire speech, which ushered in a major escalation of Cold War rhetoric and set up a howl among the political class and the chattering news media community. According to George Shultz, the speech was designed to let the Soviets know we knew what they were up to in preaching for a freeze.

"The Soviet leaders have openly and publicly declared that the only morality they recognize is that which will further their cause, which is world revolution," Reagan began. "They must be made to understand that we will never compromise our principles and standards. We will never give away our freedom. . . . I would agree to a freeze if only we could freeze the Soviets' global desires. A freeze at current levels of weapons would remove any incentive for the Soviets to negotiate seriously in Geneva and virtually end our chances to achieve the major arms reductions which we have proposed. Instead, they would achieve *their* objectives through the freeze. . . . (L)et us be aware that while they preach the supremacy of the state, declare its omnipotence over individual man, and predict its eventual domination of all peoples on the earth, they are the focus of evil in the modern world. . . .

"If history teaches anything, it teaches that simpleminded appeasement or wishful thinking about our adversaries is folly. It means the betrayal of our past, the squandering of our freedom. . . . In your discussions of the nuclear freeze proposals, I urge you to beware the temptation of . . . blithely declaring yourselves above it all and label both sides equally at fault, to ignore the facts of history and the aggressive impulses of an evil empire, to simply call the arms race a giant misunderstanding and thereby remove yourself from the struggle between right and wrong and good and evil. . . .

"I believe we shall rise to the challenge. I believe that communism is another sad, bizarre chapter in history whose pages even now are being written."

Three weeks later, on March 23, President Reagan introduced SDI in a speech televised to the nation.

"Let me share with you a vision of the future which offers hope," he stated. "It is that we embark on a program to counter the awesome Soviet missile threat with measures that are defensive. Let us turn to the very strengths in technology that spawned our great industrial base and that have given us the quality of life we enjoy today.

"What if free people could live secure in the knowledge that their security did not rest upon the threat of instant U.S. retaliation to deter a Soviet attack, that we could intercept and destroy strategic ballistic missiles before they reached our own soil or that of our allies . . . ?

"Tonight, consistent with our obligations under the ABM [Antiballistic Missile] Treaty . . . I'm taking the important first step. I am directing a comprehensive and intensive effort to define a long-term research and development program to begin to achieve our ultimate goal of eliminating the threat posed by strategic nuclear missiles. This could pave the way for arms control measures to eliminate the weapons themselves. We seek neither military superiority nor political advantage. Our only purpose—one all people share—is to search for ways to reduce the danger of nuclear war."

The president appointed a past director of the NASA Space Shuttle Program, Air Force Lieutenant General James Alan Abrahamson, to oversee the Strategic Defense Initiative Organization (SDIO). I worked with SDIO to help draft a policy "to ensure the security, integrity, confidentiality and mission availability of all SDI assets . . . in the face of direct attempts to degrade, disrupt, destroy, or usurp the various elements."

At Lawrence Livermore National Laboratory, a scientist named Peter Hagelstein and his team called the O Group began efforts to design a nuclear explosion-powered X-ray as SDI's initial focus. The system they envisioned combined ground-based and space-based sensor units, orbital space platforms, and lasers to shoot down incoming Soviet intercontinental ballistic missiles.

A news article published by the *Washington Post* the day after Reagan's speech introducing SDI quoted Senator Edward Kennedy of Massachusetts describing the president's proposal as "reckless Star Wars schemes." His reference was to the George Lucas *Star Wars* movies still running in theaters nationwide. In my opinion, in this real-life drama, the United States played hero Luke Skywalker while Russian leaders assumed the role of villain Darth Vader.

Reagan's critics used the "Star Wars" tag derisively, implying it was impractical science fiction fantasy. The American media's mockery did much to damage the program's credibility in the public mind. The Soviets, however, took it seriously. They viewed SDI as an effort to seize the strategic initiative in arms control by neutralizing the military components of Soviet strategy. The Kremlin released statements condemning SDI, saying space-based missile systems made nuclear war inevitable.

Through DCI William J. Casey, I obtained secret plans the Soviets intended their KGB agents and other officials to use in discrediting, penetrating, or otherwise destroying SDI. It was a hefty document that revealed much not only about the structure of communism and its worldwide goals and activities but also about Judas goats hidden inside the West. Clearly, the Soviets were concerned SDI might interfere with their aim of subjugating the world to the "working man."

The missive began with a cover paragraph stating, "As a part of the continuing effort by ruling circles in the United States to achieve dominance and prevent the achievement of the peaceful objectives of the Soviet Union, in March 1983 President Reagan announced a new program aimed at disabling Soviet strategic peacekeeping forces and emplacing strike weapons in space.

"This program envisions the development of a multi-layer array of weapons operating over the homeland of the USSR, over the oceans where our seaborne forces operate, and in U.S. territory to nullify the effectiveness of our strategic deterrent forces. It will require highly advanced technology, will cost enormous sums of money, and will extend the arms race into space, destroying the hopes raised by present international arms-control treaties and agreements. In the interest of mankind's progress, the Soviet Union is obliged to resist this development by every means. . . .

"The proposed Star Wars systems are vulnerable in all stages of their development. The purpose of this study is to identify those vulnerabilities and outline means, excluding direct military attack, for exploiting them.

"The first and most fundamental vulnerability is political, primarily within the U.S. governmental system. . . . Clearly, if ways can be found to cause the defunding of Star Wars, our central objective will have been achieved without any need for other, more costly and risky, countermeasures on our part. Therefore we attach high priority to political measures against Star Wars. An example of such measures is discrete support of anti-Star Wars scientific and popular groups in the U.S. . . . In parallel with such public, high-profile activities as our "Star Peace" program being presented to the world via the United Nations, we must continue to identify reliable and respected Western opponents of Star Wars and do what we can to advance our cause. Direct sponsorship of such people is out of the question because it would destroy their credibility in internal U.S. debates. Therefore, we must use more indirect methods as discussed later below."

The document then listed some of these "indirect methods," to include:

- Propaganda through both overt and covert channels
- Diplomacy by injecting the issue into all negotiations with the U.S.
- Organizing protests against it through sympathetic organizations such as the World Peace Council, International Organization of Journalists, World Council of Churches, United States Peace Council, World Federation of Teachers Union, and others
- Influencing the U.S. Congress by working with students, journalists, scientists, lawyers, clergymen, physicians, and others to effect policy change in Washington
- Activate deep-cover agents under KGB and GRU control to leak forged documents to the press implicating illegal transactions between SDI representatives and "the military-industrial complex."
- Participation by the Communist Party of the United States (CPUSA), the missive emphasized, "will be held to a minimum, as this fraternal party is unfortunately too closely identified in the U.S. public mind as an arm of Soviet foreign policy."

The entire thing was a masterful exercise in subterfuge and deceit. These guys were good at what they did.

The report concluded with, "Emphasis must be placed throughout that this sad waste by a misguided U.S. government . . . is occurring at a historic moment in the superpower relationship—a time when the current leadership of the Soviet Union is consciously and obviously striving to eliminate the climate of mutual distrust and fear which has led to the superpower arms race. . . .

"Again, 'Star Wars' must be presented to this 'soft' audience in the context of 'peaceful' Soviet proposals for cooperative, 'progressive' uses of high technology, like space exploration, and advanced medical research. [The search for a cure for AIDS is a subject which surveys have shown meets with high levels of approval across most ethnic, cultural and educational achievement lines]. . . Absence of U.S.

collaboration in worthy causes which should benefit mankind should be lamented, caused by diversion of huge amounts of funds, talent and energy into the useless 'Star Wars,' which has impeded the social, medical, and nutritional benefits that modern-day technology rightfully should be achieving."

Even while the Soviets were mouthing platitudes of "peace" and "cooperation," Secretary General Yuri Andropov continued to pursue the same agenda as previous Russian leaders had in their quest for world domination, stirring up insurgencies, funding rebel communist guerrillas, suppressing revolts against communism as in Hungary, keeping satellites like Poland and East Germany encased in the Soviet iron fist.

Conflict between the West and communism repeatedly brought the world to the very brink of nuclear war. On the night of August 31, 1983, Russian fighter planes shot down Korean Airliner Flight 007, killing all 269 passengers, including a U.S. congressman and sixty other Americans. Andropov claimed the Boeing 747 was on a "spy mission" over Soviet territory. Like the biggest bully on the block, he refused to back off his accusations.

I believed more and more that Reagan was on the right track.

Incredibly, some at the Pentagon claimed an all-out nuclear war with the Soviets was "winnable." I knew there were Soviets who thought the same thing. One day CNO Watkins returned from a briefing at the White House with President Reagan, Cap Weinberger, and General John Vessey, JCS chairman. The briefing centered on a U.S. plan for defense in the event of a surprise nuclear attack before we had an adequate deterrent. Essentially, the plan was another take on MAD. The CNO wanted my opinion.

"What you've described," I replied, "could lead to the end of civilization."

Barbara and I watched *The Day After* on TV, a movie in which a nuclear strike wiped out Lawrence, Kansas. Scenes from it burned themselves into the minds of millions of Americans. Armageddon like that was appearing more frequently in movies and books. People were jittery, uncertain, afraid.

Watkins nodded grimly at my response. "The president said the same thing. He thinks Star Wars is the answer to saving the planet."

CHAPTER SIXTY-THREE

SOVIET REPRESENTATIVES CONTINUED TO walk out on arms control talks. Or Soviet leaders died unexpectedly.

General Secretary Andropov sent Reagan a letter proposing another meeting. He died a week later, on February 9, 1984. Konstantin Chernenko took his place. He died on March 10. Mikhail Gorbachev took *his* place.

"How am I supposed to get anywhere with the Russians," Reagan complained to Nancy, "if they keep dying on me?"

Gorbachev insisted the United States halt work on SDI as a prerequisite for future nuclear arms talks. Reagan refused. I recalled a poem JFK was fond of reciting:

> *Bullfight critics ranked in rows*
> *Crowd the enormous plaza full,*
> *But only one in there who knows*
> *And he's the man who fights the bull.*

Ronald Reagan was the man who fought the bull.

In early November 1985, Secretary of State Shultz returned to Washington from a meeting with Gorbachev to talk about *talking*. From what the CNO passed on to me, Shultz found the Soviet leader intelligent, sure of himself, and fully in charge of the USSR.

"But he's full of anti-American, anti-capitalist propaganda," Shultz said. "He thinks arms manufacturers spread anti-Soviet propaganda to keep the arms race alive in order to profit from it."

Later that month, Reagan and Gorbachev met in Geneva. Reagan offered to share SDI and open the laboratories for Gorbachev's inspection. Gorbachev was suspicious. He seemed to believe the U.S. was using SDI as subterfuge for an offensive first-strike capability.

Reagan sent Gorbachev a letter a week after he returned from Geneva: "The truth is that the United States has no intention of using its strategic defense program to gain any advantage and there is no development under way to create space-based weapons. Our goal is to eliminate any possibility of a first strike from either side. This being the case, we should be able to find a way, in practical terms, to relieve the concerns you have expressed."

CIA analysts like my wife Barbara uncovered evidence that the Soviet economy was in dire straits as a result of the arms race. Many of us in the Pentagon as well as at the CIA felt, as Reagan did, that a Soviet economic tailspin would force Gorbachev to come around on an arms reduction agreement.

In the meantime, mayhem kept the rest of the world in a tailspin.

On April 5, 1986, terrorists bombed the *LaBelle* discotheque in West Berlin, killing three people, one of whom was a U.S. serviceman, and injuring twenty-nine. Intelligence services traced the act to Libya.

Libya in North Africa and its leader Muammar Gaddafi had become a major concern to the U.S. after Gaddafi aligned himself with the Soviet Union and expressed ambitions of establishing a new caliphate of Arab and Muslim states. According to the CIA, the little nation was infested with terrorist training camps.

Not only that, Gaddafi was obsessed with becoming a nuclear power and had moved in on nearby Chad and occupied it. Chad was rich in uranium.

President Reagan had already proved himself a leader not to be trifled with. On April 15, he ordered airstrikes against Libya in retaliation for the nightclub bombing in West Germany. The primary target was Gaddafi's own palace. A cheer erupted throughout the Pentagon.

The Soviets remained uncharacteristically quiet about it.

Less than two weeks later, an explosion and fire at the Chernobyl nuclear power plant in the Ukraine spread radiation into the atmosphere and over much of western Russia and Europe. It was the worst nuclear accident in history, killing thirty-one people. Radiation fallout was expected to last into future generations.

The accident brought to front pages around the world the dangers of nuclear power. President Reagan used it as an opportunity to propose to Gorbachev a sweeping new arms summit. The meeting between them occurred in a waterfront home overlooking the Atlantic in Reykjavik, Iceland, in October 1986. Present with the leaders were Secretary of State George Shultz and Gorbachev's Minister of Foreign Affairs, Eduard Shevardnadze.

Everything went along fine until, with a smile on his face, Gorbachev said, "This all depends, of course, on your giving up SDI."

That was when Reagan realized this meeting was all a charade, an attempt to put the U.S. in an awkward position.

He blew up. "I've said again and again that SDI wasn't a bargaining chip. I've told you, if we find out the SDI is practical and feasible we'll make that information known to you and everyone else so that nuclear weapons can be made obsolete. Now, with all we have accomplished here, you do this and throw in this roadblock and everything is out the window. There is no way we are going to give up research to find a defensive weapon against nuclear weapons."

We in the Pentagon knew from daily intelligence briefings that the Soviets were secretly researching a missile defense system similar to SDI. Their technology was inferior, but if the U.S. halted work on SDI we could all wake up one morning to find the USSR now possessed the defense we had given up on. SDI was an insurance policy to guarantee the Soviets kept their word should Reagan and Gorbachev make commitments.

Angry, the president stood up from the table. "The meeting is over. Let's go, George. We're leaving."

Before, the Soviets had always been the ones to walk out.

Gorbachev's continued resistance through most of 1987 were busy months—the Iran-Contra affair; conflicts between Israel and her Arab neighbors; the continuing war between Iran and Iraq and their attempts to close the Persian Gulf to shipping; new efforts by Democrats in Congress to cut U.S. military programs essential for continuing Reagan's policy of peace through strength; a mistaken attack by Iraqi warplanes against the USS *Stark* patrolling off the coast of Saudi Arabia that claimed the lives of thirty-seven U.S. sailors.

After a year of stubbornness and continued expenditures on weapons his country could ill afford, Gorbachev sent Reagan a letter indicating a desire to work out their differences. Prior to their meeting scheduled for December, wily old Reagan played a little night fighter psyops of his own that would definitely catch the attention of Soviet intelligence groups.

Two articles appeared in the November 23 issue of *Aviation Week & Space Technology*:

(T)he Strategic Defense Initiative is starting final preparations for its most ambitious flight test to date, the $200-million-dollar Delta 181 mission set for launch by NASA in early 1988 to obtain data critical for development of multiple SDI satellites planned for the space-based layered defense system.

The Strategic Defense Initiative Organization plans to test two kinetic energy weapons concepts—the space-based interceptor and exoatmospheric reentry interceptor subsystem . . . to demonstrate their economic and technical ability to serve as the kill mechanism for a first phase Strategic Defense System. . . .

On December 7, 1987, the forty-sixth anniversary of the Japanese attack on Pearl Harbor, Mikhail Gorbachev and Ronald Reagan signed the Intermediate-Range Nuclear Forces (INF) Treaty. Each leader made brief remarks. Reagan ended his with an old Russian maxim: *"Dovorey no provorey*—trust but verify."

Gorbachev said, "You repeat that at every meeting."

"I like it."

Reagan observed later how he considered the most important reasons for the historical breakthrough in nuclear talks with the Soviets was SDI and America's overall modernization of our military forces. What few of us foresaw was that in trying to keep up with the U.S. in the arms race the USSR had expended its last resources on weapons systems and spent itself into bankruptcy and exhaustion. The Evil Empire was on its last legs.

CHAPTER SIXTY-FOUR

TIME. SOMEONE ONCE CALCULATED that God gave a person about twenty-five thousand days to spend if he lived an average life span. Each day spent was like taking a seed out of a jug containing that number and tossing it out the window as you sped down a highway. That seed was gone forever and you seldom knew if it sprouted new seed or if it withered.

Dad used his seed the best he could. He died between my time at the CIA and my return to active naval duty. Died of heart failure at the age of seventy and lay buried at Arlington National Cemetery. Mom stayed on at Virginia Beach and eventually married Dad's old classmate, Joe Briggs, from the Naval Academy. She too was ailing from a heart problem. I made every effort to see her often. She always welcomed Barbara and me with a warm hug and that big tolerant smile of hers that she wore all her life. With her I always felt the little boy again nibbled by something in the surf, afraid to go back in the ocean until she proved to me it was all right.

"You *participate* when you are young," I remember Dad saying. "When you grow old, you step back and *watch* others participate."

I was over sixty years old now. I figured I had about four thousand seeds left, more or less. I was weary, had more lines in my face, my height was a bit stooped, my steps were a little more deliberate, but otherwise I was in fair shape. Sometimes I thought I was at that stage

Dad talked about, no longer a participant in great events but instead an observer. Perhaps that was part of acquiring wisdom, that you could look back and make some sense of it all.

Former communist Whittaker Chambers in his 1952 autobiography *Witness* expressed his belief that communism would ultimately triumph because of the "intensity of faith" communists invested in their cause. He wrote that, in order to overcome the dark clouds of socialist collectivism, "the Free World must discover a power of faith which will provide man's mind at the same intensity, with the same two certainties: a reason to live and a reason to die."

President Ronald Reagan seemed to possess that certainty. When I shook hands with him that time, it was like shaking the hand of history itself. He had somehow been allotted more than his share of seeds and used them wisely. His bold, straightforward attack against communism shocked Americans as much as it did the Soviets. After all, we had been pussyfooting around the Russian bear and kowtowing to it since World War II and before.

"Russia's postwar position in Europe will be a dominant one," predicted Harry Hopkins, an advisor to President Franklin Roosevelt's White House. "With Germany crushed, there is no power in Europe to oppose her tremendous military forces. The conclusions from the foregoing are obvious. Since Russia is the decisive factor in the war, she must be given every assistance and every effort must be made to obtain her friendship."

"They expect us to play doggie, turn over with our paws in the air, whimper, piss on ourselves, and play dead," I remarked to CNO James Watkins in one of our many discussions during the tense and controversial period of Reagan's standoff with the Soviets. "Many of us are like an old whore ready to spread our legs for appeasement and peace."

"This is a high-stakes game," Watkins said. "The president is one tough old sonofabitch. I'm betting Gorbachev blinks first."

All these communist leaders, from Josef Stalin right up through Mikhail Gorbachev were the same—bent on dominating the world.

The Soviet Union began aggressively building an empire from 1917 on. Under Lenin, Russia forcibly annexed the Ukraine, Belorussia, Georgia, Armenia, and Azerbaijan. Stalin added Lithuania, Latvia,

Estonia, Bessarabia, and parts of Bukovina and Finland. As WWII ended, new Soviet seizures were executed in Bulgaria, Romania, Hungary, Poland, East Germany, Czechoslovakia, and Yugoslavia. Opposition leaders and groups were imprisoned, exiled, or executed.

Communist revolutions erupted in China and Indochina. Communist-fomented civil wars broke out in Greece, Malaya, and the Philippines. Reds attempted to stage general strikes in France and Italy, while in the Balkans and other parts of Eastern Europe populations faced a choice of either fascist or communist dictatorships.

There seemed to be no stopping the Red tidal wave. The Korean War ended in a draw, with the Soviets maintaining influence over North Korea. The Red Chinese seized the helm in China, the most populous nation on earth, and promptly murdered as many as sixty million of their own people and one million Tibetans. Ho Chi Minh announced communism in Vietnam.

The United States refused to intervene in the 1956 Hungarian uprising against Soviet rule. Cuba turned communist under a Castro takeover, the first Soviet-backed regime in the western hemisphere. East Germany erected the Berlin Wall. Communist regimes sprang up in South Yemen and Africa. South Vietnam, Cambodia, and Laos fell to communism. Hundreds of thousands of South Vietnamese fled the country while an equal number ended up executed or in labor and "reeducation" camps.

Henry Kissinger, President Gerald Ford's secretary of state, proposed detente with Russia by proclaiming that "we cannot prevent the growth of Soviet power."

Marxists came to power in Nicaragua, the Seychelles, and Grenada and initiated other "popular front" uprisings all over Latin America. The Soviet Army invaded Afghanistan. Terrorism supported by Soviet Russia as well as Islamic jihad increased dramatically. President Jimmy Carter lifted the ban on travel to Cuba and North Korea.

In a speech of May 22, 1977, Jimmy Carter exhorted Americans to abandon their "inordinate fear of communism."

Many "progressives" in the West cheered for a world communist victory. Cradling the Marxist agenda under their bonnets, they insinuated themselves into the heart of American democracy, claiming to have glimpsed the future in which, with a few breaking of eggs, an omelet could be made.

Shortly after I went with the CIA, I obtained an FBI memo that listed known contacts between representatives of the Soviet Intelligence Services and members and staff personnel of the U.S. Congress. The list included hundreds of Congressional staff members and at least thirteen senators and representatives.

Disgust for these people filled my throat with bile. We seemed to be on a downward spiral of American susceptibility to communism's false promises of a collectivist Utopia. It spread moral uncertainty across the heartland while much of the world remained sealed behind an iron curtain of repression, an impenetrable barrier that impounded at least one billion people while untold numbers of others were killed, tortured, or imprisoned with no hope of rescue or outside help. What people seemed not to understand was that communism was the ultimate manifestation of terrorism.

Few U.S. presidents starting with Woodrow Wilson put up any significant resistance to the advance of world communism. Until Reagan, the West seemed to hunker down in fear to accept the inevitable, like Churchill's story of the monkey who makes a deal with the crocodile on the condition that he be the last one eaten. Reagan posed the world's first substantial challenge to communism since Lenin was a pup.

It came as no surprise to me that he faced a formidable array of critics as he continued to press the Soviet Union during his presidency's last months leading up to the 1988 elections. He abandoned completely the "sweet talk" temerity of Cold War presidents before him in his ideological, economic, and geopolitical offensive to draw the Soviets into a battle of systems in which they could not compete and that he predicted would leave them on the "ash heap of history." No political figure since the American Revolution had so boldly expressed the tone of what freedom meant or entailed.

Reagan was deemed "reckless," accused of "provoking the Soviets into war." Media described him as "dangerous . . . simplistic . . . crazy . . . illiberal and provocative." *American Journey*, a freshman history textbook, mocked him, saying he "considered the Soviet Union not a

coequal nation with legitimate world interests, but an 'evil empire'"—
which, in fact, he did. The *Washington Post* shouted, "McCarthyism!"
The Law Center for Constitutional Rights echoed with, "A move back
to the Dark Ages."

The people who viscerally understood what he was most about
were trapped behind the Iron Curtain. His "Evil Empire" speech res-
onated inside the Soviet gulag. Political prisoner Vladimir Bukovsky,
who was expelled from the Soviet Union and emigrated to America,
recalled how Reagan's words were "incredibly popular" among the
Soviet Union's political prisoners.

Natan Sharansky, a Jewish dissident inmate at Permanent Labor
Camp 35, jumped for joy when news of the speech filtered into his cell.
He passed it on to other inmates.

"Finally," he exclaimed, "the leader of the free world had spoken
the truth—a truth that burned inside the heart of each and every one
of us."

Not even John F. Kennedy understood as well the concept, principles, and practices of waging unconventional warfare as well as Reagan. Reagan was a political night fighter who played for keeps and
toward a single purpose. Sovietologist Sewery N. Bialer explained it
in this way: "(His) self-righteous and moralistic tone, its reduction of
Soviet achievements to crimes by international outlaws . . . stunned
and humiliated the Soviet leaders. . . . [Reagan seemed] determined
to deny the Soviet Union nothing less than legitimacy and status as a
global power [which] they thought had been conceded once and for all
by Reagan's predecessors."

Harvard sovietologist Adam Ulam observed how the only way
Soviet expansion could be blocked was to be confronted with a "power
strong and determined to make Soviet adventurism too risky and
expensive."

I understood what Reagan was doing. I had practiced it myself in
one form or another since the Naval Academy forty years ago. It was
war "by other means." Both clandestine and overt at varying times.

Reagan installed Pershing missiles in Europe to deter further
Russian expansion. He pressured the Soviets with a massive military buildup in the United States and introduced "Star Wars," which

threatened to make Soviet nuclear weapons obsolete. He provided military support to anti-communist movements around the world and, as at Grenada, stood ready when necessary to go to war against communist encroachment. He and Pope John Paul II cooperated in destabilizing the communist regime in Poland, which led eventually to the nation's freedom. On June 12, 1987, he delivered his famous speech at the Berlin Wall.

"We welcome change and openness," he said, "for we believe that freedom and security go together, that the advance of human liberty can only strengthen the cause of world peace. There is no sign the Soviets can make that would be unmistakable, that would advance dramatically the cause of freedom and peace. General Secretary Gorbachev, if you seek peace, if you seek prosperity for the Soviet Union and Eastern Europe, if you seek liberalization, come here to the gate. Mr. Gorbachev, open this gate. Mr. Gorbachev, tear down this wall."

The Soviet Union's efforts to counter the United States militarily over that past two decades had led to its economic decline and finally to this ultimate confrontation in an arms race it could not win. It was Reagan who led the final assault that wrecked the Soviet economy and overwhelmed its technological capabilities. Overextended, hampered by economic and social stagnation that set the stage for its own dissolution, it began to withdraw into itself and abandon its aspirations for world domination.

Socialism had, in fact, collapsed in Russia on a number of occasions. Whenever the State is the single producer and distributor of goods, the results must inevitably be shortages, corruption, and political tyranny. Each time before, when confronted with breakdown, it survived only because it briefly compromised and permitted the free market to make a rescuing adjustment, such as Lenin's New Economic Policy (NEP) in the 1920s.

But as soon as things were going good again, Lenin or Stalin or Khrushchev or whoever else happened to be in charge jumped back in to re-impose full-blooded socialism. This time, however, the Iron Curtain was cracking. Backed into a corner, Gorbachev blinked first and signed the Intermediate Range Nuclear Forces (INF) treaty. While the treaty offered relief from economic decline due to fierce competition with the United States, Gorbachev still found it necessary to temporarily release the free market and the people for another "rescuing adjustment."

"Do not be concerned about all you hear about *glasnost* and democracy," he reassured the Politburo. "Those are primarily for outward consumption. There will be no serious internal changes in the USSR other than for cosmetic purposes. Our purpose is to disarm America and let them fall asleep. We want to accomplish three things: 1. Get America to withdraw conventional forces from Europe; 2. Get America to withdraw nuclear forces from Europe; 3. Get America to stop proceeding with the Strategic Defense Initiative."

Forced democratic reforms resulted in unintended consequences. Reagan's victory over the "Evil Empire" became all but complete as internal USSR institutions began to fall apart and satellite slave nations declared their independence and broke away from the Soviet. The USSR was negotiating its own surrender as Reagan's presidency drew to a close. It formally dissolved itself on Christmas Day 1991. Mikhail Gorbachev was out the door. Boris Yeltsin became the first president of the New Russian Federation.

The long Cold War was over. Ronald Reagan won. Chalk one up for the good guys.

I retired from the Navy and public service and collected the pet dog I had long coveted, a Kerry blue terrier pup. President Ronald Reagan retired to his California ranch with his horses. Gorbachev received the Nobel Peace Prize. But then so had President Jimmy Carter and PLO terrorist Yasser Arafat.

"Miss it all?" Barbara asked me.

"Yes," I said. "But it was a good run. Some of the seeds were good and strong and brave."

She frowned, not understanding. "What?"

I grinned at her. "Honey, you are the best of the seeds."

AFTERWORD

I'M EIGHTY-EIGHT YEARS OLD. There are a few who remember me, who let me know when a big operation is going down, who discuss with me and solicit my advice as sort of an elderly statesman of unconventional warfare and counterterrorism. I'm just an old warhorse now, out of harness and casting my last daily seeds into a wind that seems to grow harsher.

I'm not so steady these days. I fall. Clumsiness, old age, blacking out sometimes. Four times so far, which meant trips to the emergency room. It's a hell of a way for an old night fighter to end up. Maybe that's why I can't remember so much anymore, all the falls.

But I remember who the enemy was and who he still is. And I remember the brave men who fought to win the Cold War, to stop communism, tyranny, and terror: Beckwith, Boehm, Rodriguez, Fane, Kauffman, Bucklew, Howard Hunt, Marcinko, McCone, Ashcroft, Mad Mike Hoare. Most of them are dead now. I close my eyes sometimes, and my memory returns and I see their faces and I see white crosses in ranks at Arlington.

My mother is buried there next to Dad. My brother, Frank, and I are the last of our family's generation. Barbara retired from the CIA in 1993 but continued contract work for the Agency several more years before finally retiring. I bought her a Mercedes, which she still has.

We packed up and moved to the sunny suburbs of Tucson, Arizona, as though to escape to the center of the country and away from wars and terrorism with which we had both invested much of our adult lives.

On Tuesday morning, September 11, 2001, with the sun barely risen, I took my dog for a walk through the quiet residential streets of our neighborhood. Barbara was in a tizzy when I returned.

"They're bombing us! They're killing people!" she cried.

I watched with her, live on TV, the second airliner fly into New York's Twin Towers. We huddled around the TV for the rest of the day as the 9/11 drama played out, horrified by scenes of collapsing buildings, panicked people fleeing through soot and smoke. It reminded me of Hiroshima and Nagasaki in 1945.

Total loss of lives—2,996, including 343 New York firefighters and 72 police officers. It was the greatest loss of American lives in an attack since Pearl Harbor.

Militant Islamic terrorism takes center stage. In the wake of 9/11, President George W. Bush declared a War on Terror, which was to become the longest war in U.S. history, extending into the Desert Storm clash of 1991 and on and on through wars in Afghanistan and Iraq, and then into Syria and the rise of ISIS.

At the CIA and at the Pentagon those years ago I tried to warn against the rise of international Islamic jihad so often I sometimes felt like Chicken Little. "The sky is falling!" I watch now from the sidelines, feeling helpless as the entire world unravels.

On a recent visit to the Pentagon, I met Major General Vernon Chong, an air force surgeon and commander of Willford Hall Medical Center at Fort Sam Houston in San Antonio. He later used parts of our conversation in an essay.

"Our country is now facing the most serious threat to its existence, as we know it, that we have faced in your lifetime and mine (which includes WWII)," General Chong warned. "We can definitely lose this war [on terror]. It would appear that a great many of us think that losing the war means hanging our heads, bringing the troops home, and going on about our business, like post-Vietnam. Not the truth.

"The attacks will not subside, but, rather, will steadily increase. Remember, they want us dead, not just quiet. If they had just wanted us quiet, they would not have produced an increasing series of attacks against us over the past eighteen years. The plan was, clearly, for terrorists to attack us until we were neutered and submissive to them. . . .

"They will pick off the other non-Muslim nations, one at a time. It will be increasingly easier for them. They already hold Spain hostage. It doesn't matter whether it was right or wrong for Spain to withdraw its troops from Iraq. Spain did it because the Muslim terrorists bombed their train and told them to withdraw their troops.

"The next will probably be France. It may already be too late for France. France is already 20 percent Muslim and fading fast. Without our support, England will go also. There are now more mosques in England than churches.

"The radical Muslims fully know what is riding on this war, and are completely committed to winning, at any cost. We'd better know it too, and be likewise committed to winning at any cost."

I agree with my friend Rear Admiral Albert M. Calland III, until recently the Navy's top SEAL, when he said, "The fight against this dispersed and elusive enemy requires a small, flexible, responsive force supported by a robust intelligence capability. . . . This concept of 'SOF [special operations forces]-centric warfare' is built on the foundation that in order to stop future terrorist acts from happening effectively— to stop the emergency before it occurs—we need to be a preemptive force."

Barbara and I moved back from Arizona to Virginia Beach to be near where we spent so many years of our lives. I walk my dog. I visit SEAL Team Six headquarters down at Dam Neck Annex south of Virginia Beach. The wars have been long and tiring on special operations people. I find the guys, *my* guys, looking battered physically and mentally. An old man, I feel like tottering off somewhere, sitting down on my butt and crying my eyes out for what we are doing to them when we need them most.

I like the old movies. Turner Classics on TV with John Wayne, Randolph Scott, Jimmie Stewart, Henry Fonda, Robert Mitchum, Susan Hayward. . . . *The Night of the Grizzly, God Is My Copilot, Bend in the River, The African Queen* with Humphrey Bogart and Katherine

Hepburn on Lake Tanganyika where I fought Che Guevara. They are the enduring symbols of when giants who walked the earth stood up for honor and principle, with real guts to call a spade a spade and not apologize for it, who knew the enemy and were bound to kill the bastards, not preach and whimper and grovel to them.

But what the hell? I'm an old man mumbling in my soup. I'm off the main battle line now. All I can do is rage about it. And take my dog out for a walk. Slower now, pondering. . . .

So I walk my dog. My seeds thrown out the window of the speeding car are blown away. But sometimes I still see those faces in my mind—night fighter ghosts. I close my eyes and my memory returns in brief glimpses. I see faces looking at me with tears in their eyes.

"Bone? Bone, wake up. We still have a job to do."

ABOUT THE AUTHORS

William H. Hamilton Jr. graduated from the US Naval Academy in Annapolis in 1949 and served as a fighter pilot in the Korean War. Fascination with unconventional warfare led his involvement in underwater demolition teams. In 1961, he became the commander of UDT-21 in Little Creek, Virginia, where, with Roy Boehm as his operations officer, he was responsible for developing the Navy SEAL program. Hamilton subsequently conducted missions with SEALs and CIA in Cuba, Vietnam, Latin America, and Africa. After the Iran Hostage Crisis, he worked in counterterrorism, and was one of two men responsible for developing SEAL Team Six. He also advised the Reagan White House on the security of the Strategic Defense Initiative. Hamilton retired from the Navy in 1986. He resided with his wife in Virginia Beach, Virginia, until his death in November 2016.

Charles W. Sasser is a full-time freelance writer, photographer, and journalist with more than sixty published books and thousands of magazine articles in publications from *Reader's Digest* and *Time/Life* to *Soldier of Fortune* and *WWII History*. A former Navy journalist, then an Army Special Forces (Green Beret) soldier, he is now retired from the Army (active and reserve). He also served fourteen years as a police officer in Miami, Florida, and Tulsa, Oklahoma, where he was a homicide detective. He has taught history and other subjects at universities, lectured nationwide, and traveled extensively throughout the world.

His bio is included in *Who's Who in the World*, and he was awarded the organization's 2019 Lifetime Achievement Award. In 1986 he was a finalist to fly into space with NASA's Journalist-in-Space Project; in 2001 he set a world's record by making the first transcontinental flight in an ultralight powered parachute aircraft; he has sailed a forty-foot sloop across the Caribbean, solo-kayaked Canada's Inside Passage, climbed Africa's Mt. Kilimanjaro; guided missionaries into Algeria; ridden horses across Alaska, and dog-sledded the Arctic.

His published books have been translated into Chinese, Russian, Serbian, Thai, French, Spanish, and other languages. His most recent and successful books include: *Crushing the Collective*; *Two Fronts/One War*; *One Shot–One Kill* (with Craig Roberts); and *The Night Fighter* (with Bill Hamilton). He lives in Chouteau, Oklahoma.

LTC William Craig Roberts, USA (Retired), is a US Marine veteran of the Vietnam War, where he served in a line company in the 9th Marine Regiment. After leaving the Marines due to combat wounds in 1968, he later enlisted in the Oklahoma Army National Guard and served in a reconnaissance (Scout) platoon first as an NCO and later as an officer. Graduating from OCS in 1975 as an infantry officer, he rose through the ranks and served in both command and staff positions. He later transferred to the Army Reserve and served as a Ground Liaison Officer (GLO) to an F-116 fighter squadron. An internationally published author, Lieutenant Colonel Roberts is a graduate of the US Army Command and General Staff College and is also a veteran of the Tulsa Police Department where he served as a patrol officer and later police helicopter pilot with over 3,500 flight hours in helicopters and fixed-wing aircraft. He is the author of more than a dozen books, both nonfiction and fiction. He lives in Locust Grove, Oklahoma.